SHIFTING SANDS

By

T.L. McCOWN

To Mrs. Betty —
Thank you for your
support of my creative
endeavor. There is just
nothing like a wonderful
Perry neighbor.
With love,
T.L.

For details on how to schedule T.L. to speak to your group,
for additional information about T.L., to email T.L.
or to order additional copies of *Shifting Sands,*
please visit **www.tlmccown.com**

Editor: M.J. Matthews

ISBN: 1-58597-220-7

Library of Congress Control Number: 2003112558

□

LEATHERS
PUBLISHING

A division of Squire Publishers, Inc.
4500 College Blvd.
Leawood, KS 66211
1/888/888-7696
www.leatherspublishing.com

Dedication

I give these words with love to my dear family for all the love and support they have given me, and to my princess for the special memories.

ॐ Introduction ॐ

Countless hours of soul searching preceded the writing of these pages. On the one hand, I wanted to protect the privacy of the princess I came to know and my other Arab friends. Yet, on the other hand, I wanted to share what I learned and experienced with the Western world. After living and working in the Kingdom of Saudi Arabia for a decade, I knew that I had experiences people would want to read about.

I have been back in the United States for almost two years. I have read claims about the Kingdom and its people that make me cringe. Almost nightly, I hear reports from supposed authorities, and the majority of the statements I hear make me angry because of their lack of validity. For these reasons, I was compelled to share the following pages.

I do not claim to be a scholar of Islam, and I do not wish to demean the Islamic religion with the writing of this book. I do not know or claim to know everything there is to know about the Saudi people. I doubt many Americans could make this claim. When the decision was made to carry forward, I made a promise to myself that only what I experienced personally would be included in the pages. Judgment and opinion, I leave to the reader.

To assure individual safety and to satisfy my need to keep the privacy of the princess and other friends, all names have been changed, including my own. Consequently, the pictures I could include are limited to protect privacy as well. However, every event that follows is true. Because of the amount of time covered and feedback received, *Shifting Sands* is divided into two sections for ease of reading. The first section is chronological, revealing how and why I went to Saudi Arabia and the events that led to my employment with the princess. Section two topically approaches the aspects of living in the Kingdom as a Westerner and life with a princess as my employer and my friend.

Not all of the words I share about the Kingdom are pleasant, but I would assume if someone wrote about America or other countries, the same would be true. If I offend, I apologize to my Arab friends. I only want to share the truth about what I saw and experienced. Hence, this begins my story of life with a princess in the Kingdom of Saudi Arabia.

ॐ *Contents* ॐ

ॐ *PART ONE* ॐ

ॐ Chapter One ॐ

Looking Back

I guess I always knew. I guess it could be said that I never attempted to see the big picture, to see the truth. I knew from the beginning that our cultures were different, and rightly so, but I never dreamed *where* the differences were or where the cultural divergence would surface. I was shocked to discover how these differences could pervade the most fundamental values and beliefs of human beings, fundamental differences on how people from different cultures and religions look at the world around them, fundamental differences on how friends treat each other.

Essentially, the acts of daily life clouded my view. All expatriates in Saudi Arabia had heard the rumors of the potentially fickle nature of Saudis, but I chose not to believe them. I even defied the rumors because my perceptions were skewed. As I reflect, twelve years later, I am still mesmerized by the adventures I had and in awe of the things I witnessed. It is as if I lived a dream that lasted a decade. Conversely, it is still difficult to believe the subtle things that occurred along the way, and eventually, the blatant events that took place as the years unfolded and my dream ended.

With the recent terrorist attack on America, all of these memories have flooded back into my mind and my heart. It was the event on June 25, 1996, that changed our lives in the Kingdom of Saudi Arabia. Prior to September 11, the Khobar Tower bombing, a tragedy that killed nineteen American soldiers on foreign soil, was considered to be one of the largest terrorist bombings ever. However, it was June 1996 when our daily existence in the desert changed forever. We faced armed gates, Consulate Warden messages, and additional threats of terror. Instead of community town meetings to discuss satellite television and playground equipment as before, we had community seminars on personal security measures, surveillance recognition, attack recognition, and improvised explosive devices. Our idyllic life quickly turned into a nightmare.

Until June of 1996, the Kingdom had always been regarded as one of the safest places in the world because their punishment of criminals is swift and severe. Never before had we felt fear, until the twenty-fifth of June.

No one can understand the meaning of terrorism until they experience it first hand. The fear looms in the back of your mind. With one bomb, the terrorists of Khobar Towers were able to captivate an entire community of expatriates in the Kingdom, an entire community of Westerners. And now, with four of our own planes, terrorists have been able to do the same thing in America — captivate an entire nation.

After the Khobar Tower bombing, we conducted our daily tasks with an ever-present fear looming over us, holding residual fear in the back of our minds. Just when we felt relaxed we would see a water truck, which is a typical sight in a desert climate, and we would flinch just a little. Is it a bomb? Does the driver look like a terrorist? What in heaven's name does a terrorist look like anyway? We would ask ourselves all of these questions and more as we tried to snap back to reality, to some sense of normality. A delivery truck, an unfamiliar face on the compound, or a suspicious wrong number would bring to the forefront feelings of suspicion and fear that became a part of our daily existence.

After the Gulf War in 1991, my husband, David, and I made our way to the sands of Saudi Arabia to learn and adventure. Loving our life there, we spent a decade in the Kingdom. During our years in Saudi Arabia, our relationship flourished and we started our family, welcoming the blessing of two beautiful children: a boy and a girl. Through a turn of fate, I enjoyed an insight into the Saudi culture that very few expatriates have ever had the opportunity to enjoy. Shortly after my arrival, I was employed by a Royal family from the House of Al-Saud where I developed a deep friendship with Princess Madawi, which enabled me to see life through her eyes. Within my expatriate community of over five hundred American women, I was one of only three women to my knowledge who had the privilege to develop a profound friendship with a Saudi princess.

My experiences were rare, even within the Kingdom. However, as much as I was fortunate to experience over the years, I was not of their world. I am still a Christian American with different values and beliefs looking into their world; nevertheless, my seat at the theater of Saudi culture was extremely close to the stage. I was honored to experience the Royal family's inner circle first hand, which allows me the opportunity to share insight into the Saudi culture that has never been revealed to the Western world.

Fortunately, the threat of terror was not always present in the Kingdom, and I prayed that life would be as it was before Khobar Tower. For the most part, the Kingdom was a wonderful place to live, and most of the people were wonderful as well. This is not to say that Saudi Arabia is a utopia. All cultures, societies, and countries have their faults and their merits. All cultures have parts of their history they would like to exalt and parts they would like to erase. All societies have good and bad people. All countries have allies and enemies. However, on the whole, the Kingdom was a good place to be — in the beginning.

From their nomadic tradition, the Saudi people are a very hospitable breed, kind and welcoming to strangers. Some Westerners perceive their traditions as strange, but this is just semantics. They are not "strange," just different from what Westerners are accustomed. Throughout the years that I lived in the Kingdom, I met many people, most of whom were kind to me.

It was one Saudi, in particular, whom I came to know and love. Perhaps it is because of her that I loved the Kingdom the way that I did and failed to recognize the fundamental differences that would eventually tear us a part. Perhaps, it is because of her that I wanted the terrorist nightmare to go away and life to return to normal. Unquestionably, it is because of her that I have been left with this feeling of disillusionment.

It is certainly because of the princess I want to share my story so that the West will have a better understanding of the Saudi people, their thoughts, their values, and their way of life. To understand the fundamental differences in our cultures is essential to acquire a basic understanding of each culture's perception of reality, and how these perceptions cause us to act and react to each other in personal relationships and global events.

I can only offer my observations and experiences in this foreign land, and I leave judgment to someone else. Because Princess Madawi and I shared many similarities — two women who could love, hate, laugh, and cry — our friendship nurtured understanding, acceptance, and compassion in the beginning. However, because the deeply rooted differences in our perceptions of reality eventually surfaced, hurt and humiliation ultimately overwhelmed our friendship.

ॐ *Chapter Two* ॐ

A Little History

The decision to move to Saudi Arabia was made years before the day came to actually fly there. After my husband, David, and I were married and completed our university degrees, our sole purpose and goal for the next stage of our lives was to live and work in the Kingdom of Saudi Arabia. The desire to travel and understand this distant land was passed to us by my parents who had been expatriates for many years in the capital city, *Riyadh.* Inspired by their stories and adventures, we fell in love with the idea of experiencing the Kingdom. Just before graduation, David applied to a major U.S. company for a project manager position supporting a foreign military sales contract in Saudi. While negotiations were being made for his employment, disaster struck.

Kuwait was invaded by Iraq, and our plans were put on hold, but only temporarily. The company that had hired David to work in Kingdom called immediately following the invasion in September of 1990 and told us they would be in touch in March the following year. "In March?" we questioned. The war had not even started yet, so how did they know they would contact us in

March? Disappointed, with the desire to go to Saudi still in the back of our minds, we accepted temporary positions, and I used my idle time to learn more about my future home.

I wanted to know more and to learn as much as I could. What is the climate like? I knew it was a desert, but I had never lived in a desert and thirsted to learn. What are the regions of the Kingdom? Was it like the United States or different? Where did these people come from? What is their history? Who rules the country? How is the country ruled? Why is the country like it is today? I felt it was important for me to find answers to these questions so I could appreciate the rich heritage of the region, appreciate its culture and antiques, and most importantly, understand its people. Even though I had heard stories about the Kingdom from my parents for years, I was amazed by what my research uncovered.

Many times when people think of Saudi Arabia, they picture an endless, dry desert with *Bedouin* tents scattered about and camel trains on the horizon. Pictured probably because Saudi Arabia is home to two of the largest desert areas in the world: The *Rub al Khali,* also called the *"Empty Quarter,"* in the south and the *Great Nafud* in the north. Contrary to popular belief, Saudi does embrace a variety of climates and subcultures. The country is divided along geographical lines into five regions, each with its own terrain, climate, and way of life. Consequently, the people of each province reflect these differences.

The Western Province, known in Arabic as *Hijaz,* is

the location of the two Holiest cities in Islam: *Mekkah* and *Madinah*. Also located in *Hijaz* is the major port city of *Jeddah* on the Red Sea. People of this region are fairly accustomed to foreigners and their ways because of early camel caravans that frequented the area and because of the enormous number of pilgrims that visit the Holy cities each year for the Islamic duty of *Hajj*.

The *Asir*, or Southern Province, is a popular vacation spot due to its year round mild climate and pleasant temperatures. Located on the Red Sea, the *Asir* is home to the cities of *Khamis Mushayt, Taif*, and *Abha*. The area is dotted with towering escarpments and vegetation, marveling the eye with its magnificent views. In *Khamis Mushayt*, wild bands of baboons can be seen among the foliage. The people of this region are colorful and their clothing styles reflect the influence of neighboring Yemen, with the men still adorning double-edged daggers around the waist when they go to market.

Riyadh, the capital city of Saudi Arabia, is located in the Central Province, also known as the *Najd*. This province is the home of the ruling Al-Saud family, the founders of Saudi Arabia, and it is probably the most conservative of all of the provinces regarding dress and behavior. The Central Province is usually the hottest and driest populated area of the country, with temperatures commonly rising above 120 degrees Fahrenheit in the summer.

The Eastern Province, which would be my home for ten years, is the major oil-producing area of the country. *Dammam*, capital of the province, is where oil

11

well # 7 is located, the first well to strike oil in the region in the 1930s. In addition to its importance in the oil industry, *Dammam* is also a vital seaport and industrial center. Located nearby are the cities of *Al-Khobar,* a commercial and residential area, *Dhahran,* the major oil production area, which houses Saudi Aramco, and a bit further away, the cities of *Qatif* and *Hofuf,* the one-time the capital of the province. Because of the international influence in the area, the Eastern Province is much more liberal for Westerners than the rest of the country, yet the native population remains very traditional with its beliefs and Bedouin customs. Being that they are both coastal regions, the Eastern and Western Provinces of the country are much more humid than the Central area, with humidity reaching as high as 100 percent in the summer months, but without rain.

The fifth region of the country is the Northern Province. Although strategically important, the province is mainly agricultural. Its capital city is *Tabuk* located in the *Great Nafud* desert region. At night, temperatures can drop as much as twenty degrees. The region is plagued by fierce, sandy windstorms, known as *shamaals,* which often are so powerful that they shift the landscape. Where one day a sand dune can be 100 feet tall or more, following a *shamaal,* it can be completely flat. The sands shift continually, completely changing the face of the desert.

Originally from the southern part of the United States, the climate of the Kingdom was not as intimidating for me as it was for some. After learning about the regions and their climates, my desire to go there was peaked by the diversity the country held.

The history of the region dates back to some of the very earliest known civilizations, some as old as the first millennia B.C. *Madain Saleh,* an ancient city in the *Hijaz* region, dates back to the time period of Petra in the country of Jordan. As travel expanded with the domestication of camels, the peninsula became the land of major trade routes for spices such as frankincense and myrrh, silk, and pearls.[1]

The current ruling monarchy, the Al-Saud family, traces its roots back to the fifteenth century. In the eighteenth century, Saud Ibn Muhammad ruled the country outside of *Riyadh* in the city of *Diryyah.* It was his son, Muhammad, who made an alliance with a religious reformer, Sheikh Muhammad Ibn Abdul Wahhab, who preached a return to the message of the *Quran* and the teachings of the Prophet Muhammad *(PBUH).* Twenty years passed, and there was strife among the citizens who believed that the teachings of Muhammad (PBUH) were too strict. This forced Sheikh Muhammad to join with the Saud tribe who supported his movement. It was at this point that the two houses, the Sauds and the Wahhabs, became allies and their union was integral to the unification of the country. The two houses formed the first state in the *Najd* only to be cast out by the Ottomans. Shortly thereafter, the House of Saud returned to form a second state in *Riyadh,* only to be exiled to Kuwait by the Rashid family in the nineteenth century.[2]

Abdul Aziz bin Abdul Rahman Al Saud, the founder

of the modern Saudi Arabia, grew up in exile. When he was in his early twenties, he returned to *Riyadh* with a band of forty men to reclaim his homeland from the Rashids. He succeeded. Over the next thirty years, Abdul Aziz skillfully used diplomacy to unite the tribes of the peninsula by taking a bride from each of the twelve warring tribes. In 1932, the country of Arabia was renamed the *Kingdom of Saudi Arabia*.[3]

King Abdul Aziz continued to rule until his death in 1953, leaving his forty sons to rule the country and his eldest son, Saud, to become king. In 1964, his brother, Faisal, who made major advances socially, technologically, and economically in the Kingdom, replaced King Saud. King Faisal, inheriting his father's gift of diplomacy, was eager to modernize the Kingdom. It was he who led the Kingdom to become one of the richest countries in the world by the time of his assassination by a deranged cousin in 1975. Following King Faisal's lead, King Khalid, Faisal's half-brother, continued the progressive economic policies and social reform that King Faisal had begun and launched the Gulf Co-operation Council in 1981. Today, the Kingdom is ruled by King Fahd, who prefers to be known as the *"Custodian of the Two Holy Mosques,"* referring to his responsibility for the two Holy Islamic cities *Mekkah* and *Madinah*.[4]

With a basic understanding of the Kingdom's history in hand, I became even more anxious to respond to the call to come and experience a chance for adventure in this mysterious, foreign land. However, with the Gulf War just beginning in January of 1991, things looked doubtful for March.

[1] The American Women of the Eastern Province, *Marhaba: A Guide to Life and the Pursuit of Happiness in the Eastern Province of Saudi Arabia*, 2nd Ed., (Saudi Arabia: 1994 and 1998).

[2] William Facey, *The Story of The Eastern Province of Saudi Arabia*, (London: Stacey International, 1994 & 2000).

[3] *Ibid.*

[4] William Facey, *The Story of The Eastern Province of Saudi Arabia*, (London: Stacey International, 1994 & 2000).

ॐ *Chapter Three* ॐ

Arrival

Night after night, I watched the reports of the battles of the Gulf War, fearing for friends I had yet to meet. Glued to the television, I was completely consumed with the progression of the war and prayed that it would end. As I continued to monitor the development of the war, my hopes dwindled that my dream to live in Saudi Arabia would ever come true. Then, just as predicted, the telephone rang early one March morning … it was the company. When I knew who was on the other end of the line, my heart dropped, fearing the worst. Then it leapt.

It all happened so fast. Within three months, David completed his contract formalities, picking up from where we had left off before the war. We got our passports renewed, endured the required medical examinations, had various inoculations for travel, and we compiled the paperwork package required by the Saudi government for employees in the Kingdom, which included copies of David's bachelors degree, our marriage certificate, and our birth certificates.

Before we knew it, David was on the plane to serve the required ninety days before I, David's "dependent," could mobilize. During these ninety days, I was anxious, excited, and terminally bored. Finally, the day came for me to leave Georgia and fly to a site unseen to live in a mysterious, foreign land that I would soon call home.

There are no words to completely describe my feelings. Numerous emotions encompassed me as I entered LaGuardia for the first time. I was a young woman from the south, who had never experienced New York, much less flown half way around the world alone. I was excited, scared, and experiencing something akin to the "cold feet" of a nervous bride. With my accepted wardrobe of conservative clothes packed, passport in hand, and all the advice I had been given by my Mom charging through my mind like a racehorse, I stepped onto the Boeing 747 to transport me to a completely different world.

My initial arrival in *Riyadh* was as if I were in a dream, perhaps due to lack of sleep or anxiety over the strange environment. I was taken aback by the beauty of the enormous, marble-laden airport and mesmerized by unfamiliar smells and sounds. From my research, I knew that this was the largest airport facility in the world, and after looking around, I concluded that it was probably the prettiest and most expensive as well. My excitement heightened, only to be bridled by my fear of the unknown.

As we were herded into one direction to clear customs, obviously being kept in a group, I became anxious as I looked around. In contrast to the beauty and modernization of the airport, the ambiance seemed anything but beautiful at that moment in time. The smells were strange to me, and I felt the glare of stares from every direction. Although I was dressed very conservatively in a calf-length skirt and long sleeve, tunic blouse, I was still uncovered ... in their eyes.

As I stepped up to the customs counter, the uniformed man spoke to me in Arabic, gesturing to my luggage. He seemed to bellow as he spoke to me, which gave me the feeling that he was angry. Later, I learned that I just misunderstood his tone. The utterances of the Arabic language tend to sound angry to English speaking people, even when they are not angry.

Unsure of what to do, and unable to understand the custom's official's request, I hesitated, but only for a moment. Remembering advice from my Mom, I promptly unzipped all of my baggage to show that I had nothing forbidden and nothing to hide. I wanted to appear calm and collected as he rambled through my belongings. I smiled the entire time attempting to make friends from the beginning.

A few hours after clearing customs, which was a feat in its own, I was escorted into a secluded room where I found other American women and their children whose husbands worked for David's company. After what seemed like forever, we were escorted as a group down a long corridor and onto a domestic flight that would take me to my final destination, *Dhahran,* where David anxiously awaited my arrival.

Once on the ground, along with the other company women, we were grouped together and shuttled onto a bus to clear customs again in the international terminal in *Dhahran*. I have yet to figure out why we were subjected to an additional customs experience; however, clearing customs the second time was much easier.

Departing the airport became the next challenge. All of the women entering under the sponsorship of the company were pulled aside yet again to await claim by their husbands, as if we were possessions rather than people. After what seemed like hours, I tried to leave our confined room and was stopped by a uniformed officer. After motioning for me to return to the room, he left without a word. Anxious and frustrated, I knew then it was time to draw on my Mom's advice: *"They will not touch a woman ... they aren't sure how to deal with a demanding American woman, and if all else fails, cry."*

Seeing that no other company wife was taking on the "demanding American woman" role and all of them seemed happy to just sit for days waiting to be collected by their husbands, I scanned the adjoining room through the huge glass window for anyone who looked official. Once targeted, I went to a uniformed gentleman and asked why we were being held. He informed me that we were being held until our husbands came so that we could be admitted to the country under their *Igamas*.

Well, this was fine and dandy, after all regulations are regulations. However, the big question that emerged in my mind was "how can our husbands claim us when they believe we are in the *domestic* terminal?" We arrived in *Dhahran* from *Riyadh* on a domestic flight into the domestic terminal, and then we were transported by bus to the international terminal, separating us from the other passengers and our waiting husbands. "How can they claim us if they don't know where we are?" I asked the officer. He disregarded me and my further questioning as if I were not important. The only information he continued to offer was that I had to wait and essentially be quiet until my husband arrived.

Hence, it was time to throw on the Southern charm and implement the *"they won't touch a woman"* portion of my Mom's advice. Taking a deep breath for courage, unsure of what the outcome of my action would be, I headed for the exit on the premise that I was doing them a favor to locate the husbands, and, in turn, rid them of the bothersome group of company women and children. It worked. I was free from the customs area to look for help.

When I turned the corner to look for David, I saw three women standing along the wall completely veiled, completely covered in black. I was taken aback literally. Yes, I had seen pictures. Yes, I knew the women veiled, but, to see it for the first time in person, I was almost nauseated by fear, exhaustion, or perhaps the heat. Simultaneously, I was hit with the smells of various people of different nationalities awaiting their arrivals and so many different languages that my head spun. Perhaps, my bold venture was a big mistake. Maybe we should not have come to this strange, distant land. I doubted our decision as fear hit me. My eyes raced around the room for the familiar face of my college sweetheart. "Where could he be?" I thought. "Why wasn't he here to save me, to *claim* me?" All I wanted to do was run, just run. And then, I felt the most overwhelming calm when I saw him. Everything was okay, even though we could not embrace because any public display of affection between a husband and wife is forbidden by Saudi law. This tore at my heartstrings, particularly after being apart for three months, but I compliantly held my emotions until we were alone.

"Is she yours?" the official questioned looking solely at David. My big eyes that David has always felt could talk, darted at him. David knew what I was thinking with my piercing stare, "Yours?"

"Yes," David calmly replied as I heard the echoing pounds as stamps went into his *Igama* marking my arrival. The idea of being "his" had always been a loving thought to me until I heard it in this way. In the Kingdom, "his" not only meant my heart, but every part of my being. I was a possession now. My fiery independence wanted to speak, but my fear and exhaustion kept me silent.

Finally, we were allowed to exit the airport and go to our temporary quarters, my new home. A place I warmly referred to at first as "the motel," and later contemptuously called "the cave." With all of the preparation and paperwork to move, the anxiety of travel and arrival, and David officially claiming me, we had undeniably crossed the threshold to our new life in the Kingdom of Saudi Arabia.

ॐ *Chapter Four* ॐ

The Motel

The drive to the "motel" seemed endless and, for days that followed, I would have sworn our destination was at least fifty miles from the airport. In fact, it was only five. As we talked about my trip and the challenges of my arrival, I could not sit still for gazing at the land of my new home from the passenger window. Because my arrival time was 12:30 a.m., which expats in Kingdom refer to as "O dark thirty," I could hardly see a thing in the black of the night. I did, however, notice an endless number of solitary lights reaching to the night sky above the flat sea of city lights. These lone lights mesmerized me, drawing my attention like a magnet. Now I know that it was the minarets of the many mosques that I saw. The towering structures peaked with the crescent moon symbol of the Islamic faith reaching up to the heavens as if watching, somehow guarding the land below. Finally, the car stopped.

My eyes were wide as we entered the gate of my new home, the "motel." I eagerly took in everything, noticing every detail as if I would not see it again. Unsteadily, due to sleep depravation, I trailed David to apartment #20. Adapted to the nocturnal life of the

Kingdom, five company women sat outside our apartment by the pool. The "whale club," as they were later known, sat pompously hashing over the day's gossip with their noses in a twitch to see the new incoming wife. Determined to start off on the right foot and make friends with all of my fellow countrymen and women in this distant land, I kindly, in my Southern way, greeted each of them, only to be disillusioned later as to their cordial intent.

At the time, the motel was temporary housing for married couples until our new compound, known as DM 18, was complete. The motel consisted of twenty nice but small, very small, efficiency apartments. However, after three months apart from my sweetheart, I could not have cared less. I was home. My new little love nest, the start of a new life, a new beginning and a new adventure.

Although my international airline ticket indicated my destination as *Dhahran,* our compound was not located there. *Dhahran* is actually an area which includes Saudi Aramco, Dhahran International Airport, the United States Consulate, and King Fahd University of Petroleum and Minerals (KFUPM). While Westerners refer to living in *Dhahran,* most Western compounds are actually located in either *Al-Khobar,* which is where we lived, or *Dammam,* the capital city of the Eastern Province. Our compound and our daily lives revolved in *Al-Khobar.* Starting as a small fishing village, *Al-Khobar* truly came into its own when oil exploration began. Today, it is home to a large international community with a cosmopolitan image.

My pillow gold, a tradition for the much-missed incoming wife, greeted me. Heart-shaped earrings and a pendant of 21-karat gold were spread upon the bed with roses all around to welcome me to my new home. I was ecstatic After exhaustion-induced babbling and buzzing around the new apartment, fatigue finally overcame adrenaline and we slept.

The next morning brought the first of a thousand pretty days in the Kingdom. Being a desert climate, we rarely had clouds. We rarely saw rain or felt cold. You would think living in a place where nine months of the year the climate is like paradise, you would be grateful. Because we are human, however, we were not. It was not long before I prayed for a stormy day, to have just one without incessant sunshine.

In time the saying, "another pretty day in the desert," held strong contradictory meanings for me and for many on the compound. On the one hand, we enjoyed the pretty weather, the cloudless sky, and the carefree, ostentatious life in Kingdom. On the other hand, it represented the superficial beauty of life in the Kingdom, and the stress that results from continual adherence to suppressive regulations and lack of freedom.

The unfamiliarity of what faced me in this distant land was hard to comprehend. Little did I know that I had stepped into a world of contradictions and change. We often laughed and said, "The only thing that is constant in the Kingdom is change." A world where one minute you must behave one way and the next you must behave entirely different. It all depended on where your feet were at the time. This is probably the most difficult thing for new wives to become accustomed to once they arrive. However, in time, the pendulum swing between east and west became second nature for me.

Whether it was a result of my personality or my deep desire to understand this foreign land, adaptation to the Saudi culture came easy to me. It was adapting to the Med One/*Peyton Place* compound life that was most challenging. In the beginning, the life of leisure was fun and exciting. Almost daily there were coffee mornings on one Western compound or another where bored ladies would get together and talk. Bingo, for jackpots as much as $1,000-plus, was available on Sundays and Wednesdays, company ladies' club meetings on Mondays, International Wives' Group meetings on Tuesdays, occasional craft bazaars, and sunbathing when time permitted. What a life! It was first class all the way with no worries, only coffee and more coffee. A life "to die for," which became a literal feeling rather than a figurative one after only a few weeks of this.

After all of the initial introductions and several weeks of the good life, I woke up and really started listening to the ladies at these events. They were constantly talking about each other, degrading their husbands, and complaining about the company as if they had ever had it so good. Most of the expats I met over the years appeared to come from "the other side of the tracks," only to come to the desert and instantly become debutantes with an aristocratic lineage. At the infinite coffee morning gatherings, I would hear of university achievements by individuals who could not even speak using correct grammar. I would hear of mansions they owned in the States, but no one was able to produce pictures for one reason or another. I would hear of the huge amounts of money people had, only to see them wearing the best Wal-mart can produce. It sounds crazy, but as I was once told and have never forgotten, "These people believe God can't see them in the desert!"

Not only did my Mom give me advice about the new culture I had entered, she gave me invaluable council about compound living. "Find one really good friend that you can trust, and be cordial to everyone else." But how could I find a true friend in all of these coffee mornings? How could I find a friend to trust when the common practice was to talk about each other, their husbands, your husband, and every other husband? How could I follow my Mom's wisdom that was vital to compound survival with these women?

Without a doubt, my husband, David, is wonderful to me. He is my best friend. But there are things, ideas, and feelings that all women feel and that a man just simply cannot understand. Even women with the best of marriages need female companionship, a girl friend to talk to, laugh with, and share private feelings. Little did I know that only a few weeks would pass before I would meet her.

ॐ Chapter Five ॐ

Extreme Boredom

Long before I arrived, the plan was already in place to consolidate the company's employees and their families. Rather than five temporary compounds around the city, it would be much more cost effective for the company to place us all, along with the incoming employees, on two larger compounds: DM 16, which was already built and the center for most entertainment in the beginning, and DM 18, the new, 184 villa compound on the edge of the Arabian Gulf. Fortunately for us, DM 16 was already full, and we were slated to move to DM 18.

Within two months of my arrival, the company community was buzzing. In the dining hall at one temporary compound, around the pools at others, and on the shopping buses, everyone was talking about the new compound, DM 18! The community rumor mill was in full swing with knowledgeable whisperings like: "The husbands will start choosing the villas next week"; "Our compound will pick first"; "No, the husbands have to choose by their *INCO* number"; "I want a waterfront villa"; or "I want a villa with blue carpet," and on and on and on.

Even though I knew most was a product of the community rumor mill, I could not help but get excited. Despite its less palatable effects, the rumor mill usually produced a lot of excitement though little truth. Yet, this time I believed that it must be true because everyone was talking about it, not just a few. The idea of moving to our new villa was exhilarating. Three thousand square feet with three bedrooms, three baths, living room, dining room, kitchen, luxury furniture and washer/dryer, all for just David and me to enjoy. I could hardly wait. Finally, I had a chance to get out of "the cave," our efficiency apartment, and fill my time with decorating our new home.

Then, my spirits were shattered and my bubble burst. It turned out that the word of our move had all been rumor mill — no truth. We were not moving, yet. Consequently, depression consumed me, and I had no idea how much longer I could stand the confines of the cave or the isolation that enveloped me. I had to think of a way to pick my spirits up again, a way to fill my time until the eventual move. My answer? Decorate. I soon determined that I could start decorating before we moved, and I decided to try shopping to get me out of the cave while David was at work.

I was petrified my first day out. Not only did I have to utilize the company's mass transit system, which was composed of Coaster buses with curtains on the windows so the unveiled, "sinful" Western women could not be seen, but I had to make my way without David, without a man. In retrospect, the event was comical. Never before had I had to catch a bus, and to make matters worse, I am inherently late. Plus, I did not know a word of Arabic. I had no clue where I was going, and I did not know my way around town once I got there. Further, I was not comfortable with the currency exchange, and I had no idea if I even had enough money to return home if I missed the bus, assuming I could figure out which direction home was. I was so frightened and apprehensive. However, I did not feel that I could endure yet another coffee morning, so I had to try. The first day, my fear was so great that I rode the bus for its entire run and got off where I had begun, the motel. Although my first shopping attempt could not be considered a successful venture, at least it was better that the alternative of being trapped in the cave or the coffee morning gossip circles. Because I had seen where the shopping bus went, the next day it was a little easier to try the shopping idea again. Success! I shopped until my feet hurt.

Soon I became a pro and began each day by hopping the shopping bus, clad in my *abaya* with a copy of David's igama in hand, which was required by Saudi law. Relishing my newfound freedom, I set out to find new and unique treasures.

It is important that I clarify that Westerners are not required to wear the traditional *abaya,* headscarf, or cover our faces like the Saudi women do. We were only required to dress conservatively in respect of the culture, covering from elbows to knees, showing no shape. Yet, I found that when I did not wear at least the *abaya* to cover my form, the merchants and Saudi men would stare excessively to see a women uncovered, which was very uncomfortable for me. Some of the American women I knew refused to wear the *abaya*, feeling that it changed them in some way, and as Americans they should be "free" not to wear it. Many times their impertinence to the culture and refusal to wear the *abaya* only resulted in catcalls and confrontations with the men in the market.

One lady on the compound was particularly indignant about the *abaya* and publicly refused to wear it, announcing to all of the ladies on the shopping bus that, "she would never be caught dead in the black bag." A few weeks after her announcement, she encountered a *Muthawen* downtown and passed her sentiments on to him. As a result, the company, who had received notice of the altercation from Saudi government officials, reprimanded her husband. The next time we saw her on the bus, she had on a "black bag."

Never did I feel that wearing the long black covering changed who I was inside. Yes, it was an inconvenience, but it did not change the way I looked at myself. To me, it only represented respect for my host country. After all, "when in Rome …"

In the quaint little downtown shops, I found treasures of all kinds: Persian carpets, antique pots, clay pots, incense burners, and *qhawa* pots. In my travels to the old *souks*, I found things that I will always cherish. Each time I look at each of these unique pieces, I can close my eyes and remember the store, the shopkeeper, the sounds and smells. *Souking,* as the Westerners fondly called shopping in the Eastern Province of the Kingdom, is a wonderful adventure. The store keepers, usually dressed in their country's traditional attire, are very polite, always saying, "Madame this and Madame that." The level of respect and kindness shown to Americans after the Gulf War was incredible, but that, too, eventually changed. However, immediately following the war in 1991, everyone in the Kingdom was still appreciative of America and its role in the war. Once the shopkeeper distinguished me as an American, the praise would begin, beating his heart and bowing, saying "Americee number one, very good." With more head nods, he would praise, "Yes, Americee very good." If an agreement on the price could not be made, a little tea is served to discuss a middle ground. Tea, served by "tea boys," as we referred to them, is offered in small, cylindrical cups while you shop.

And then there are the gold *souks*. Words cannot do justice to describe the gold souks in the Kingdom of Saudi Arabia. A deep, yellow gold color completely consumed the shops as it dripped with gold necklaces, breastplates, bracelets and earrings, all displayed on velvet backgrounds to enhance the luster. Most Westerners do not even know what 21-karat gold looks like, much less be able to imagine it hanging from floor to ceiling in stores. The amount of gold in one gold store is mind-boggling. For the longest time, I had to tell myself that it really was not real. But it is real, with 18 karat being the cheapest you could find.

To purchase gold, you choose your selection and then the shopkeeper places it on a scale. You pay by weight, with the per gram price fluctuating daily with world markets. It was funny to see the old-timers around the compound when someone would show off their newest gold purchase. They always wanted to hold it, to determine how much was spent. Over time, I became quite adept at estimating gold jewelry weight, usually guessing within a gram or two. Hours could be spent just looking at the different designs of this wealth, all in stores with no guards and no alarm systems. Even so, theft, was extremely rare. In the Kingdom, strictly following *Sharia* law, stealing is punished by amputating the left hand. Obviously, with laws such as this, theft is not a temptation for the sane.

As fascinating as it was, I soon tired of shopping. A person can only shop so much. Plus, the coffee morning ladies rode the same bus, always intent on drawing me into their gossip. Escape from the rumors seemed impossible. Soon, I began to spend most of my days and nights in the apartment, quiet and alone, only to jump on David the second he came home from work, desperate for some sort of conversation and news from the outside. My little love nest soon became like a prison, a self-imposed barrier to the coffee morning ladies and shopping boredom. I began rearranging furniture on a regular basis for something to do. I even began to try to cook, which was laughable because I am anything but domestic. In spite of my optimistic, outgoing personality, the normal depression that attacks anyone experiencing adaptation to a new culture and a secluded environment, was hitting me full force. I began to feel as if I were drowning. Something had to change. Something had to lift me over the natural culture shock curve. Work was the only answer. After all,

I had spent seven years at the university. I had to get a job and find work to occupy my time as well as my mind.

Having decided my new path, my spirits were high. With my Masters degree in hand, I began to actively seek employment. Unfortunately, classified ads were unavailable. Most employment for company wives was achieved through word of mouth, under cover so to speak. English language tutoring, the U.S. Military Base Exchange, or a compound job were my choices, and I immediately ruled out a Base Exchange position. At only 115 pounds, I work better with my mind rather than my brawn. Lifting boxes and loading trucks for the Base Exchange did not seem a viable option. I made call after call and sent out resume after resume, all to no avail. It became apparent that my new endeavor would take more effort than I had anticipated. Legally dependent expatriate women are not allowed to work in the Kingdom without their own *igama,* their own sponsor and company support. Hence, publicly advertising myself was out of the question, particularly since wives on their husband's *igama* really were not supposed to work. My spirits quickly began to drop. Nightly, David assured me that something would come through, that I would find the perfect job, the perfect place for me to spend my days in this foreign place.

"Just keep looking and be patient," he would say. Patience — a virtue with a whole new meaning in the desert, something that I would come to understand in time.

ॐ Chapter Six ॐ
The Move

I believe that when God closes a door, He opens a window. Finally, my window opened and my depression lifted. It was March 5, 1992, and the promised moving day arrived. The community was filled with excitement. Trucks, vans, any vehicle people could find to move their belongings were coming from different directions, different temporary quarters, laden with personal items for each new home. The villas on our new compound, DM 18, as advertised on the rumor mill were large, about 3,000 square feet and exquisite. David and I were so happy to have room, so happy to have space, so happy to be able to whisper and not have the other one hear. The motel had been so small and confining that one of us could not shower while the other brushed his or her teeth. Finally, we had space. Finally, we could actually whisper without hearing each other.

The compound was breathtakingly beautiful with palm trees, manicured landscaping and ground lighting. Yet, the compound was for our enjoyment only, surrounded by a fifteen-foot wall (for privacy, we were told) and equipped with only one manned gate for entry. No one entered or departed without receiving clearance from the gate guards first. In the beginning, I believed what I was told that the wall was for our privacy, allowing us to dress in our traditional American clothing of shorts, swimsuits and short-sleeve shirts. But as the years passed, the wall served a more substantial purpose and the gates became equipped with machine guns as well as military men.

The villas provided to Americans working for large companies in Kingdom were not only exquisite, but they were equipped with everything a family would need: designer furniture, televisions, wire whisks and everything in between. Expats know these as F&E items (Furniture & Equipment), all provided to each villa, assigned to the employee upon occupancy and rechecked on departure. The items you add are solely for your individual decorating style.

We often laughed and said that if the people back home could see our villas ... our compound and the *Med One* life we led in the desert, the company might revoke the hardship pay that was added to our husbands' salaries each week, approximately thirty percent of your base salary, completely tax-free. Not only were our villas fantastic, our new compound was great. It had bowling facilities, a theater for dances and plays, a little grocery store, a library, a weight room, racquetball courts, saunas, tennis courts, swimming pools, a dining hall that resembled a five-star restaurant, and a snack bar overlooking the pool.

Moving day kept me busy, and I remained busy for the several weeks that followed. I was on a natural high settling us into our new home. In less than four short months in the Kingdom, I was already becoming extremely spoiled. By simply calling an extension on the compound, I could have pictures hung, light bulbs changed, or any service I could think of. A man, of course, from another country performed all these tasks — an expatriate, like myself, only from simpler beginnings.

These Third World Country Nationals, TCNs as they were known, worked on the compound to serve us, to do the jobs that were deemed unfit for or beneath the Americans. Personally, I felt pity for these men. They worked extremely long hours, six days a week, and were not allowed to return to their home countries for at least two years, if then. Typically, when men from countries other than the West worked in the Kingdom, they signed a two-year contract that did not allow travel from the country during their employment. Unfortunately, many Saudi employers would take advantage of this situation and force the men to stay longer than the agreed two years until they provided them with transportation funds to leave. They lived in camp housing provided for them that commonly housed six men in a six by eight foot space. They worked hard and were proud, always showing a smile no matter what anyone asked them to do. It was always, "Yes, Madame" or "no problem, Madame," with their eyes usually lowered and their head bobbing in agreement as they spoke.

During the first week of our move, something comical happened. To this day, I still do not understand it, and I am almost embarrassed to share it. As with any new structure, there were problems, things that needed to be repaired. Our villa had a small leak from the bath on the second floor into the wall socket in the kitchen below. To handle the problem, I naturally called the maintenance extension and requested assistance. Within twenty minutes — it never took them long to respond — a little man from India, the compound electrician, arrived on his old bicycle and knocked on my door. I refer to him as a "little man" because none of them are large in stature and definitely not overweight, although they are very large in character and pride.

Communicating the problem was a touch difficult as I still was not used to speaking with people from India, and he had the same problem with English. However, through a lot of acting, head nodding and pointing, I finally conveyed the problem to him. Looking up and down the wall at the leak, agreeing the entire time, he finally smiled and responded *"Insha Allah,"* and off he went with a smile as I returned to the kitchen to continue sorting our new F&E items. He went up the stairs and came back down numerous times, working diligently to complete the task. On one of his visits to the kitchen light switch, it so happened that I turned and knocked a glass plate from the counter that crashed onto the floor, striking my toe as it fell. Naturally, I screamed. The little man came running to the rescue, speaking to me rapidly in one of the many Indian languages. Trying to assure him in English that I was okay, in spite of the blood running down my foot, he persisted. He fell to his knees, grabbed my foot and began to suck my toe! I continued to back away and pull my foot from his grasp, while trying feebly to assure him again and again that I was okay. *"Tieeb,"* I repeated, *"tieeb,"* as I hopped to find a paper towel on the counter. Yet, he persisted and persisted. Within a minute, the bleeding had stopped. The gentleman stood and smiled. "Good now, Madame," he uttered, grinning with pride that he had made everything okay. I guess he had performed some sort of Indian first aid!

As the days passed, I stayed busy. Making flower arrangements, adding decorative painting touches to the white walls, and other decorating projects kept me going. However, it was not long until I decided that we needed to add a traditional flair to our décor. We needed some Saudi accessories to tie it all together, so we decided to travel to *Hofuf* to do some shopping with the locals.

Hofuf is located in the *Al Hasa* oasis, which is the largest oasis in the world and is about an hour and a half drive from *Al-Khobar* where our compound was located. Hence, it is not nearly as Westernized or modernized as *Al-Khobar.* No signs in English were posted, and very few people spoke our language. Truly, it would be a trip into the real Saudi Arabia. Excitement rose and plans were made with friends. In the Kingdom, as their ways are different and the drive across the desert somewhat barren, it was always best to travel with others when leaving the sanctuary of our little village. In that the work week in Saudi Arabia runs from Saturday to Wednesday because of the Muslim Holy day, Friday, we decided to go the following Thursday, the traditional shopping day with husbands. Thursday was always the much-anticipated shopping day, as I could go with David rather than using the compound shopping bus. A sense of freedom always encompassed me when I shopped with him.

Thursday came and, thankfully, it was another pretty day in the desert. With snacks and beverages loaded into our company-provided Suburban, fondly known as the *"Bedouin Cadillac"* (most Saudis drive them due to large families and desert sand), we were off on a real adventure. Never having been out of the *Al-Khobar* area, this trip promised to be exciting and full of new sights. I was not disappointed. The plan was to visit *Hofuf's* Thursday morning market, known as *Souk Al Khamis,* a traditional place for the locals to sell their wares. Additionally, we would explore the covered market on *Share'a Al Khabbaz* Street, see the old Turkish fort located there, visit the local camel market, and travel to see the wind-carved caves outside the city during the noon prayer.

As a result of the *Bedouin,* nomadic history of the Saudi culture, each city has a Thursday morning market in the town center, as they have done for hundreds of years. Clad in our *abayas* and our headscarfs in our handbags, we meandered through the little pathways of the *Hofuf* open market. My nose came alive with the smell of various incenses that filled the air, my ears perked to the chatter, close and distant, of the Arab tongue. With every turn through the market we found interesting trinkets, traditional carpets, camel saddles, camel bags, antique wood doors, and baskets, baskets and more baskets. The locals seemed uninterested in the antique items and more interested in the latest products brought from the west, from other cultures and environments. However, we were drawn to the antique veils laden with coins and detailed embroidery, to the antique pots that could tell a tale if only they could talk. I was mesmerized by the traditional and the unique.

Laden with our new treasures, bought for almost nothing in American money, we headed down the street toward the Suburban to store them. On the way, something of interest caught David's eye, and he wandered across the small street with a friend while my girlfriend and I continued strolling along the street. Shortly, a very clean-cut gentleman dressed in thobe and guthra stopped us. He spoke to us in exceptional English, obviously having been very well schooled, and asked if we had made any purchases. Excited to share my treasures, I began opening my bags to reveal each purchase. Cordially complimenting each and every one, as is the Arab way, he soon asked if I had purchased any gold.

Still excited, yet somewhat curious by now as to his query, I replied, "Oh, yes, some earrings."

"May I see them?" he asked.

"Of course," I replied. Piling all of my other packages at my feet, I dug out the small plastic box from the gold *souk* bag that is always used to hold a gold purchase. I opened the box to reveal the contents.

"May I hold them?" he asked. Curious, I agreed. We stood there and watched as the gentleman "weighed" the earrings with his hand, looking at them intently. There was a long pause.

"May I asked what you gave for them, Madame?" he questioned.

"150 SR (about $40)," I answered, still curious as to why he was getting so personal with my purchase. There was another long pause.

"Very nice purchase, Madame," he said as he handed my earrings back to me and bid us good day.

Later, I learned that he was the local gold inspector. Since gold is sold by weight in the Kingdom and the prices fluctuate daily with the world's market price of gold, each gold *souk* shopping area has a gold inspector. It is his duty to watch and regulate gold sales and to make sure that all are receiving a fair market price. If you feel you did not receive a fair price, that you were cheated in some way or that your item was misrepresented, you can see the local gold inspector and he will take care of the problem.

Since Saudi Arabia is owned by a family — the House of Saud — they are extremely proud of their family lineage and forefathers. Their respect of the people who came before is evident in their names. A Saudi's name is their given name followed by their father's name and his father's name and so on, ending with the name of their house or tribe. For example, a common name could be Nora *bint* Abdullah *bin* Mohammed *Al-*Naif, meaning Nora "daughter of" Abdullah "son of" Mohammed "from the house of" Naif. However, it is very peculiar to me that a society such as this that prides itself on its family lineage would be so haphazard with and disinterested in its historical sites.

In the center of *Hofuf* sits an old Turkish fort. There are no markings, no apparent upkeep, and no lines to enter the site. It just sits, looming over the village with villagers passing as if it did not even exist, eroding with wind and rain. Now we Westerners found the fort intriguing, but we were unable to enter and investigate, as the government forbids entry, a fact we never understood. When was the fort built? Who lived there and why? What were the lives like of the people who inhabited it? So many questions with the answers forever lost.

"Allah Aakabar, Allah Aakabar, Allah Aakabar," the noon prayer call began, a majestic sound ringing from every direction. The clamor of closing doors, merchants packing their wares until next week, and people bustling soon rang in tune. Closing time came much too soon for my adventuring pleasure. As the remaining shops continued to close and the mass of men in white *thobes* meandered toward the nearest mosque (which was not too far as there is one on practically every corner in every city in the Kingdom), we piled into the Suburban and headed toward the desert, specifically the camel market where the "ships of the desert" are bought and sold.

After wandering around for almost an hour, unable to read the Arabic signs for the camel market, we concluded that the best idea would be to follow one of the numerous little white Toyota pick-up trucks with a live camel or sheep as its cargo. The plan would work as long as the driver was going to sell, rather than driving home with his recent purchase! Sure enough, the plan worked, and we found the market spread across the sand, stretching for miles. Little shacks and lean-tos scattered with fence after fence, marking territory. Each owner had his own area with a fence for the camels and a shack for the laborer who lived there and tended the stock. As a highlight to our tourist experience, the TCNs were more than happy to let us ride a camel for a fee of 10SR ($2.67), smiling the entire time as we cumbersomely mounted and rode these enormous beasts.

The air was filled with stench and swarming flies. The most disheartening sight was to watch as the purchased camels were hoisted by crane into little white Toyota pick-ups for transport to their new destination, perhaps someone's dinner table. These large animals were shackled, bellowing as they were put into the beds of the trucks. In the distance, you could hear the baby camels' cries as they were separated from their mothers. Other camels, still in their pens, were shackled on the front ankles with either metal shackles or rope, unable to hobble more than a foot or so at a time. It upset me to know that these animals, once the lifeline for travel in this barren land for these nomadic people, were now treated in such a seemingly inhumane way. Their big brown eyes with long layers of lashes seemed to speak. As we were leaving, a dead camel lay by the dirt road covered with flies, obviously having been there for a while. I felt sick. Silence fell over the Suburban as we passed the carcass. I never returned to the camel market again.

After a flurry of conversation about what we had just experienced, we wound around the village toward the infamous caves, another long lost place with no significant historical remembrance, upkeep or value except to Western tourists. These magnificent caves, reportedly made by the wind, are housed within enormous escarpments that surround *Hofhuf.* They stand tall around the oasis as if guarding this hidden paradise in the desert. After wandering past numerous date farms, we located the entrance to these famous caves.

We clamored from the Suburban with our picnic lunch in hand and began our climbing adventure. We climbed the side of the escarpment, approximately 200 feet in the air. The climb was treacherous, particularly in a calf-length dress covered with the full length black *abaya.* Every step had to be taken with care, as a person could fall down, perhaps one hundred and fifty feet or more, through the cracks that had formed over time. Once on top, we sat in awe as we overlooked a sea of palm trees nourished by the precious oasis water. The view from the top of the caves is one that is burnt into my memory. With the warm breeze on our faces, we could see for miles in every direction. Toward *Hofuf,* we saw nothing but green and more green. The tops of the trees lay at our feet like a carpet. In the other direction, we saw nothing but the deep reds and browns of the desert sand, with the sun creating familiar mirages on the horizon. It was breathtaking.

After hours of climbing over and crawling through these wonderful works of nature, it was time to head back to *Al-Khobar.* Because of the rather barren trip across the desert, it was not a good idea to travel after dark. Before leaving the caves, I was drawn to a little, old man, a *Shabah,* standing off to the side of the sand parking area, surrounded by hand-made pots, each one irregularly shaped and unique. I could not resist. I approached *Shabah* with obvious interest, and it seemed as if he was looking through me. His face was worn with time, wrinkled, brown and dry, and his eyes were deep and penetrating. He was a short man with dusty feet and a wrinkled *thobe.* In my feeble attempt to speak Arabic, I began bargaining for a pot. After much to-do and a lot of hand motions and facial expressions, our bargaining came to a momentary impasse. I wanted to pay 15 SR ($4), but he wanted 20 SR ($5.33). We continued to barter as David approached the event. *Shabah* slowly sized David up and then looked back to me. He was firm, 20 SR for the pot, no more, no less. Although I wanted to get my price, I wanted the pot more and agreed to 20 SR. David reached into his pocket and gave the man a 20 SR note. The old man fumbled with his roll of bills, paused, and then turned to me and handed me a 5 SR note, the difference between our prices. Again, another long, soul-touching stare, and he said *"Shukran* Teresa" as he smiled. I was stunned that he knew my name.

The encounter with *Shabah* was touching to me and revealed so much as well. *Shabah* was willing to take from David, a man, but willing to give the difference to me, a woman. The event was the highlight of conversation for the ride home. All the while, I wondered how he knew my name. Little did I know that he had read my gold Arabic name necklace. From his appearance, I would have never guessed he could read. Exhaustion from the heat and exercise at the caves overcame us all, and we slept as David took us across the desert in the rocking Suburban to home. We marked this outing as our first big adventure in this foreign, distant land.

ॐ Chapter Seven ॐ
The Interview

The excitement of Thursday soon passed. It was Saturday morning and David was back off to the airbase. Although it was another pretty day outside, I felt alone again. The newness of the villa had expired and the same feelings felt before in the cave pervaded my spirits. Real depression had returned. Even though it is not in my nature, I had almost given up on the idea of working, and I had no idea how many more pretty days I could endure meandering through the huge, empty villa in solitude. Then, the phone rang. It was David.

"Would you be interested in tutoring the children in one Saudi family?" he questioned before even saying hello. I heard his voice, heard his words, but could not believe it. I was so excited I almost dropped the receiver.

"Of course," I exclaimed with mixed excitement and reluctance. Details, details, I needed details. A flutter of questions flowed from my mouth. "How many children? What levels? How often? What is the pay?" David could not get a word in edgewise. Then I took a breath and allowed him to finish.

"Dick, the company's Personal Support Services

supervisor, just asked me if you would be interested in tutoring the children of a Saudi family in English. If you are, he'll set up the interview." I could not answer yes fast enough.

When he came home from work that afternoon, he told me the interview was set for Sunday, the next day, in the evening. He said that Dick would pick me up around 7 p.m. and drive me there and introduce me.

"Who is the family?" I asked, as if I actually knew any Saudis anyway.

David replied, "I don't know. Dick wouldn't say. He seemed fairly cloak and dagger about the whole thing." In a way, it all seemed rather sneaky and suspicious. However, that is something I now know as "normal" because everything in the Kingdom is either behind a wall or secretive in some way. Privacy is of the utmost importance in the Saudi culture.

It was April 5, 1992. Dressed in my best suit, as I would be for an interview in America, I waited for Dick to collect me for the interview. The entire day had been spent on the phone with my mom stateside trying to decide what I should wear to interview with a Saudi family. We debated and finally decided that a business suit would be the best approach. I had no idea that I was about to meet a princess and interview with a Royal Saudi family.

When we arrived at the gate of the palace, I still had no knowledge regarding whom I was about to meet. The gatekeeper opened the gate, and we entered a private, elegant brick driveway surrounded by a sanctuary of beautiful shrubs and flowers, brick walks, and a beautiful home hidden from the outside world by its towering walls. A Filipino woman opened the enormous wooden doors and asked us to wait. As I looked around, I was amazed. The floor was covered with expensive hand-made Persian carpets, larger than my entire downstairs. I later learned that one of the hand-made Persian carpets on the floor was a gift to Madawi's father from the Shah of Iran and estimated at about $650,000. A full-size, hand-carved mahogany eagle statue, surrounded by a garden of indoor plants, guarded the entrance to the enormous room. Sofas lined the walls, as is the Saudi way, with large gold-tipped coffee tables placed comfortably in front of the sofas. The wall opposite the entrance was all glass, with long closed draperies. Later, I learned that it covered an indoor rock waterfall and atrium.

"You may go in now," the Filipino woman's voice broke my trance, and we followed her down a marble hall.

We entered a salon and there sat a man, obviously the father, and his wife. They cordially rose to greet us.

"Colonel Awad," Dick said, "this is Teresa McCown."

The Colonel shook my hand and we exchanged cordial greetings. His English was impeccable. Dressed in traditional *thobe* and *guthra,* he looked dashing. His dark eyes, rounded face and masculine, military posture permitted him command of the room. Yet his gestures and comments made me feel immediately comfortable. The woman then stepped forward, dressed casually in blue jeans and a long tunic top. So graceful and so personable, she extended her hand

"I'm Madawi," she said, as a warm, elegant smile broke across her face.

Her English was also impeccable, and her smile was both alluring and welcoming. Madawi was a tall, slender woman with large black eyes that twinkled when she smiled. Her hair was jet black and silky and swung fluently when she walked. She was elegant that evening even in blue jeans, and in any other country in the world she could have been a model. Even though I had heard David mention Colonel Awad's name (he also worked at the airbase), I had no idea at the time that I was meeting royalty, meeting the daughter of a King! She seemed so natural, so down to earth, and so real. She was not at all pretentious as I had imagined royalty might be. She seemed genuine.

Then, even in a room of mixed company, we separated. Dick sat on the sofa to the right of the Colonel, and they began to talk. I sat on the left sofa by Madawi's recliner, and we began the interview. At first, things were a little formal. She explained to me that she wanted someone to tutor her five children in English. She was looking for someone part-time, perhaps 20 hours per week, to meet with the children after school Saturday through Wednesday.

I gave her the resume I had brought, and she reviewed it silently for several minutes. Then Fahad entered the salon, the oldest child (and only son) who was named for Madawi's father. He sat down beside me, dressed in his *thobe,* but with no headdress. He was such a handsome young man of 14 years. He was quiet, yet I could tell that he was dying to ask me many questions. His big dark eyes seemed to penetrate to my soul. Madawi introduced him and told me how well he had been doing in school. Fahad blushed a little. He then proceeded to ask me a few general questions, acting far older than his years, and then he excused himself. Before leaving, he and his mother exchanged words in Arabic. I sat quietly and waited.

After Fahad came Nora, the oldest daughter of 12 years. She had her hair tied back and seemed somewhat shy, at that awkward age all preteens experience. Tall and slender, like her mother, she glided across the floor. We, too, exchanged a few questions before she rose to leave. Again, the exchange of Arabic between mother and child followed. It then became obvious that the whole gang was interviewing me one after another, from oldest to youngest.

Fatma came next. The stocky little ten-year-old won my heart from the very first moment our eyes met. She was fiery, full of imagination, energy and spice. Her build was more like her father's, and she walked more like a tomboy than did Nora. Her hair swung, silky and black, fluttering in front of her huge black eyes so like her mom's. Her smile was just as genuine, yet mischievous. She bounced into the room and looked at me as if she were sizing me up. Later, I learned she was. It was because of Fatma that I was the fifth English tutor in half as many years!

Maha, a precious, chubby five-year-old, followed. Her toothless grin made me smile with its sincerity. With big black eyes and wavy black hair like Nora's, Maha scooted up close to me on the sofa. As her mother introduced me, she looked up with the most longing look, and after a few minutes asked me, "Are you going to teach me English?"

I answered, "Maybe. Will you study very hard?"

She responded in the cutest way, "Verrrry hard!" she exclaimed, as her eyes glowed when she rolled her r's as she enunciated in spite of her missing front teeth.

Bandari, a three-year-old and the youngest at the time, followed her brother and three sisters, looking as if she were a smaller version of Nora. Her English was obviously not as good as her older siblings; however, she attempted to communicate all sorts of things to me, but I understood very little. She was adorable, and soon she won my heart as well.

After the entourage of interviews, Madawi and I were left alone. We began talking about our opinions on various topics, our general likes and dislikes, with one starting where the other left off. Periodically, a Filipino woman would appear with hot tea (the Arab favorite) or an iced fruit beverage. Then came snacks and more snacks, tea and more tea, as the conversation continued. Before I knew it, I discovered that we had been talking for over four hours! Dick had long since left without our notice, and our flurry of conversation was relentless. Around 11 p.m., Madawi noticed the time and mentioned that she had to get ready for an engagement that evening. The Saudis, being a desert people, are nocturnal by nature, and most of their parties and get-togethers occur late at night rather than in the heat of the day. Frequently, they will entertain until the wee hours of the morning.

This was a way of life to which I would soon become accustomed.

I correctly assumed that the Arabic conversations preceding each child's departure earlier in the evening indicated that I had been approved for the position. Turning back to business, we negotiated a salary and she called for a driver to take me home with the understanding that he would return for me the following day at 2 p.m. to begin my new post.

As the car swayed through the black of the night toward my compound, I reflected over the evening, still unaware of Madawi's noble position. A warm feeling pervaded my thoughts as I remembered our conversation. It was as if we were united, connected in some way. We seemed to share the same opinions on everything we discussed. I smiled, feeling blessed because I knew then that I found the friend that I so desperately needed to survive in this land. It was a delightful evening that I will always cherish.

ॐ Chapter Eight ॐ
The Tutor

All day as I cleaned the house, I continued to say Madawi's name over and over. With my Southern tongue, the name Madawi was difficult for me at first, and I did not want to show up at the palace and start off my new adventure by mispronouncing her name. Time passed as I cleaned and got ready to go. Excitement overwhelmed me. I called David more than usual that day just to touch reality and make sure all of this was really happening. During one of our conversations, David passed along a story with me that Dick had shared with him.

Before Dick worked at the airbase for the Royal Saudi Air Force (RSAF), he had been the private security lead man for a powerful prince. Somewhere along the way, the relationship went bad and Dick was removed from the prestigious life of traveling the world with a Saudi prince and was reassigned to an office cubicle on the base where he handled mundane housing assignments for American workers on behalf of the RSAF. The details of the story are foggy, but I vividly remember David saying that Dick cautioned me to "watch my step with the princess as things can end as quickly as they start when it comes to the Royal family. One minute you can be in their favor, their golden child, and the next, you can be out of the country bearing an exit-only visa," which means that you cannot return. I took this advice with a grain of salt. Nine years later, however, his words of warning would unfortunately become my experience.

Two o'clock came and went. I sat anxiously at my kitchen bar. Had I misunderstood Madawi? Did I really get the job, or was I supposed to start another day? Did the driver remember where I lived? I calmed myself and waited. Around 2:45 p.m., the doorbell rang. I opened it to see a very black man, dressed in *thobe* and *guthra*. He was stocky with the kindest eyes, Kenyan by birth. I would have never guessed that this man would turn out to be one of my most treasured and truest friends in the years to come.

In broken English, Saleem said, "Mrs. Teresa, please come. Princess waits you." He opened the back door of a new model Buick for me to enter, and off we went to the palace, slowly through the compound and out the gates as the guards snapped to attention with our passing. Conversation was absent for lack of ability to speak the other's language. However, this fact was overshadowed by Arabic music playing loudly on the radio. As I looked out of the window over the sand speckled with weeds, mosques lined the horizon and the car rocked with speed and lane changes. I thought to myself, "Is this real ... am I really going to work for a *princess?*"

We arrived at the familiar gates from the night before; Saleem honked the horn, and we entered the huge wooden gates. Met at the door by yet another Filipino woman, I followed her to the door of the salon in which I had met the family the night before. The salon was the most private family room in the palace. Beautifully yet comfortably decorated, the room felt cozy and personal. On the large wall behind his and her leather recliners were large portraits of Arab men, a pictorial family lineage hung with reverence. The oldest patriarch, Abdulaziz, hung higher that the rest. This was that special, intimate room found in each home where the family gathers to talk, watch TV and share life together. When we reached the salon entrance, I went bouncing in to where Madawi sat. I did not take notice that the Filipino woman did not enter. I plopped onto the sofa beside Madawi as she nibbled her lunch, which was on a silver tray and small table beside her. Because a half an hour remained before the children would arrive from school and Bandari, the toddler, was still napping, we continued our conversation from the night before. Already feeling quite at home and comfortable with the princess, I even reached over and helped myself to some of her lunch. Her look welcomed the gesture, and we continued to talk and laugh.

When the children arrived, I left Madawi in the salon and went upstairs with the girls to the girls' quarters. Each child was excited to show me her room and their communal salon where they would watch television, play games and hang out. The room was sparsely decorated with a Western-style sofa, two end tables, a table with four chairs for studying, and an entertainment cabinet. The salon, centrally located between

Bandari and Maha's bedrooms, was light and airy with lots of room for play. Unlike Americans, Saudis do not adorn their surroundings by hanging many pictures and displaying knickknacks around the room. The necessities were there, perhaps even the extravagant in terms of electronics, but there were not many items displayed in the way of decorative touches, as Americans know them. Each daughter's bedroom was somewhat more decorated, but again, not in the manner of a Westerner. Beautiful bed linens and necessary furniture adorned each room with its adjoining bath.

After the grand tour, the girls pulled me with excitement into their little kitchen to join them in their after-school lunch, a pattern that continued for the next two years. The daily lunch included delicious Arab dishes and at least three Filipino servants to serve it! The days spent in this little kitchen sparked my love of Arab food, as the girls would always take the time to tell me the names of the dishes, the ingredients, and other interesting facts they could think of that related to a particular food. During this special time each day, I believe they learned more English than they did during their individual study times. It was during this time that we learned each other's likes and dislikes, shared dreams and became like family to each other. They would share with me events that had happened in school during the day, both the good and the bad. Over time, they got to where they would ask my advice about friends, relationships and other aspects of their lives. Conversely, they also began to inquire about the details of my life. The 30 minutes at the little kitchen table after school each day soon became very special to me, and I always looked forward to it with great anticipation.

After stuffing ourselves with Arabian delights, I would start with Bandari, the youngest at that time. We began with alphabet flash cards and moved on to simple worksheets. We sang English songs and learned English rhymes. Before long, her English had improved tremendously. She loved to study with "Mrs. Teresa" and always yearned for more. After a year with me, Madawi actually pulled me aside and asked that I slow down with Bandari's English lessons as she was becoming better in English than in her native Arabic language.

After Bandari, I would study with Maha. At first she loved to study, but as time passed, her desire to study English dwindled to only completing the required work from school. Any additional traditional study attempt was an enormous effort for both of us, but we managed.

Fatma followed, and as I suspected the night before, she truly turned out to be my greatest challenge. She had driven the other tutors away, and if I were to stay, it would be Fatma that I would have to win over. Self-determined and somewhat defiant at first, Fatma hated to study but did so under duress from her mother.

In the beginning, she would say to me as we studied, " I hate you, Mrs. Teresa," and then follow it with choice words in Arabic.

I would always calmly respond by saying, "No, you don't hate me, you hate studying English, but we have to do it anyway." I would then always pause, give her my tilted brow look and say, "By the way, the Arabic doesn't bother me because I don't know what you're saying!"

At this, she would just dart those big black eyes at me, sigh loudly, and we would continue the lesson. Fatma hated traditional school and seemed to prefer a more Montessori approach to learning. As I got to know her, I learned that it was her immense creativity and imagination that made her hate the traditional style of studying. Realizing this, I used alternative methods to reach Fatma. We would swing on the playset as we practiced her spelling words, or splash in the indoor waterfall of their atrium. We would play various games incorporating her English studies as we played. And when all else failed, I would bribe completion with the promise of a fun day at my house on the compound, with no studying! Little did she realize how much English she practiced as we read English recipes and baked delicious cookies. Covered in flour and the kitchen a mess, we had a ball. Once I understood her and she me, we got along beautifully and our friendship deepened as the years passed.

Nora, like Bandari, was easy to teach. She was such a responsible, focused young lady of twelve. Nora was the picture-perfect princess child. She was always ready to show me her required work, always ready to learn more. From the first day we studied, she told me she wanted to continue with school, go to the university and then run her father's company one day. Upon graduation, she, in fact, did go to the university, and she did excel as she said she would.

After studying with the girls, I would return to the downstairs children's salon to study with Fahad. Essentially a mirror image of the upstairs girls' salon and decorated comparably, this salon was for all to share, even Fahad, and was also equipped with a small kitchen. From this common area, you could access Nora's and Fatma's rooms, each with their own baths like the bedrooms upstairs.

After the tour of the older daughters' rooms, each showing me a little something that represented their favorite Western star or singer, I settled back to the little table to study with Fahad. Fahad was such a smart young man, but he was aware of his intelligence and did not always seem receptive to my instruction. In spite of this, he seemed to enjoy studying and would never reveal that I had taught him something new. A normal response, I suppose, for a royal teenage boy still trying to find his way, particularly one raised in a society dominated by males.

During the first year, our time together was very special until Fahad felt he no longer needed to be taught by a woman. It was during this special year that he shared with me many of his likes and dislikes, his dreams and wants. Being a young man of fourteen, he naturally loved cars and told me how one day he would buy his own red Ferrari. He revealed his love of music and art and his fear that his father would not want him to be anything but a military man. Daily, between our English studies, he would discuss the latest music star, song or Hollywood movie. He knew all the stars, all the new releases. He would even have the latest videos shipped in to him, a privilege we Westerners did not have, and he would let me borrow movies on the weekend. He had so much pride in his family, his country and his customs, as he should, and he shared these with me with amazing excitement and vigor.

On my second day of work, everything proceeded as the day before and for the two years that followed. Saleem, the driver, arrived to collect me and transported me to the palace. I continued to visit and nibble some lunch with Madawi, and we would share ideas, feelings and thoughts before the children arrived.

Only a few days into my time with the family, I began to notice that the Filipino women would always stop at the doorway to the salon. I also noticed how the various Filipino women would address Madawi as *Amity* and the Colonel as *Amir* every time they wished to enter the room. As a result of these observations, I awoke with a start from a deep sleep on the fourth night of my employment, as if I just realized these subtle things occurring around me. I was flooded by panic, believing that I had done something that was incorrect, something out of step. Worried, I did not sleep a wink the rest of the night and decided to confront the issue the very next day during my afternoon chitchat time with Madawi.

For the entire ride, as Saleem swerved between lanes and the Arabic music played, I rehearsed in my mind what I would say to Madawi about what I had observed. This day, I entered the salon differently, asking to come in. She seemed curious about my behavior change but said nothing. After idle conversation, I mustered the nerve to inquire.

"Madawi," I asked with hesitation because I did not want to be offensive, "what should I call you?"

With an even more curious look she paused and responded, "Madawi." "And ..." I wavered, "... what should I call the Colonel?"

With her look even more puzzled, she paused longer and responded, "Colonel."

With an internal sigh of relief, I shared with her my observations and my fear of having done something to offend. She explained that what I had observed with the Filipino women, essentially servants, "did not apply to me." I countered that I wanted to make sure that I had not offended anyone, as I was not accustomed to interacting with royalty. After all, we do not have a royal family in the United States. I explained that the closest thing we have is a President, and if we do not like him, we impeach him! She chuckled and reemphasized that it "did not apply to me." She then assured me that she hired me for who I was, not what anyone would change me to be. It was then that I understood the strict societal hierarchy that exists in the Kingdom. There are the Royals on the one hand and the *TCNs,* such as Filipinos, Sri Lankans, and Bangladeshi on the other, and never the twain shall meet. I was the fortunate one. The American expat who could float between the two classes with ease and be accepted by both. Whether I was in the salon with Madawi and the Colonel or in one of the little kitchens with the Filipino nannies, I was "Mrs. Teresa." And that was okay.

My special time in the afternoon with Madawi continued as the years passed. Some days we would just sit and watch the news, and other days we would talk insatiably. There were even days when we would sit on the floor of the salon and thumb through Western clothing catalogs and magazines like *Cosmopolitan* or *Mademoiselle,* showing each other what we liked and what we did not, critiquing each other's taste as to whether the outfits we saw would really look good or not on each other.

"You know, Mrs. Teresa," she started one day in the middle of our catalog shopping, "you are different." She continued with hesitation as if trying to decide how to express her feelings.

"With you, I can be me. You don't want anything from me." Then she paused, "You just want to be my friend."

It was at that moment that it truly hit me the responsibility she had as a princess. It was not an official job, but it was work. In her society, most times when women would come to her, they would have a hidden agenda, always desiring something from the princess. With me, it was different. And it was in this way that I began my life with a royal family, my life with a princess as my friend.

ॐ *PART TWO* ॐ

ॐ Chapter Nine ॐ
Peyton Place

From the moment I stepped onto the Boeing 747 bound for Saudi Arabia, I knew that I would face new challenges and adventures in my new home. Culture shock, a normal event when you move to another country, was expected. I knew it would be a challenge to adapt to living so far from the place of my birth. I faced these challenges head on and mastered them in stride and in time. It was the unexpected challenge of learning to live in a confined community of fellow countrymen which threw me for a loop. I had no idea that I had stepped into a modern day *Peyton Place* community.

When I first arrived, I was talked about by the existing compound ladies simply because I was new and younger than most. The fact that David was the youngest manager with the company, a "white shirt" who worked directly for Colonel (Prince) Awad (Madawi's husband) made us frequent topics of conversation as well. Out of the 400-plus employees with the company in the Eastern Province, only about 15 were "white shirts," the employees who worked directly with the Royal Saudi Air Force commanders. The remaining employees were referred to as "green shirts," men who physically worked on the jets. David's private office, his direct influence with the Saudi commanders, being on a first-name basis with most colonels and generals, and a company-provided Suburban to boot, made us irresistible lunchtime chit-chat material. This flurry of gossip soon diminished as new wives and new topics of conversation entered our community, but it was a short reprieve.

Shortly after I started working for the princess, the gossip started to race again, a fact that I was startled to learn. One day, deciding that I needed to get out and enjoy another pretty day, I headed for the luxurious dining facility provided for us on the compound to enjoy an early lunch before the driver, Saleem, came for me. It was always good to nibble before I went to the palace, just in case I did not care for the Arab cuisine of the day.

Music played in the background, Italian tile flooring was configured in a black and white geometric design, and long white curtains hung from floor to ceiling on windows that looked out over the finely manicured landscaping, which enhanced our restaurant's aesthetic appeal. The dining hall, as we called it, complete with white tablecloths and upholstered chairs, was an exquisite dining experience even for lunch. After a few smiles and hellos, I made my way through the crowd and found a table off to the side and ordered.

As I sat, the waiters, all men from third-world countries dressed in black pants and white shirts, attended to my every need. I sure was roughin' it in the desert! It was so easy to become accustomed to five-star service all the time. Breakfast, lunch, or dinner, it did not matter. The compound restaurant was great and extremely affordable. A shrimp cocktail and soda cost me only 15 SR ($4), and a huge taco salad, enough for two people, and soda only 10 SR ($2.67). I could not prepare it myself for that price, and I surely could not enjoy it with this kind of service at home. Quickly, in every respect, I, as well as every other Westerner on the compound, became spoiled — spoiled rotten.

Shortly after I ordered, I saw my neighbor, Gay, come in and head my way, stepping more quickly than usual, smiling as if she were about to burst. Gay, a delightful friend and neighbor for five years, stayed a true friend the entire time, which was a rare find in this distant community. When others were my friend one day and my executioner the next, Gay held steady, always ready to share her feelings with me whether I liked them or not. She always understood that I knew her feelings were sincere.

Settling onto the chair beside me, she leaned close to fill me in on the latest scoop — me! It had happened in spite of my efforts to keep my employment secret. Understanding that the Saudi people revere their privacy, I had only told a few close friends about my new position. Honestly, I think that the villa walls had to be bugged. Over the years, there were numerous times David and I spoke in confidence in our own villa, pillow talk so to speak, only to go to the recreation center or dining hall a few days later to hear a misconstrued version of our private conversation. Basically, if you were constipated, the compound knew it. No secrets here.

I was the latest topic on the rumor mill. Gay told me that I was the hottest topic on the compound bus and around the pool since the move to the new compound. Everyone was buzzing with the fact that I was working for the princess. Obviously not wanting me to achieve anything that they could not attain, the whale club, the group of overweight ladies who lounged by the pool the night I arrived in Kingdom, came into play again by telling everyone that I was working for the princess as a nanny! Gay said she could not believe it when that woman actually had the nerve to announce this misrepresentation in front of seven eager-eared, loose-lipped women. Robert, Gay's husband and also a dear friend to this day, did not appreciate the whale club and their tactics in the first place, and he could not hold his tongue when that comment came out.

"Nanny?" he began, "where in the world did you get that idea?" He continued before the loose-lipped ringleader could retaliate, "Since when does a person with a Master's degree wipe noses and change diapers?" Breathless, he continued, "The fact is that she has been hired by the princess as the family's English language tutor."

"Nanny?" I clarified with Gay, "they said I was a nanny?" I truly could not believe my ears. Now this is not to say that I have anything against, or lack respect for, any individual who is a nanny. I respect what they do, and I am not really sure that I would have the energy to do it myself. However, in the Kingdom, nannies are usually from third-world countries, and it is a position that does not require any level of education. The rumor got under my skin because I had spent seven years at the university, and I felt somewhat offended that these ladies would be so vicious as to take someone else's fortune and turn it into their daily gossip. Whether it was the Arab-dressed driver entering the compound unabated and coming to my villa or the new hours I was keeping, the word was out that I worked for royalty.

Still upset about being the topic of the latest gossip when I returned to my villa, I called Mom.

"Now, honey," she began, "I told you about what happens when you confine a lot of women with nothing to do."

"I know, Mama," I continued, "but I never thought they would make up things if they had nothing factual."

"Just treat it like water on a duck's back," she said rather firmly to pick up my spirits, "and let it just roll on off."

Mama always has a way of making me look at the picture from another angle. "Think of it this way," she shared, "if they are talking about you, then they're not talking about someone else. You are strong, others may not be. Just go on about your business and let them talk. Talk is cheap and it won't last long. They'll be on to someone else next week." Again, Mama had come through for me; however, they were not on to someone else and it did last long.

At first the rumors were relentless. Rumors about me, David, me with the princess, David working for Colonel (Prince) Awad, David with the base commanders, it went on and on. However, no one ever talked to us directly, never where we could defend ourselves. One particular time when I entered the dining hall, a practice I soon avoided or searched for a remote table when I did go, I spoke to ladies along the way as was expected, or my lack of cordiality would be the next day's topic. It was around 9 a.m. As I entered and I greeted, one lady, in a sneering sort of way, declared in front of the entire table, "My, it's amazing to see you out and about so early since you didn't get home until 3 a.m.!"

How in the world had she known that I had gotten home at 3 a.m.? True, I had attended a Saudi ladies' party the night before, and, true, I had gotten home around 3 a.m. But how did she know? Didn't these people have anything better to do than sit up and see what time I got home at night? I was amazed, completely stunned.

It was the more brazen women who would speak up with a comment of this sort. Most, however, would be nice to my face and then talk about me all afternoon. Whenever I entered the dinning hall, the community store, the bowling alley or any other place people gathered, I faced a dilemma. If I stopped and spoke, anything I said would be misconstrued and regurgitated incorrectly later in the week. But if I did not stop and visit as I entered where the whale club ladies were, the next rumor would be "what a bitch that Teresa is ... she thinks she's too good to speak to us." Either way, I felt like I could not win.

It was because of this that David and I soon became somewhat reclusive. We had acquaintances, but not real friends at first. We attended and helped organize compound social activities and participated as active community members, but we tried to keep our personal lives a secret from most. We made only a few close friends in the Western community over the years, sharing with them concerns about our family, worries about children, and other aspects of our American lives. Yet, even with these very few friends, five couples or less, did we ever reveal or share any personal experiences or information about our relationship with the Awads, our royal family. It was a schizophrenic life, yet required for survival. As my experiences and adventures with the princess grew, I remained one of the hottest topics of conversation on the compound until the day I got on the plane to leave nine and a half years later and, perhaps, after.

Looking back, it seems only natural that compound life was as it was. After all, we were all confined in the same space, behind the same wall. As nice as it was, we were still confined. In this environment, the same people worked together, ate together, swam together and socialized together — everywhere the same people. It was almost like 500 siblings imprisoned in one home.

In spite of the gossip, which soon fell on deaf ears with David and me, some sense of community developed, which I suppose is normal in that we were all in the same boat. We were all a long way from home, a long way from family. Essentially, we stuck together in times of trial and pulled together when the going got tough. As explained, word traveled quickly on the compound, and when the scoop was that someone had a family emergency, an illness, or perhaps a happy occasion with their family, we all jumped in to morn, help or celebrate. This aspect of our community life was so strange, almost schizophrenic as well. One minute, you could feel so much dislike for something he or she said about you, and then in the next moment you would participate in a prayer vigil over their misfortune or take care of their pet while they left the country on emergency leave or holiday. We just seemed to stick together. Like brothers and sisters, we fought and we cared.

During my years in Kingdom when my parents lived there with me, my mother had a heart attack while they were on holiday in the states, and we immediately flew back to the U.S. for her open-heart surgery. While I was holding vigil at the hospital with Mom, I received numerous calls from compound friends and Arab friends. I even heard that the entire compound had held a candlelight prayer vigil at the exact time of her surgery in the states! A few years later, my father had an aneurysm and had to have brain surgery. Again, the community banded together in our time of need, and helped us pull him through with their prayers and concern.

If ever we saw another Westerner on the side of the highway with car trouble or in some sort of disagreement or confrontation downtown, we went to his or her aid. Even if it were the one individual that we feuded with the most on the compound, we would still help him or her. Whenever one of us had an emergency stateside, a death in the family, or a critically sick loved one and needed to leave the country as soon as possible, everyone would do what they could to expedite the somewhat lengthy process of getting paperwork ready to leave. Saudi Arabia is a closed country where you must have the government's permission to enter, an entry visa, and their permission to leave as well, an exit visa. Without the help of fellow Westerners pulling strings where they could, and the help of company-employed Saudis who were our Government Relations' officers who empathized with our needs, an exit/re-entry visa could take up to a week to obtain. With help, good fortune and God's blessing, it could be done, remarkably, in as quickly as twenty-four hours. In a sense, the Kingdom was a prison without bars.

After understanding how the rumor mill worked, I soon learned what to say and what not to say, when to say it and when not to say it. And even though I do not miss this aspect of compound life, I learned to handle it as time passed. Conversely, I do miss the camaraderie, the sense of family that compound life afforded. In America, most barely know all the families on their street, much less all the families in their neighborhood. Nowhere in America have I ever felt the sense of community that I felt behind the wall in Saudi Arabia.

ॐ Chapter Ten ॐ
For the Women

In the Saudi culture, nothing is more anticipated or prepared for than a wedding. A wedding, any wedding, is seen as a huge event — the union of two families, a merger in a sense. Unlike marriages in the West, the family decides the union, and it is based on enhancing the family's status in some way. The bride and groom rarely meet on a formal basis before the event. No accepted form of dating exists in the Saudi courtship. However, the younger generation has found a few ways to circumvent this illicit act. Fahad once told me that some teenagers do attempt to date. One way of contact is for the girl to stroll through the grocery store until she attracts the attention of a young man. She will then conspicuously leave a piece of paper on a shelf with her cell phone number written on it. The boy who sees this will follow, take the paper and give her a call.

Another way that teenagers who are experiencing the natural emotions of adolescence attempt to contact each other is done on the highways. The boy will post a sign in his car indicating that it is for sale, listing a telephone number to call clearly on the sign. The girls, who are cruising under the guiding hand of their drivers, will call the number listed. Although most of this prohibited act is via telephone, the teenagers are attempting to make some sort of contact with each other.

Contracts between families dictate the official courtship in the Saudi culture, with the eldest male of the bride's family essentially making the decision with some feedback from the female members of her family. At first I thought the bride had absolutely no say in the arrangement; I later learned that she does, but objections rarely occur. I also learned that a Saudi woman never takes her husband's name as women do in the West. Rather, she continues to be known by her given name and family lineage.

When I was more comfortable asking Madawi private questions about life as a Saudi woman, I asked her how these marriages worked? What about love? She replied by saying that "love comes after respect and commitment." She explained that because of the instructional yet strict rules put forth by Mohammed *(PBUH)* in the *Quran,* there are certain ways specified on how to treat your spouse, how a man should treat a woman, and the woman the man. Supposedly, the love grows over time, if you can call it "love."

On one particular afternoon, only one month into my employment, Fahad met me in the hall as I entered the palace to tutor for the afternoon. He was excited to the point of exploding with a special surprise.

"Mrs. Teresa, we want you to attend the wedding," he exclaimed.

Trying to get him to slow down a little, I moved toward the children's salon to discuss the excitement further.

As he followed, he continued, "I want you to come to my Auntie's wedding in *Riyadh* and see what our weddings are like!" he explained. From previous afternoon chit-chats with Fahad, I had learned how important a Saudi wedding was and knew from other Western ladies how unique and rare it was to be invited to one, particularly a royal one.

With Fahad's immense love of his culture, the invitation to attend the wedding just spilled out of his mouth like the rush of a waterfall. He wanted so much for me to experience this wonderful event and seemed overjoyed when I said I would be honored to attend. It was set. Both David and I would attend the royal wedding as guests of the family! Then the rush began. When was the wedding? What would I wear? When would we go? So many details had to be arranged.

Thanks to my mother, I had known to take cocktail dresses for compound events such as Christmas parties (known as holiday parties because we were not really supposed to celebrate the Christian holiday of Christmas in the Kingdom), New Year's Eve and Valentine's Day parties. But I never dreamed I would be invited to a royal Saudi wedding, and I would need a formal evening gown. In ten years, I personally only knew two other Western women, out of over a thousand I came in contact with, who were privileged to attend even one royal wedding as the personal guest of a princess. Because of Madawi, however, I was honored to attend two royal Saudi weddings.

With my first royal wedding only two weeks away, the idea of getting a long dress shipped to me from the states was not an option. I shared my problem with Madawi.

"*Mofie Mushkala,* Mrs. Teresa," she said with her special smile. "I have several dresses, and we will find one that will work."

Now this concerned me a touch as I am much more petite than Madawi. With her towering 6'2" stature compared to my 5' 5-1/2," I could not see the connection, but I trusted her that it would work. After studying upstairs with the girls that day, I returned to the downstairs children's salon to find a stack of evening gowns waiting my approval. Madawi joined me as I tried each one on, modeling for her and the girls. The room buzzed with excitement. Nannies ran about to help me try on each in Fatma's bath while Maha and Bandari jumped on the sofas with glee. As I modeled each dress for my audience, Madawi gave her opinions. "No, that one won't do," or "That one is a possibility." And then, I tried on a black and gold printed tea length with a black bodice, which was strapless and revealed a slit up the front.

With no hesitation and her already familiar smile, Madawi exclaimed, "That is it!"

Although the dress was beautiful, I thought to myself, "It?" It was a little big. Somehow sensing my concern, she immediately sent for her tailor, who lived on the palace grounds, to make the dress perfect for me. A week later, the dress arrived at my villa via one of the palace drivers, wrapped in a garment bag and tailored perfectly to me.

With my dress ready, I became anxious that I needed some sort of nice jewelry set to wear, something fitting for a royal wedding. This notion was naïve to say the least. Never would I be able to afford any jewelry that could come within reach of the jewelry the women wear at a royal Saudi wedding. Because I had not been in the country long, I had not acquired one of the magnificent gold pieces seen strung in all of the gold stores. This is not jewelry as we Westerners know jewelry. I am talking about huge gold necklaces, at least several ounces of 21-karat gold, with many of the pieces being like breastplates that seemed to drip gold. It was off to the gold *souk* for me. After much deliberation and frustration, I found what I thought to be the perfect set that fit my budget. It was a 21-karat gold chain, completely encircled with small coins, approximately an ounce of gold. To top off the necklace, I bought matching coin earrings with seven coins dangling from each. I just knew I would fit in. With the dress and the gold, I was ready.

Instructions were sent to the villa that David and I should be ready to leave at 5 p.m. on Wednesday. A driver would take us to the palace first and then on to the airport with the family to fly to *Riyadh*. This sounded simple enough, but we could not have imagined what was to follow.

Wednesday came, our bags were packed, and we sat anxiously waiting for the driver to arrive. Right on time, he placed our luggage in the trunk, which we did not see again until we were in our hotel room in *Riyadh*. Embarking for the palace, the mesmerizing, adventure-enhancing Arabic music played as we weaved through traffic. As expected, David and I rode in the backseat as the special guests of the princess. Once at the palace, we were shown to the salon and served the customary tea in small cylinder-shaped crystal cups with saucers. We were then offered a variety of blended fruit drinks and traditional dates while we waited. We talked with the children as each ran in and out of the salon frantically preparing for departure. Excitement filled the air. After a while, Colonel Awad joined us as Madawi and the girls continued their preparations. He and I exchanged greetings, some small talk, and then his attention turned to David. I continued to talk to the girls as they came and went, but I could not help overhearing David and the Colonel's conversation.

"The wedding," the Colonel paused in his officer kind of voice, "is for the women."

Although there would be a men's wedding party for David to attend, the Colonel explained that it would not be like the women's wedding party. However, he did talk about the traditional sword dancing done by the men at many celebrations, and David looked forward to the possibility of witnessing the event.

Abruptly, Madawi appeared and it was time to go. The entire entourage went to a long line of waiting cars with engines running and formally dressed drivers in *thobes* and *guthras,* all lined up waiting for the family. Madawi assigned cars to each of the children and their nannies. David and I, too, had our own as-

signed car and driver. We loaded ourselves, and away
we went as our huge motorcade exited through the big
wooden gates. To our surprise, our driver did not take
us to the domestic terminal at the airport where we
would have gone had we not been traveling as the
guests of a princess. Rather, he took us to the royal
terminal located off to the south of the regular termi-
nals that everyone else uses. As we approached, we
were grinning like Cheshire cats, and our senses
heightened at the thought of entering such a beautiful, unreachable place for the ordinary Saudi or expatriate. The exterior of the royal terminal was magnificent with marble everywhere, manicured landscaping
and a private drive that took us straight to the door.
The driver looped our car through the circular drive,
stopped, and then opened the door for David and me to
depart. Saleem always got upset if we tried to open
the door ourselves. It was his honor to do so, his job
that he took pride in doing.

I was all eyes as we entered the terminal, trying to
take everything in without looking like some kind of
small town girl who had never seen anything like this
in her life, even in pictures. I tried to be cool, but my
heart was racing and I just could not see enough out of
my casual, nonchalant glances to satisfy my curiosity.
We approached no ticket counters, no lines, no baggage checks, nothing normally found when you enter
an airport to depart. Rather, we followed a long, beautiful corridor to the royal waiting lounge. Decorated in
a manner, naturally, fit for royalty, the floors were covered in expensive, hand-made Persian carpets, enor-

mous crystal chandeliers hung from the huge vaulted ceiling, sofas lined the walls of the vast waiting area, and coffee tables accompanied each sofa offering expensive chocolates and tissues for the weary traveler. The entire back wall was one-way glass for the royals' privacy, which I should have guessed, and was draped from floor to ceiling with gorgeous curtains. Through this portal, a beautiful view of the airport and runway was revealed to us.

As we entered, Madawi met us. It was an exciting time and everyone was talking at once about what was to come. As the chatter continued, we were again served tea. Pretending as if this was a normal everyday event for me, I sipped the tea and enjoyed the company. Shortly, one of the drivers, the head driver, Abdullah, who also acted as a concierge, arrived at the door. *"Amity,* it is time," he said to Madawi.

The bustle began with everyone adorning their *abayas* and veils and collecting their handbags, leaving the teacups on the tables for unseen faces to collect. The girls' nannies grabbed their carry-on pieces of luggage, and we followed as Madawi led the way through the door to the runway. Once outside, David and I almost flipped as we were given our own white, new model Cadillac to ride in to the airplane, only fifty yards away! It was just too cool. The driver opened the back door for us to be seated in the already running, cooled car. We drove down one side of the plane, around the tail, and up to the side where the steps were to enter. Again the back door opened. Once inside the plane, we were seated in first class, of course.

Beginning with the Islamic travel prayer announced over the plane intercom, as is customary before a flight on *Saudia Airlines,* we settled into our first class seating complete with blended juice cocktails and dates for refreshment. The flight seemed shorter than the expected hour, as our time was filled with exciting talk about the weekend ahead.

When we landed in *Riyadh,* Madawi and the girls went one way, as yet another driver was waiting to collect David and me to take us to the hotel. No baggage claim, no customs, no terminal — nothing. We just waltzed through the building, escorted like diplomats. We simply followed the new driver, made our way through another lounge and exited to a waiting car. As before, our first-class transit included an open door to the back seat, which was encircled with drapes on the windows that could be opened or closed by the passenger.

The familiar Arabic music played as the BMW 750SL wheeled its way into *Riyadh,* about an hour's drive from the airport at an excessive speed. I was entranced with the beauty of the desert surrounding the capital city. As we traveled down this magnificent, well-kept interstate, we saw billboards in Arabic for Rado, Givenchy and other designer wares. In the distance, we could see the hundreds of minarets reaching to the sky marking the mosques of the city, and at ground level, the more mundane, regular square stucco buildings of the past. As we approached the more populated area, the driver spoke.

"Mrs. Teresa," he hesitated, almost embarrassed, "you must wear your *abaya* and head scarf whenever you are in public here." He continued, "And you cannot smoke in public," he paused, "but it is okay in the car behind the curtains."

At this, I looked at David; our glances said it all. In spite of the royal treatment and the beauty of the desert, we still held no control of what we did or said in this land. The car rolled on.

Within an hour, we pulled up to the Intercontinental Hotel in downtown *Riyadh*. The hotel was magnificent, complete with a circular entrance, fountains and plush landscaping. Actually, everywhere we looked we saw magnificent modern buildings of marble and glass reaching to the heavens. Mingled throughout the old, the new stood out as shining lights in the desert sun. I never expected such modern buildings, such elaborate structures in this mystical land.

When a Saudi says you are their guests, they mean it in every sense of the word. The airline tickets, our food and our hotel were all paid for by the princess. Additionally, no wedding gift was required. Actually, when I had asked Madawi for an idea of what gift to purchase, she quickly explained that in their culture the guests are given a gift for attending and are not required to bring one as it is in the West.

As we entered the hotel, the driver, who had already been there to check us in and collect our room key, offered the keys to David and told us to order whatever we wanted and just sign it to the room. We were like giggling school kids by the time we reached our suite.

That night we enjoyed a wonderful dinner in the hotel's five-star restaurant, followed by intense conversation and excitement about the day's events before we slept in our luxury suite.

My mom, who had lived in *Riyadh* for five years, had always talked about the *Bata* in the old downtown section of the city, and I wanted to go see it. With the touch of the telephone, the driver arrived around 9 a.m. the next morning to take us to the infamous *Bata*. Clad in my *abaya* and headscarf, we were off. The *Bata* was all that my mom had said it would be. I felt a rush of excitement as I meandered through the passageways of the open-air market while my senses heightened to everything around me. With Arabic chatter all around, the strong smell of incense, the bustle of haggling over prices, and Arab men in traditional attire sitting on carpets enjoying their tea and *sheesha* pipes, known to Westerners as "hubbly bubblies," it was as if we had stepped into a place that modern time forgot. As I shopped, with David a few feet behind to watch over me, my eyes went from one treasure to another. Piles of old silver and copper pots waited for me to sift through to find just the right one. I could close my eyes and picture these pots over an open fire in the desert as their owners enjoyed each other's company over a traditional Arab meal. Baskets were everywhere with the women sitting on the ground, completely veiled, selling their art. Treasures and more treasures. The perfect place for the antique lover! We shopped until we could carry no more, until we could shop no more. *Allah Aakabar, Allah Aakabar, Allah Aakabar,* the familiar noon prayer call began, and we made for the driver who had waited for us the entire time we had shopped.

After taking a few minutes to freshen up at the hotel while the driver waited, David stayed behind to rest, and I headed to see the family who was staying at Mama Raja's house, the Colonel's mother's palace, for the weekend. Again with *abaya* and headscarf on, the doors were opened for me, and the Arabic music played as the BMW crowded into the bustling traffic of downtown *Riyadh*. Recalling from my mom's advice that it is customary to take a gift when visiting an Arab's home, I asked the driver to stop at a flower store on the way. Considering this was after the noon prayer and most stores remained closed until after the afternoon prayer around 4 p.m. each day, this was a feat that he did his best to fulfill. After about an hour of riding around to every flower store he knew, only to find them locked up tighter than Dick's hatband, we stopped at a local grocery market. Fortunately, the markets in Saudi usually have fairly nice floral departments, and I was able to purchase a beautiful bundle of orchids for only 100 SR (approximately $25). With my gift in hand, we were off to our original destination — Mama Raja's.

As we approached the neighborhood near the diplomatic quarters where most of the royal family lives, I was completely amazed at the enormity of these homes, most of them seriously dwarfing our White House in Washington, D.C. Surrounded by tall privacy walls, each estate is essentially a compound in and of itself. Unique, intricately woven marble designs adorned the privacy walls, and large entry gates with brass handles and towering entryways were strewn across the rolling desert landscape as if an architect had dreamed his wildest dreams of beautiful mansions and erected them there. Soon we turned and entered the gates of the King's sister's palace, Mama Raja's home. Once inside the privacy walls, again I could not help but gaze in amazement. A huge circular brick driveway around a beautiful fountain lay ahead. The doors to the main palace were inset with glass and had to be at least twenty feet tall as if watching over the inner sanctuary. As my car rolled to a stop, the girls came running. Again, the excitement of the event was everywhere.

"Come on, Mrs. Teresa, Mama and *Baba* are eating," I heard one say.

"Let me show you my room," said another. "I want to show you the pool," and "I want to show you the garden." Their chatter was utterly endless with their excitement of my arrival and their desire to share their world with me.

"Guess what, Mrs. Teresa, I get to walk with the bride," Maha blurted out.

"Okay, I will see it all," I told them as we hugged. "But first let me say hello to Mama."

They led me to a second house off to the left of the palace where my royal family was staying for the weekend, a guesthouse of a mere 4,000 square feet.

When I arrived, Madawi and the Colonel were eating lunch and asked me to join them. I presented her with the flowers. She smiled genuinely and thanked me.

"*Shukran,* Mrs. Teresa," she said, as she smelled the bouquet. "Will you join us?" she asked graciously,

93

motioning to the chair beside her. She then beckoned in Arabic, and a nanny appeared to arrange the flowers in a vase she carried in and put on the table.

"Yes, Mrs. Teresa," the Colonel interjected with a mouth full of rice. "Please join us, eat," he said most emphatically as he swallowed.

"Have some *sambusha*," he offered as he handed me the platter piled high with the flaky, cheese-filled pastries, knowing that it was one of my favorite dishes.

Oh, how I learned to love *sambusha,* Basmati rice, *hummus,* and many other traditional Arab dishes. To this day, my mouth waters to think about them. Over a delicious lunch, Madawi asked how I was enjoying my trip so far. I proceeded to tell her how much fun I was having, and my excitement from the *Bata* experience came pouring out.

"You went to the *Bata?*" she asked as we ate, smiling her usual sincere, heartfelt smile in the direction of the Colonel. She seemed to approve of my desire to see and learn more about her land.

"Yes," I answered enthusiastically, and I went on to explain for at least a half an hour about all I had seen and done.

After a brief time with the girls, Madawi highly recommended that I go back to the hotel and rest before the evening's festivities.

"Oh, Mrs. Teresa," Madawi began dabbing her mouth with her linen napkin, "what a day you have had! Really, you should go and sleep now." She continued as she stood from the table. "We will talk more tonight."

Since this was essentially my first ladies' event, I was unaware that it is a good idea to rest beforehand and put your sunglasses in your evening bag. Most Saudi parties, particularly their wedding parties, begin around 11 p.m. If you can last long enough, the party will end with breakfast when those dark glasses can come in handy. After telling me when to be ready and that someone would come for me later in the evening, the driver was summoned, and I returned to the hotel, still on the natural high that had been with me since I left my villa on Wednesday. Unfortunately, I did not heed Madawi's advice, and I spent the remainder of the afternoon telling David all about the beautiful palaces I had seen. Not resting would prove to be a big mistake.

So as not to waste any natural beauty prep time, we ordered room service for our dinner. All showered and dressed up, I felt like a princess myself, dripping with gold ... or so I thought. Then a knock came at the hotel door. It was Sheryl, Nora's nanny who had been with the family since Nora's birth. Smiling, she beckoned me to come, and David left for the men's wedding party in another part of the hotel. With little conversation exchanged, she led me through the huge, elegant lobby to a large side hall. When we turned the corner, several women were guarding the enormous ornate doors, checking *abayas* as each lady entered, in a fashion similar to how Westerners check coats. When I approached, the women spoke to me in Arabic, which I was unable at that time to understand. Their mannerisms and tone seemed as if they did not want to let me in, as if I did not belong. Sheryl responded in Arabic, and immediately the doors swung open for me.

Lined in front of me were at least a thousand ladies, dressed in more traditional female Arab clothing of long, ornate dresses. Each woman wore elaborate jewelry literally dripping in gold, dwarfing my little necklace. All around were huge television screens. The Arabic tongue filled the air with excitement, and they all stared at me with their dark black eyes as we made our way through the crowd. I could tell that I was the new topic of conversation. Thinking this was the wedding party, I followed Sheryl with some hesitation through the crowd, wondering where we could be going. The answer quickly became evident as we turned yet another corner.

Again, several ladies guarded huge doors, and yet again, Sheryl stepped to my defense in Arabic. Suddenly, we entered the most elaborate party hall I could ever imagine. It was at least 200 yards long and fifty yards wide. Thousands of chairs lined each side, at least forty chairs deep, all facing a center aisle. At the opposite end of the aisle was a huge stage decorated with thousands upon thousands of beautiful flowers: orchids, lilies, and roses. I followed Sheryl, and we walked in the direction of the stage, down the aisle lined with the rows and rows and rows of chairs filled with ladies, young and old. The magic had begun. Arabic music played so loud that you had to yell to speak to a person right next to you. As we walked, ladies stared — again. I later learned that I was one of only three Western women attending the wedding party of over 3,000, and the other two were British women whom I did not know. The air was filled with sandalwood incense, which I was told could be a "gift fit for a King" costing about $250 a kilo.

As we made our way, I soon saw Madawi walking up to greet me, her gait revealing her beauty as she walked. She was stunning, simply elegant. Her long flowing gown accented her beautiful figure and height. Around her long, slender neck hung a simple diamond, the size of a walnut, gently cradled at the base of her throat. Her hair and makeup were flawless. She was perfect, a princess in every sense of the word.

"Welcome, Mrs. Teresa," she shouted over the music as she approached. "You look beautiful tonight."

"Oh, Madawi, " I gasped, "you look wonderful! And this," I began as I motioned my arm around the room, "this is fabulous!" She smiled with pride, and I believe happiness, that she had included me.

Putting her arm around my shoulders, she encouraged, "Come, Mrs. Teresa. We will find you a seat."

Madawi led me through a maze of strange faces to the edge of the stage where I saw Madawi's daughters, my girls, waving for me to sit with them. As the evening progressed, I felt more and more like a housemaid rather than an honored guest. Not because of the way I was treated, rather because of the way I was dressed. Of course, my dress was nice as it was one of Madawi's, but the jewelry I had so painfully selected and been so proud of earlier was nothing compared to the jewels I saw: diamonds, rubies, emeralds, and sapphires glistening everywhere. The little royal girls present wore more diamonds than I could ever dream of owning. I was encircled by beautiful Italian gowns worn by beautiful Arab women with flawless olive complexions, dark eyes, jet-black hair, and make-up to rival any I have ever seen an American woman wear. I actually pinched myself to make sure everything was really happening, to make sure that I was really experiencing all of this.

From the moment I sat down, I quickly learned not to get up or lose my seat. In the Saudi way, filled with grace and hospitality, I was served tea, juice, dates, petite sandwiches, expensive chocolates, and much more, all on silver trays passed by Filipino and Sri Lankin maids. As I sat and ate, I watched and the music played. As I looked around, I noticed women running cameras, as if in a television station, spaced strategically around the room on risers. Curious, I looked more closely, and then I put it together. They were televising the event so that the ladies who were important enough to be invited, but not important enough to be included in the main party room, could see the action on the huge television screens I had seen earlier in the evening.

On the stage were mostly the younger girls, laughing and dancing in the most beautiful, sensual way — the Arab way — while the older ladies sat and visited, relaxing and enjoying themselves. It was mesmerizing. Chatter of the Arabic tongue filled the room and incense continued to fill my senses. Periodically, the girls would run to me and talk a few minutes, pointing out this Auntie and that Auntie, this cousin and that cousin, and then off they would go to dance on the stage again. Back and forth they went all night, sometimes bringing a little cousin or friend to meet "Mrs. Teresa."

As I sat, one particular event captured my attention. To my left, a bit closer to the stage, I saw someone's Filipino nanny take a picture. Within a minute, a lady approached her, beautifully dressed with incredible jewelry. Although I was not close enough to hear, as if it would have mattered in that I did not yet speak Arabic, it was clear what was going on. After an exchange of words, the Filipino lowered her head and handed the lady her camera. The lady gracefully opened the camera, removed the film and handed the camera back to the nanny. Later, I learned that the woman collecting the film was the mother of the bride. Obviously, the strict code of secrecy by the royal family forbade pictures that could reveal to more common people the opulence of their wedding celebrations. It was then that my senses heightened even more. I did not want to miss a blink. If I were lucky enough to experience something like this again, it was obvious that I would not be able to record it. I vowed to let this evening burn into my memory forever.

It was around 1 a.m. when the mood in the enormous room suddenly changed. Ladies started bustling around, moving for some reason. My senses stood on end, and I began to scan the room even more eagerly. The older ladies began wrapping their headscarves, while others completely veiled to cover their faces. The younger girls began leaving the stage, giggling all the way. Something was happening. The lights dimmed and a spotlight shown on two huge, brass-laden doors at the end of the aisle opposite the stage. The music changed, and the doors opened.

There stood the most beautiful bride I had ever seen. Naturally, she was in all white, literally beaming. With her groom by her side, handsomely dressed in the traditional white *thobe* and red and white *guthra,* they stood and smiled for a moment as the crowd of women went wild. The older ladies began to make a high-pitched shrieking sound that somewhat startled me. Their cry was a traditional sound made somehow in the back of the throat, an art I never mastered, that showed their excitement and expressed their joy. As the music continued, the bride and groom proceeded down the aisle, which took about 15 minutes, as the aisle was so very long. Little Maha walked in front of the bride and groom, as she had told me she would earlier in the day, grinning with pride and trying her best to stay in time with the music. As the wedding party drew closer to my seat, I saw bright beams of light streaking from the bride's neck, which was encircled with a choker five rows high of diamonds. Each diamond was at least a karat. For me to be able to see them from my seat, suffice to say, they were big stones. To match, her tied raven-black hair was dotted with large diamond hairpins that glowed like stars from beneath her bridal veil. It was incredible.

While our attention had been on the couple, a faceless someone had placed a beautiful settee on the stage, encircled with flowers and ribbons for the newlyweds to sit. Once at the stage, they took their place in front of the crowd, still beaming. One by one, beginning with

the bride's mother, ladies approached them to, I assumed, wish them well and bless their union. Some
younger ladies, however, began to dance on the stage
in front of the couple. Fatma explained that they were
dancing to honor the couple. One by one, the closest
relatives of the couple danced before them. When they
danced, it was if their whole body moved in unison, in
a rhythmic, meaningful way. The way they danced was
so sensual, so elegant. After about an hour, the groom
stood, waved and departed down the aisle, greeting a
selected few older ladies as he went. The bride was left
to enjoy the wedding party "for the women," just as the
Colonel had said. As soon as he left the room,
headscarves and veils fell. The party was cooking again.
In came the incense, and up went the music.

Shortly, the atmosphere changed yet again. All the
ladies began to rise and bustle, but this time no one
veiled. Thanks to Maha, I learned it was time to eat
dinner. It was 2:30 a.m.! Led by the mother of the bride
and her daughter, the remaining royals followed. Not
exactly knowing where I fit in, I hung with the girls so
they could "show me the ropes."

We entered another enormous room to find a huge
buffet and seating for everyone. All the different foods
you could imagine were laid out for us, displayed and
presented in the finest manner. Ice sculptures, cascading arrays of fresh fruits, and dish after dish of goat,
lamb, beef, chicken, rice and more rice. Scrumptious
desserts of every design and flavor were laid out for
the taking. As we went through the line, Nora delighted
in telling me what each was and which ones were her

favorites. When we sat to eat, each place held a gift for the guest. As Madawi had said, each guest gets a gift. A little brass book with Arabic writing lay before me to take home as my keepsake from this unforgettable evening. Nora told me that the book held a blessing for the newlyweds, listing their names and marking the date. It was very special.

Completely stuffed and overwhelmed by the evening, my lack of rest as Madawi had suggested caught up with me. Even though I did not want the evening to end, I simply could not hold my eyes open anymore. It was almost 4 a.m. It took me about a half an hour to locate Madawi in the crowd. As I approached, she smiled her special smile, and when I reached her. she simply said, "You must sleep." We said our goodnights, and I made my way through the crowd and various party rooms and lobby to reach my suite, leaving the Arab women still going, still laughing and still dancing. I learned the next day that the girls went to bed around 8 a.m.

When I reached our suite door, I met David, returning from his adventure. Although exhausted, I could not help but tell him some of what I had seen, and I was so curious as to his night. Had it been as exciting as mine?

"Oh, David, you just won't believe," I began, "the women, thousands of them, and the jewelry, and the food," I continued as I began to change into my pajamas.

"There should be guards around this hotel with the amount of wealth that is in those two rooms," I stated in a matter-of-fact way.

"There are," he replied. "The hotel is surrounded by military men."

Although utterly exhausted, neither of us could release the evening to sleep. Even after we crawled into bed, only a minute or two would pass before one of us spoke up with more details of the evening. After half an hour of this, we gave up on the idea of sleep, ordered room service and sat cross-legged in the middle of the king-size bed recapping the evening, one and then the other. As I had witnessed the ladies' party, I was extremely anxious to hear about the men's.

After leaving the suite, David was escorted through the magnificent hotel lobby to a large party hall by one of the family's drivers, dressed respectfully to the hilt in his finest *thobe* and *guthra*. As he entered, he saw men sitting, as is the Saudi way, in lavishly upholstered arm chairs lined against the walls of the room, all facing each other with a large open center. As is the custom, he was instructed to proceed around the room, greeting each guest along the way, and then he took his place in an open chair. With all the men talking to guests on either side of their chair, they enjoyed tea served by the male servants.

After about a half an hour, the men began to move about. Of all the guests, he was the only Westerner and the only one not wearing *thobe* and *guthra*. Unsure of what was to come, David fell conspicuously into the crowd and followed the more than 500 men out of the lavish room to an outside multi-level garage. As the garage doors opened, he was amazed at what he saw. Lining the parking deck were the latest models of

Mazaradis, Lamborghinis, Ferraris, Porsches, Jaguars, and Rolls Royces in every color imaginable. Millions of dollars worth of cars encircled the perimeter of the parking deck Whereas the women had their jewelry, the men had their cars!

In the center of the cars was a long line of Persian carpets, about 300 feet long, topped with plastic table-cloths, so to speak, that are always used when eating on the ground. This plastic tablecloth, although dis-posable, was cloth-like on the bottom and plastic on the top, adorned with a rather tacky floral pattern. On top of the plastic tablecloth were huge silver trays of *Kebsa,* the traditional meal for Arab celebrations, with one every ten feet down the line of carpets. Each sal-ver held one quarter of a goat sitting on a bed of rice. Surrounding each huge platter of *Kebsa* were mixed matched bowls of greens, grapes and olives, coupled with platters of rolled grape leaves, *sambusha,* and plastic liters of water. As the crowd entered, they dis-persed around the meal, each finding his own place to sit in front of a platter. Before stepping onto the carpet topped with plastic, however, they removed their shoes, leaving them on the garage floor behind them. Over the years, David learned how important it was not to wear socks with holes to a men's wedding party!

Once seated, with no one waiting for others to sit, the men began to eat. David watched intently as this was his first traditional Arab meal. The traditional way of eating is with the hands. Saudis eat with only their right hand, seeing the left as the unclean, bathroom hand. Communally, they ate from the platters, reach-

ing with their hands under the layers of fat to dig deep
for the tender meat. To eat the rice, a handful was
worked into a ball with the right hand and then popped
into the mouth. As David was new to this, his balling
and popping of rice was slow and slightly unmanage-
able at first. Before long, he got the hang of it.

After everyone had had their fill, the crowd began
to move from the carpet.the party of men moved
through the hotel and out into a lavishly landscaped
courtyard. The courtyard was open in the center with
two five-foot incense burners burning sandalwood, the
"gift fit for a king." It was said at the party that over
$25,000 worth of sandalwood was burned throughout
the evening.

As they entered, the men formed multi-centric circles
around the open center and then sat on the ground
shoulder to shoulder. Again, tea was served and conversations continued while drums about four feet in diam-
eter stretched with goatskin were played. After a while,
movement began, obviously marking the beginning of
something. As David curiously surveyed the group, the
men began to sing Arab songs, tribal songs of the Al-
Saud tribe. Everyone joined in, and the tea continued
to flow. Later, after David had been to several non-royal
weddings, he learned that the tribal songs vary from
tribe to tribe, family to family. The singing continued
for almost an hour as the men would finish one song
and then another gentleman would begin another.

During the course of the evening, David had noticed that about thirty of the men were not only dressed
in *thobe* and *guthra* but adorned swords as well. After

the singing, the group of sword-bearing men entered the center of the circle as the remainder cheered them on. The musicians reheated their drums over the open fire to tighten them before the next round of songs, the honored songs of the traditional Arab sword dance. The dancers formed a line, shoulder to shoulder, and the fun began. Moving in unison to the beat of the drums and chanting in Arabic, the men began the preset movements of the sword, up, down, and side to side. They executed the dance that has been passed down through generations, just as long ago warriors once did when they prepared for battle. The dance continued, mesmerizing David with the movements of these enormous three-foot silver swords.

After the sword dance concluded, the men cheered and more tea was passed as the dancers rejoined the circles. More conversation, laughter and songs followed while the musicians reheated their drums for the next event — more dancing. This time, it was not only the sword dancers, but everyone joined the fun. The entire crowd, David included, locked elbows and began to move to the beat of the drums. Still in multi-centric circles, the men moved left and then right, to the center closing the circle, and then out again. In the majestic, dreamlike atmosphere, David had no idea how long they danced. Soon after, he, too, was struck by lack of sleep and had to return to the suite. It was a night neither of us would forget.

In the beginning I, as an American, felt that it would be strange to attend a party with all women and no men. I saw the concept as strange, and I questioned,

"How much fun could it be for a bunch of women to get together and dance?" However, from the very first of hundreds of ladies' parties that I attended, I understood. With only women together, all inhibitions are removed. We could act silly if we wished or mature, not concerned with how we look to the males in the room. We taught each other dance steps and then laughed when one of us did not get it right. We sized up each other's dresses, hair and make-up just as American women do at parties. But with the Saudi ladies, the compliments were genuine.

Although the male wedding party is a unique event to witness, Saudi wedding celebrations truly are "for the women," as the Colonel declared. It is a night filled with excitement and joy. A time for the women to dance, laugh and share their sisterhood as women. It is no wonder that it is such an anticipated event.

ॐ Chapter Eleven ॐ

The Delight of Sisterhood

Years passed before I had the opportunity to experience another royal wedding. Following the first, I always hoped that I would have another chance to step into their world in such an honored way. One opportunity had arisen, but I was busy with the birth of my daughter, literally, and I was unable to attend. Consequently, when the invitation came to attend the wedding of Prince Mohammed's daughter in *Riyadh,* I eagerly accepted.

As with all Saudi royal weddings, years of preparation and planning are required. As the wedding approached, it became the topic of conversation on our compound because of one particular neighbor who could not help but talk about it. Cecilia made it her business to nonchalantly let everyone on the compound know that she was attending "the wedding." However, rarely did she reveal why she was attending.

Cecilia's husband, Austin, was the expat in charge of media equipment on the air base for Madawi's husband, now General (Prince) Awad and General (Prince) Mohammed who was second in command of the Royal Saudi Air Force. In such, General Mohammed had requested that Austin go to *Riyadh* and be in charge of the videotaping of his daughter's wedding, all of which seemed simple enough. However, in Kingdom, such a thing is not quite so simple. Because Saudi weddings are "for the women," they are segregated by gender. Consequently, Austin could not go into the party once it had begun to change tapes and check equipment. He needed a female to do so, which is where Cecilia's purpose for attendance became clear.

Now as I was more seasoned with compound life by this time, I was on the downward slide of the learning curve regarding what to say and when to say it. I never mentioned to anyone that I, too, would be attending the wedding. The weeks passed. My lips were sealed and Cecilia's flapped.

As time drew nearer, I decided to get my hair trimmed by the compound hairstylist. Home businesses were common on the compound with most using the office/nanny's room off the kitchen of their villa as their place of business, which was a room about fifteen feet by ten feet with an adjoining private bath that suited this purpose wonderfully. Women with special talents would open home-based businesses to occupy their time and make extra money. Home businesses of every sort were there: one lady was a massage therapist and had a massage business by appointment only; one lady baked specialty cakes to order; one lady ran a Thai Foods take-out and delivery business; one ran a party business by selling balloon bouquets; one ran a video rental store complete with delivery; and the list went on. Then there was Cecilia, the hairstylist, with her poshly decorated room as her salon, complete with large wall mirrors, a hair stylist chair and the works. I called and made my appointment for the week before my departure to *Riyadh*.

The compound chatter about the wedding continued, and I remained silent. Then, the day for my appointment came. I mounted my little purple bike, a common way for women to get around on the compound since we could not drive, and headed to Cecilia's compound beauty salon. After the cordial greetings, Cecilia escorted me to her little room and began to do my hair. I could tell as we spoke that she was just dying to get around to the topic of the wedding, so for fun I continued to avoid it. Soon she began to cut, and as she continued, it was obvious that she could not stand it any more and she began.

"So," she said nonchalantly as she snipped, "why aren't you attending the wedding this weekend?"

"I never said that I wasn't attending," I cordially replied at completely the wrong moment. Shocked by my proclamation, she cut a huge chunk of hair off the side of my head! Immediately, the pace of snipping increased in a more definitive, snappy way. Without saying a word, I could tell exactly what she was thinking. We both knew that I was going as a guest of the princess while she would be attending to work, unable and unwelcome to socialize and mingle with the royals. It was not until the next morning that I realized my secrecy caused such a reaction with Cecilia. My hair was butchered. It was ghastly, and I was unable to do anything with it.

The week quickly passed and before I knew it, Saleem was at my door to collect my luggage for the trip to *Riyadh* the next day. By this time, I had traveled so much with Madawi that I knew the drill and would leave my packed luggage by the front door sometime the morning before takeoff. Saleem would always ring the bell, stick his head in the door and announce, "I have your bags, Mrs. Teresa," and off he would go, for me to find them later in my assigned room at a new location.

The next morning, Saleem appeared at the door ready to take me to the airport. As much as I grew to love Saleem over the years, he was never exactly on time. I was told it was his Kenyan nature. Anyway, this time I would be attending the wedding alone as Madawi decided, I assume, that David had already had a chance to experience a royal wedding, and an additional time was not necessary. He did, however, attend more non-royal weddings as guests of his colleagues at the airbase. With my travel letter in hand, I was ready to go. In Kingdom when any woman (Western or Arab) travels without the company of her husband, she has to have a letter from him (written in English and Arabic) granting her permission to travel.

As we drove out of the compound, Saleem handed me a folded piece of paper, an additional letter completely in Arabic.

"What is this?" I asked as I unfolded the paper.

"A letter from princess," Saleem responded.

"What do you mean, letter from princess?" I inquired. "What does it say, Saleem?"

"It says to help you," he replied. "Keep it with you, Mrs. Teresa."

"Help me?" I thought. "What in the world?" Unable to pry more substantial information out of Saleem or read the Arabic script, I refolded the paper and tucked it into my bag. Not wanting to make any mistakes, I showed the letter to anyone at the airport who stopped me: the ticket man, the security man checking travel letters, the flight attendant — everyone. Strangely, they all snapped to attention and cleared the way after reading it. Later I learned that the letter told anyone I encountered to show me the kindest of courtesy and let me pass unabated, as I was a guest of the princess. Because I was joining Madawi this time rather than flying with her, she wanted to make sure that I would not have any problems along the way. To say the least, it was a helpful letter.

The treatment was the same as before, royal all the way. In no time at all, the BMW was pulling up to the huge gates of Mama Amal's palace, Madawi's mother's home. As I entered, the girls were thrilled to see me and acted as if we had not seen each other in years when, in fact, we had been together only two days prior. Into the salon we went, and I greeted everyone before I sat, as is the custom. Then the food arrived, and we spent the remainder of the afternoon eating, talking, and preparing for the events to come. During our time, Madawi asked if I were ready for the evening. Was my dress ready? Did I have everything I needed? As always, she was gracious and hospitable. I assured her that I was prepared, but the conversation rapidly turned to my hair.

"The only thing that I'm worried about is my hair," I started. "I haven't been able to do a thing with it all week!"

"Yes," she agreed, "I have noticed."

"Oh, thanks, Madawi!" I exclaimed with a frustrated, yet serious look on my face. "That makes me feel a lot better," I said somewhat sarcastically.

She grinned, and then we both laughed.

"Where did you go for this?" she questioned with her hands flying around my head, as Madawi always spoke with her hands, referring to my cut. I proceeded to fill her in on the entire story. Madawi always enjoyed hearing the compound gossip and seemed to revel in it as if listening to a soap opera first hand. She sat and listened so attentively, hanging on to every word. She confirmed her understanding through her head nods, verbal agreements and a few "oos" here and there. When I finished with the whole story, she jumped in.

"I don't mean to make fun, Mrs. Teresa," she said as she continued to giggle, "but something really must be done." She turned and picked up the telephone by her side and spoke to someone in Arabic, smiling and nodding at me as she talked. After the call was complete, she turned to me once again.

"You will follow Nora," she told me, "at 3 p.m. with Pierre."

"Pierre?" I questioned. "Who is Pierre?"

"He is the hairstylist that I brought for us from Paris," she said very nonchalantly as she reached for her tea.

"He is only here for the day, so you shouldn't miss your appointment," she continued as she played with my hair, assessing the damage.

"He is set up in the side salon. If anyone can make this right, Pierre can," she proclaimed. Again, my current wedding problem was solved by Madawi.

Pierre fumed and grunted the entire time he assessed the damage and planned his course of action with the mess on my head. He shook his head as if in disbelief.

"Il est dommage!" he said as he showed me a three-inch difference in the length on the sides of my hair.

"I will try, Madame," he continued as he spun my back to the mirror and started to snip. An hour later, he whirled the chair around for me to see in the mirror. It was not perfect, but it was much better than before. Relieved and a touch excited, I headed straight for the salon to get Madawi's opinion.

"Much better, Mrs. Teresa," she exclaimed as she offered me some snacks and tea that were on the silver tray before her. I sat down beside her and started to munch.

"I thought you would like your privacy," Madawi began, "so I booked you a suite at the Sheraton International." The surprise on my face, as I was traveling alone, sparked her continuance.

"Don't worry," she continued, "it is just here," she said as she motioned with her hand. "Very near the house. This way, you can have your own bath and quiet to rest before," she continued. "And when you are ready to leave tonight, you can sleep." She seemed quite pleased with her offer and thought I would be pleased as well. Sensing this, I smiled and graciously thanked her for her thoughtfulness.

"Ramel will take you when you are ready," she said, "and be there any time you need the car." She paused as she stood, "Just call to the front desk for him." With that, she stretched and let me know that she was going to rest for a while. Remembering my previous wedding experience, I decided to go to my suite to rest. Settling on a time that I would return that evening, I said my goodbyes and left with Ramel at the wheel.

When we arrived at the Sheraton, Ramel opened the door to the backseat and handed me my key.

"Suite 610, Mrs. Teresa," he said lowering his head slightly as he spoke. "Call when you need me. I will be here."

With that, I thanked him and headed for 610. As it always was when I was Madawi's guest, the accommodations were first class. Knowing the custom, I knew I did not have to pay for anything. I simply signed for or requested whatever I needed. After settling down with a cup of *Nescafé* from room service, I called for a 9 p.m. wake-up call and curled up on the king-size bed to rest for a few hours, which later proved to be a good idea.

In spite of my hair ordeal, I was extremely excited about the wedding. Because I had more notice for this wedding, I had had time for my mom to send me an evening gown. It was forest green velvet with a high neckline and no back, accented by a small train that barely scraped the floor as I walked. By this time, I had acquired a bit more jewelry and planned to wear my emerald and diamond earrings and matching brace-let. Although not to the standard of royal jewelry, it was a step up from my first attempt, and I knew I would enter the wedding with my head high.

Right on time, Ramel arrived at 10:30 p.m. to collect me. Clad in my *abaya* and headscarf behind the curtained windows, we drove the short distance to Mama Amal's to join Madawi and the girls. When I arrived, the girls were already gathering in the entryway. Excitement grew by the minute. Each of them looked lovely dressed in the finest that the stores in Milan could offer.

Surprisingly, we did not wait long before Madawi floated down the spiraling staircase. As I have mentioned before, Madawi is beautiful, a princess in every respect of the word. To my surprise, our dresses were very similar in style and fabric, only hers was taupe with a sheer taupe shoulder wrap and probably cost ten times what mine did. My shoulders went a little straighter and my head a little higher in spite of the differences when I saw her. Again, we greeted as if we had not seen each other in days, admired and complimented each other as girls do, giggling somewhat as to our similarity in taste. In a flash, we were in our black *abayas* again and out to the expensive motorcade of cars, an act that I became so accustomed to over the years that I eventually did not even notice. It was the way of royalty.

Prince Mohammed's palace was about a 25-minute drive from Mama Amal's palace. Through the black of the night, the minaret lights twinkled everywhere as the motorcade proceeded to the palace. Madawi's car led the way with me by her side. Breaking our idle conversation, Madawi spoke up.

"There," she said abruptly, pointing at what looked like a compound, "Mohammed's."

I looked in the direction of her hand. Again, I saw a large walled structure, a compound for one owner, but it was big enough for an entire company of families. The wall was lined with lights every sixteen feet, revealing the intricate detail of the stone and small palms beneath each design, and it seemed to glow as we passed. Shortly, we pulled through the massive gates, each probably twenty feet high and twelve feet across with wrought iron and brass inlays on the sparkling wood. We slowed, but never stopped, as our license plate revealed that royalty was inside. The gates swung open as our line of cars entered, followed by hundreds more. All BMWs, Mercedes and Rolls, the finest of fine cars purred through the gates to an absolutely beautiful brick circular drive and inner courtyard. The shrubbery, all desert plants such as palms and pampas grass, were manicured and lit with small ground lighting and surrounded by a huge three-tiered water fountain in the center of the circle. Each car in turn stopped in front of the huge beautiful doors and ladies flowing in black exited out of each back seat. As we stepped from the car, the dry heat of the night encompassed me, which was a relief from the cold air-conditioned car. Surprisingly, even after all the things I had seen over the years with my princess, I was amazed.

As soon as we entered, we approached an *abaya* check-in as usual, but this time I had no trouble for I was next to Madawi. We each gave our *abayas* and scarves to one of the seven Filipino servants tending the check-in and received a numbered claim ticket in return. Free of the black covering, we strolled through yet another set of enormous doors into the party. Again, I was amazed. At least 3,500 women filled one massive room, and the sounds of chatter overwhelmed us as we entered. All the women were dressed in the finest designer clothes, each sporting exquisite jewelry to compliment their expensive gowns.

The room, actually Prince Mohammed's car garage, was about 250 yards long and 200 yards wide and had been transformed for the event. The ceiling had been painted like the sky, blue with scattered clouds. It was painted in such a way that it seemed to go on for miles. Floating closer to the crowd, doves were suspended as if they were flying through the room. Persian carpets lined the aisles, and along each row of chairs, one for each guest, cascading theater style from the back of the room on risers descending to the far end of the room was a large free-standing wall of fresh flowers on a huge stage. The walls, too, had been transformed to give the garage the appearance of a magical garden with painted ivy and flowers to give the guests the feeling that they were outside at an afternoon party in some remote, flourishing garden. In actuality, the event was held at midnight in a relatively barren land. Also suspended from the ceiling were numerous video cameras, the latest in technology poised among the doves to capture the event.

As we entered, we proceeded across the back aisle to the center aisle to join the crowd of women. To our right were glass walls with closed curtains and four doors spaced along the length of the structure. It was behind the closed curtains that the women who smoked could go to satisfy their vice in private. To our left was the party. Following a few steps behind Madawi, I continued to walk, greeting ladies that I knew from *Riyadh* and *Al-Khobar* along the way. Anyone who was anyone, even in the royal circle, was there. It was a kiss here and a kiss there all along the way.

The traditional greeting of Saudi women consists of one kiss on the right cheek, one on the left, and then another on the right. If the two women are closer than acquaintances, this ritual ends with two kisses on the final right cheek. If they are really close friends, it ends with three. To complicate the ritual, all of this kissing is accomplished while shaking hands and usually uttering the standard "hellos" in Arabic. This particular custom took me quite a while to master, and even after several years of practice, I would still mess up and go the wrong way sometimes, causing me and the other woman to come face to face with each other. Fortunately, each time I made this slip, we both ended up laughing and no one was ever offended.

As we continued greeting and working our way toward the stage, I suddenly felt a hand on my shoulder, which is not the Arab way. Hence, I turned around quickly. Lo and behold, there was Cecilia dressed in a nice but regular dress grinning from ear to ear. No doubt she had seen me on the cameras and come from the video room to catch me as we entered. It was an awkward moment that, fortunately, did not last long as she had to get back to work. Turning to catch Madawi, I smiled a somewhat fiendish smile; I could not help myself. I did not see Cecilia again the entire evening.

This time I was not a wallflower, as I was at my first royal wedding. Instead, I fully participated and felt no need to cling to Madawi or the girls. Because of my association with Madawi over the years, I had gotten to know all of the upper-echelon ladies, even if not all royalty, of the Eastern province who were attending the big event. As I walked, I saw many ladies I knew and offered them the traditional greeting, spending at least of few moments of conversation with each before I moved on. Consequently, Madawi and I would pass in the crowd as we each mingled. Passing each other, we would smile and continue with our greetings. Periodically, I would pass one of the girls, and they would fill me in on their evening before we continued mingling our separate ways.

Through my travels around the massive room, I could not help but notice one lady in particular who stood out from the crowd in an odd way. She was exceptionally tall, which should have been a clue to me, and she was dressed in all black. Her dress was made of a fabric that looked wet and slinky, with a black cape and cascading tiny black beads from her throat to her waist. For some reason, she immediately made me think of Cruella de'Ville from the movie *101 Dal-*

matians. It was odd. Taken aback and slightly tickled, I just had to find Madawi to point her out. I worked my way through the tight crowd searching for my tall, elegant friend. It took almost half an hour before I spotted her about 50 yards away, visiting and smiling. Keeping my eyes focused on her, I set my course, twisting one way and then the other to pass through the hundreds of ladies and chairs. Truly, if I had been the claustrophobic type, this event would have sent me over the edge. Finally, I reached her and waited patiently until she finished speaking with the latest lady who had made her way to talk to the princess.

"Mrs. Teresa," she exclaimed as soon as she was able to break conversation with the other lady, "are you having fun?"

"Oh, yes, it is just beautiful," I began. "But, Madawi," I continued, "have you seen Cruella?"

Smiling in her special way, "Cruella?" she inquired with one eyebrow raised in the way that she does when she is curious or knew that we are about to discuss mischief.

"Yes, Cruella," I continued, peering around to find her before I divulged more. When I could not find the woman, I kept going. "There is this woman who looks exactly like Cruella de Ville from the movie, *101 Dalmatians!*"

Madawi's curiosity was peaked. "Where?" she questioned as she stretched her beautiful, long neck to peer over the crowd, smiling so no one would notice what we were up to. As we started to stroll slowly through the crowd, I continued.

"Madawi, she looks just like her," I said, and then I began to tell her exactly what I had seen, black beads and all.

"It's amazing," I went on, "you must see this."

After a few greetings here and there, we continued to search for Cruella. Finally, I spotted her about 25 yards away. The moment Madawi broke with her most recent greeting, I grabbed her elbow, motioning in the direction of the woman.

"There she is, there," I whispered under my breath, as if she could really hear us or even knew that we were looking at her.

"Oooh!" Madawi exclaimed, with her face saying it all as her eyes widened.

"Mrs. Teresa," again the one raised eyebrow and the mischievous smile, holding a moment to raise my curiosity, "she is the sister of the King!"

Biting my bottom lip and smiling in a harmless way, I responded, "Well, either way, she does look like Cruella." We chuckled together naughtily, and turned for more mingling.

It was not long before the bustle of women quickened. The bride was about to appear. Women started moving here and there, all vying for a seat. The older women began to veil. The music thundered as the auditorium lights dimmed, and a huge spotlight focused on the floral wall at the end of the room that began to move slowly. As it turned, the women began the traditional celebratory shrieking sound that I had heard so many times before at hundreds of ladies' gatherings. I smiled for I knew it was time and found a seat. Realizing that the stage was on top of a rotating platform typically used to display an expensive automobile, my curiosity heightened to see how the bride would appear on the other side of the floral wall.

She was stunning! As the platform rotated, it revealed her seated on a settee with her gorgeous dress draped across the length of her seat. Safa beamed as the crowd became even louder. She literally glowed, either through happiness or as a result of the enormous spotlights. Standing tall next to her in traditional dress was her groom, beaming as well. As the platform came to a halt, the ladies cheered and shrieked.

Then the dancing began to honor the new union of two people, a contract of two families. After an hour or so of dancing, it was time for the groom to depart and the real party to begin. He made his exit quickly with a wave and disappeared behind the floral wall. As the women danced, an occasional Western song was intermingled with the Arabic music. Oh, how they danced, everyone smiling, everyone enjoying herself as if she never had.

At 2 a.m., chimes rang out indicating that it was time to eat. And eat we did, a feast, literally fit for royalty. A buffet spread that would dwarf any I had seen in the 28 countries I have visited. One thing about the Saudis is that they do not do anything small. It is always the biggest, the most elaborate, and usually the most expensive. I was once told that I should never eat everything on my plate, that I should always leave something, to show that there was more than enough for everyone. I assume that this mindset is a result of their history, the way things were in the days before oil. In those times, the men ate first and the women got whatever was left. Hence, to have a wife who was a touch heavy was a sign of wealth, proof you had enough for everyone. So often the Saudi women would fuss over me, over my mere 115 pounds, as if David could not afford to feed me, and they would always plop more food on my plate throughout the meal.

At each place setting, we were given a beautiful gift for attending. That night's gift was expensive, Parisian perfume. It was held in a hand-painted porcelain flower atop a silver stem, which served as the stand for the piece. It was lovely and still adorns my bath today. After filling ourselves, we each gathered our gift and returned to the main hall to continue dancing until my feet could dance no more. Around 5 a.m. I had to call it a night. I found Madawi and she understood. I made my way through the crowd to the *abaya* check, which took almost an hour with the requirement of greeting along the way. After collecting my black attire, I stepped outside to find Ramel in the heat with the thousand other drivers waiting for their madame to exit the party. Truly, I believe the drivers enjoyed these evenings as much as the ladies. Always dressed in their best, they would all hang out together, drink tea, talk and feast on the leftovers from the women's meal, which was a special treat for them.

As we wound our way through the darkness, back to the Sheraton, I could not help but reflect on the evening. These parties truly were "for the women," as the Colonel had said, and evoked a sense of sisterhood among the attendees as I had surmised. It was their time: their time to dress up, visit and dance the night away. It was their chance to be carefree without the veils, without *abayas,* even if it was only for an evening. Even after being with these women for so many years, the evening was like a dream to me. Yet, I never lost sight of reality and how lucky I was. It was a rare privilege to share their world, share their way of life.

ॐ Chapter Twelve ॐ
Birthing Babies

A unique closeness exists among women in Saudi Arabia. It is a closeness that stretches beyond nationality and beyond religion to touch the basic fibers of womanhood. It is a bond, an understanding that unites women everywhere — childbirth. However, in the Kingdom, this privilege, this blessing, the ability to give birth to the new generation has a meaning much deeper than I have ever encountered in the West. It goes beyond that exhilarating feeling women feel when we truly understand our purpose as women, when we give birth and hear our child's first cry.

In Saudi Arabia, childbirth or the ability to do so touches every aspect of a woman's life. Because the country is essentially owned by a family, the House of Saud, it is obvious why the family entity and the ability to reproduce is so important. A Saudi man, as is allowed by Islam, may take up to four wives to increase his odds of procreation. Consequently, it is obvious why the ability to have children and keep having them is so important to the women of Arabia. If a wife cannot bear a child, even for reasons beyond her control, the husband may choose to bring another wife to bear offspring to carry on his name. If an older wife may no longer have children, a younger wife may be taken to continue the bloodline. Hence, the Saudi wife feels great pressure to reproduce. In addition to the biological pressure that many women feel to fulfill their purpose as women, Saudi women must also contend with the societal pressure to keep their husbands happy.

It was late May in 1992 when I first started to become aware of these concepts in the Kingdom. It was end-of-the-year exam time for Madawi's girls. A time treated much differently in Saudi than it is when American children have their school exams. In Kingdom, the children's exams become the entire family's concern. Everyone in the family changes their schedule to accommodate the pressure of the exams. I never really understood this, but I guess it is because I looked at the situation from an American's perspective. As I entered the girls' salon one afternoon to study with Bandari, she could not possibly focus on English until she had my sole attention about a very important matter first.

As there is always at least one nanny in earshot, she refused to speak to me until we were alone.

"Mrs. Teresa, come," she insisted. "I have a secret." She grabbed my hand and led me from the salon, down the stairs and through the back door. All along the way, I questioned the secrecy and asked why she could not just stop and tell me what was so important. Her pace quickened as she led me along the side of the palace, past the swing and to a bench in the back yard. Out of breath, we finally sat.

After a moment, her big black eyes met mine and she whispered, "A baby," giving me her most expressive look where her eyebrows move and lips adjust accordingly as if she is completely in the know.

"We are going to have a baby, Mrs. Teresa," she reiterated and broke into a huge smile.

"What?" I asked somewhat amazed because Madawi had not mentioned a word, and I thought surely she would have told me something like this. Americans tell almost everyone we know as soon as we find out we are expecting. Arabs, however, do not. Although I was never told, I believe they do not want to take a chance of jinxing anything. Perhaps they want to ward off the "evil eye" by not speaking about the pregnancy because they usually do not mention their condition until the pregnancy is obvious. I was so excited for Bandari — so excited for Madawi. What a wonderful surprise! After the relief of sharing the secret settled, we studied. Not wanting to betray Bandari's confidence, I did not mention a word to anyone. I just waited until I was officially informed.

A few weeks passed, and I was in the salon with Madawi, as I was daily, when she asked that I travel with the family that summer. We would go to Paris, Cannes, and then on to the States. I was ecstatic and accepted the invitation. It was then that Madawi made reference to the new arrival. Excited about the birth, as most Americans are, I began to ask questions. Did she want a boy or a girl? When was she due? Was she excited? The usual questions that follow the announcement of a new baby. She explained that the gender was

"Insha Allah," but I believe she hoped for a boy. With only one son and four girls, a boy would be good. Male offspring are always seen as good. Then she chuckled and explained that she thought it would probably be a girl, as "pilots bring girls," referencing the past track record of she and the Colonel. Rubbing her womb, an unconscious act of pregnant women, she said that she was due in November. She seemed to me to be strangely nonchalant. Muslims believe that life begins with birth, not conception, so to Madawi the fetus was not a baby yet. As time grew closer, she would become more excited.

I did travel with the family for eight weeks that summer, and my presence was beneficial for Madawi's family, I believe, in many ways. Not only did I speak with the children in English, teaching them along the way, but I was also able to ride rides with them at Euro Disney, ride on the banana in Cannes as we bounced over waves in the Mediterranean Sea, and participate in the other wild, fun kid activities that a pregnant mother could not do. Madawi would sit, watch and laugh as the kids and I bounced, ran and flipped.

Over the time we spent together that first summer, Madawi and I became extremely close. Our friendship grew as we shared feelings, beliefs and dreams. In fact, we shared many things that many sisters do not share. Madawi conveyed her feelings on womanhood and her experiences as a mother. She helped me realize how special it is. Focused on education, business and the act of being my own person, I was a 29-year-old woman who had been married for seven years and appeared to most as a never-to-be mom. Yet, I was fascinated to hear her talk about motherhood, which sparked deep feelings I was only beginning to address. I truly believe she always saw me in the trouser-wearing, dominating female stereotype that most American women convey to Saudi women. Most Saudi women feel that American women are more interested in work and business than family and child rearing. Perhaps it was her subconscious mission to convert me, to convert me to motherhood. It was because of this closeness that she invited me to attend labor with her in November.

For the first time in my adult life, I was involved with the daily life of a pregnant woman. I was able to see the progression, feel the excitement rise. By November, I believe I was more excited than anyone. I could hardly wait for the big moment. Starting with the first of November, I would begin our daily afternoon time with the big question "... is it time yet?" I probably drove Madawi crazy asking so much. After a week of this, as I am sure she had tired of my questioning, she abruptly responded one afternoon that she would let me know when it was time. She then paused and smiled that very special, compassionate side smile of hers.

Then the strangest thing happened, almost as if we were somehow in tune with each other. It was the night of November fifteenth, and for the life of me, I could not sleep. I was very restless and just could not get Madawi out of my mind. I kept trying to convince myself that it was only the cappuccino I had had earlier, as Madawi had been fine, completely normal when

I had seen her at the palace that afternoon. I lay there for hours, watching the clock as David slept. Then, amazingly, around 3 a.m. the telephone rang. I answered it on the first ring, knowing it was Madawi before I could say hello.

"Why aren't you sleeping, Mrs. Teresa?" she exclaimed, and I could hear the amazement in her voice.

Without answering her question, I anxiously asked, "Is it time?"

"It is time," she replied, and I could actually hear that special smile of hers.

"I will shower and then go to the hospital. I will then send the driver for you in about an hour, and he will bring you to the hospital."

"Okay, I'll be ready," I answered, so jittery that you would have thought that I was having the baby! "What should I bring?" I hesitated collecting my thoughts. "Do you need anything?" I could hardly breathe for asking questions.

"Nothing, Mrs. Teresa," she replied, "just yourself." Her calm demeanor astounded me.

Even in childbirth, Madawi was the epitome of a princess. As I entered the labor room, I was amazed at how calm and collected she was. She was royal in every respect. With her personal sheets and bedcover already there, she was composed as if she were just resting. She invited me to sit and the wait began. For almost four hours, we chatted, Madawi pausing in the conversation to ride through a labor pain. To this day, I still cannot believe how composed she was. Granted it was her fifth birth, but birth is not called labor for no reason!

Periodically, I would step from the room when the doctor would visit or when she wanted something. I was trying to be as useful as I could be. Then, around 8:30 a.m., she asked me to get the doctor, as it was time. So I did. By this time, her cousin, Princess Sara, had arrived. Together, dressed in sweat suits and wearing no make-up, we waited just outside the door as Madawi worked in the delivery room. Honestly, I felt as if it were us in the delivery room rather than her. As Sara prayed and paced, I paced also, anxiously awaiting the outcome, wanting it to end soon. Then, the nurse came out and told us that it was a baby girl. I was so exhilarated. The feeling I had was incredible. "We" had a baby. Little princess *Farah bint Awad bin Turki bin Abdulla Al-Saud* had just entered this world.

At that moment, Princess Sara pulled me aside. In a lowered voice, she asked if I would go to Madawi's room for some dates and honey, which is the Saudi tradition for women to eat immediately after birth, although modern day physicians do not recommend it.

"Mama Soha will have it ready for you," she said.

"Of course I'll go," I replied, and then she clutched my wrist with her voice even lower.

"We are not supposed to do this, but it is our way," she whispered. "Don't let the nurses see."

"*Mofie Muskala,*" I responded confidently. "I'll handle it," and away I went almost bouncing down the hall with excitement and a mission.

I wound hurriedly through the halls, searching for the royal suite, and finally stumbled upon it in a removed wing of the facility. When they said "suite," they were not kidding. Madawi's room, as princess Sara had called it, was actually four rooms connected with a bath and a small kitchen! The first room of the suite was a small sitting room with an adjoining kitchen already filled with Filipino servants to attend to the needs of the princess and her many guests on arrival. They were busy preparing tea, blended fruit juices and food to serve the guests yet to arrive. As I bounced in, they all recognized me.

"Hello, Mrs. Teresa," they began in broken English, as they all gathered to greet me. "Baby yet?" they inquired in unison.

"Oh, yes! A baby girl!" I answered with an enormous amount of enthusiasm, particularly since I was so exuberant from this enlightening experience. "I need the dates and honey," I continued. They knew exactly what I needed and had it ready for me, a small Arab cup full of strong tea and a small glass plate piled high with dates.

"You take," Salwa said as she placed the items in my hands. "Take to princess."

Before heading out, I could not help but peek at the rest of the suite. The first sitting area was connected on the left to the men's waiting area. It was conveniently located where the servants could attend to the needs of the male guests easily from the little kitchen. On the right of the little sitting area was an elaborately decorated dressing area and connecting bath, full of marble and brass, that led into the main room of the suite. The main room, where the hospitalized royal would stay, had a twelve-by-fifteen-foot hand-made Persian carpet adorning the floor, crowned on one side with a sofa, overstuffed chairs and coffee tables. Off to the other side was a single hospital bed in an area that could be sectioned off with the traditional hospital curtain if necessary. A large TV was included and additional space for more chairs when needed. Honestly, it felt as if you were in someone's home, not in a hospital. Reminding myself that I had a mission with the tea and dates, I stopped staring and headed back to the delivery room at the other end of the floor. Back through the winding hallways I went to take Madawi her post-birth tradition.

After accomplishing my mission, I called for a driver. I had to get downtown before the Dohr prayer and get a baby gift. I needed a wonderful baby gift, one fit for a princess and fit for the baby that I had helped to birth. It had to be special. With my *abaya* over my sweats, I instructed the driver to take me to the best baby goods store in town, and away we went. I looked and looked for what an American would buy as a really nice baby gift, yet keeping in mind my budget. Finally, I found it just before prayer and headed home to wrap it before I would return in the afternoon to see Madawi and Farah.

Following a long nap, as I was exhausted from being up most of the night, I showered and waited for David to come home from work. As soon as he got home, we headed to the hospital. I could not help but talk his ear off the entire way, describing the hospital room he was about to find, the royal suite — so Saudi — big and extravagant.

When we arrived, we found many people already

there, as births are a huge event in the Saudi culture, and people visit at the hospital for hours on end. Besides a wedding, a birth is tantamount. As we entered the first sitting room, we greeted a number of people we knew. As was expected, it was in the first sitting room that David and I would part, with him going to the men's waiting area to have tea, snacks and visit with the other men. Yet before I went to Madawi, I saw the Colonel. He was elated with Farah's birth, and he welcomed us to join in.

As I watched him talk, my mind wandered, remembering so many things about him as a father that I had witnessed. Shortly after my arrival in Kingdom, I had read that Saudi men do not acknowledge or care for their female offspring, but nothing could be further from the truth with regard to the Colonel. Perhaps there are some Saudi men who disregard their female children, as there are American men that do, but the Saudi men I knew were not that way. The Colonel adored all five of his girls. He praised their accomplishments and encouraged their further success. His concern for their well-being was obvious with the way he supported their education. Plus, as many fathers do, he gave them almost everything they asked for. I never saw a lack of love from the Colonel or any other Saudi man that I knew when it came to their children, males or females.

Suddenly, the Colonel's voice regained my attention as he commented that I would soon have another pupil. Agreeing, I excused myself to get to Madawi and hold Farah. After removing my *abaya,* I moved into the main salon where Madawi, the baby, and all the women sat. As I entered, I was so proud of the gift I had selected. But, my bubble was immediately burst, and I was instantaneously almost ashamed. Everywhere I looked were enormous bouquets of flowers, most of which stood four and five feet tall and just as wide! I could not believe it. I had never seen floral arrangements that big in my life. Obviously, the gift of choice is floral arrangements, big ones. I made a mental note of this for future reference.

As I greeted the girls, Mama Amal, other visiting ladies, and then Madawi, I soon forgot that I was embarrassed with my gift and became consumed with the excitement again. After a few minutes, Madawi noted the wrapped package in my hand.

"Oh, yes," I stammered, still a little embarrassed. "I got this for you and Farah," I said, as I meekly held out the box.

She broke into a huge smile as she sat in the hospital bed, also made with her personal designer linens, and she began to open my gift. Inside she found the little Peter *Rabbit*™ mobile I had brought for Farah's crib. In her truly princess way, she praised the gift. Although I know it had little significance in her culture, it had a lot in her heart.

It was because of the incredible experience of Farah's birth that I had a newfound sense of what it meant to be a woman. It was because of this experience that I wanted more than ever to become a mom. David and I had discussed the idea of having a baby before I had left with the family for the summer. Yet, it was only talk. It was not until my understanding grew and David's along with me, that we decided it was time to begin our family.

Almost two months passed and nothing happened, and naturally, I could not help but be anxious. It was late December, and I was in *Riyadh* for the weekend with Madawi, enjoying the dessert countryside with her at her uncle's farm. As the evening drew near and the sun began to set in the western sky, Madawi suggested that we walk. Oh, how Madawi always loved to walk, to stroll and enjoy the surroundings. As we meandered through the dessert brush with no aba*yas* or veils, completely revealed to the world with a cool breeze against our faces, the topic turned to my situation.

"Nothing yet?" Madawi quietly inquired.

"Not yet," I responded, and a long pause passed between us as we continued to walk.

"Perhaps it is the pills," I began, "I've been on them since we married eight years ago."

"Perhaps," Madawi agreed. We strolled further.

"You know, Mrs. Teresa, those pills can close up the system," Madawi added, and another pause followed as we pondered her conclusion.

"There is this powder," she continued, "a special Saudi powder that may help."

"Powder?" I inquired.

Madawi explained that this powder had been around for centuries and it helped women "clean the inside," as she put it. Obviously, it was a very useful powder to those unfortunate women who were unable to conceive and especially useful to those wives who felt the pressure of wife number two approaching. As we continued to stroll and watch the sun melt into the horizon, Madawi shared with me amazing stories of how the powder had helped numerous women become pregnant, some who had tried for years to conceive, but to no avail. After all the talk, Madawi decided, assuming she had my agreement, that I should try the powder. She declared that she would have some sent to me, and that was that.

As we continued to walk, the silence of the breeze was broken by the majestic, familiar sound of the *Maghrib* prayer call. We listened and slowly continued to stroll. After a moment I seized this rare opportunity to inquire.

"What do they say when the prayer is called?"

With her hands clasped behind her back, her face lit by the glow of the setting sun and lifted to catch the slight breeze, Madawi peacefully with a sincere smile explained.

"All prayer calls begin by telling us that there is one God and only one God," she paused and we continued to stroll. She then offered more, "The evening prayer call tells us to rejoice in the day that has been and come to prayer."

As she spoke, I understood how much this meant to her, how deeply she believed in her religion and her relationship with God. This touched me in a very special way. When we returned to the villa, she went to pray as the prayer call had instructed her to do.

A few days passed, and we had returned to *Dhahran* when my doorbell unexpectedly rang one evening.

There stood Saleem holding a little jam jar filled with white powder, without any labels or markings.

"For you, Mrs. Teresa," he announced as he handed it to me, "from princess." I thanked him graciously and he departed. Over the years, Madawi never ceased to amaze me with things like this. Casually, something would be mentioned and she would say that she would do something or send something; however, every time her non-verbal communication would convey that the issue was fairly insignificant, leaving me to wonder if it would really come to pass or not. Then, always as promised, the item would show up or the event would happen. I guess I was amazed that she never wrote it down to remember, as I would have to do. With so much on her plate to do and remember in her role as mother, princess and school owner (which I will explain in Chapter Fifteen), I was always amazed how she never forgot the minute details, the little things she said she would do.

I ran to David with the little jar in hand. We placed it on the coffee table and stared intently, silently. I had told David about our conversation and the powder, but we were just a little perplexed. What was it? What were the ingredients? It was white, speckled with black dots like pepper, and odorless. We were puzzled. No sooner had we begun to joke about what it could be when the phone rang. It was Madawi.

"Did you get the powder?" she inquired.

"Yes, I have it here," I answered, smiling at David to let him know that it was Madawi on the line.

"Good," she replied and proceeded to tell me how to take it.

"Start on the third day of menstruation," she began. "Each morning you should put a big spoonful in something to drink and take it," she continued. "But take it for three days, huh, even if your menstruation stops."

"Okay," I answered as I quickly jotted down the details. I proceeded to thank her again for sharing this with me and concluded with, "I'll see you tomorrow."

"Insha Allah," she replied, *"yellah,"* and again I heard that smile in her voice before she hung up the phone.

What a leap of faith! Here I was about to take some potion, and I had no idea of what it was. It was with sincere trust that I tried my first dose of the powder. Unfortunately, there was one very important detail that Madawi had neglected to share. You positively should mix the mysterious powder with something hot to drink. I, on the other hand, had selected my usual morning milk to try my first dose. I poured the required tablespoon into the milk, stirred like crazy, and shot the whole glass down in one gulp. Almost immediately, I felt as if I would regurgitate as the powder somehow hardened like cement in my mouth. I ran to the sink to spit it out before it hardened further. Gasping, I could not believe I had even tried.

That afternoon in the salon, I shared my experience with Madawi, the details poured out as I entered the room, exasperated as to how bad it was. She began to laugh as I continued and her chuckles became deeper by the moment.

"No, Mrs. Teresa," she sputtered through her laughter, "you should drink it in the morning with your tea!"

Silly me. I had not thought about the fact that Madawi always had hot tea in the mornings, not cold milk! As our laughter waned, we decided that I should try again the next morning. I did and the next two days that followed.

A month passed and my menstruation date came and went. I was ecstatic. I just knew that the powder had worked. As soon as I could get a ride to the store, I purchased a home test to try the next morning. After the suggested 20-minute wait, I could have sworn that the color had changed. Now granted it only changed a minuscule amount, but I did see change! So I zipped down to the compound medical clinic with tray and perpendicular stick in hand to gain confirmation. It was so disappointing when they told me that it was not true. I shared the news with Madawi that afternoon; I was completely crushed.

She empathized, yet reassured me. "It will come," she consoled. "Patience."

And come it did. The next month the same thing happened; I was late. Somewhat embarrassed because of my ridiculous behavior the month before, I waited a few days longer before I took the home test. This time it was clear, extremely clear. In only five minutes, the color had changed. I just knew I was pregnant. Again, away I went to the clinic with tray and stick in hand. As Madawi had predicted, the powder had worked, and I was going to be a mom.

Over the years, with Madawi's permission and her as my supplier, I shared this mysterious powder with several friends who wanted to conceive. Several of them had even undergone unsuccessful fertility treatment. Yet, every single one became pregnant after taking the powder. I asked many times what was in the powder, and I always got an answer, sometimes a lengthy one, yet never one that I fully understood. I deduced that it was made of various herbs, processed painstakingly by the "old" women in a "special way" with "special ingredients." After time, I quit trying to know and was just happy that it existed.

I could not have asked for a better place to be while expecting a baby. The Saudis truly revere the pregnant woman. Thus, I was pampered in every way, which stands to reason, understanding the basic value of family that they hold so dear. Everyone I came in contact with wanted to take care of the pregnant lady, shopkeepers, compound workers, all of the Arabs. Weekly and sometimes daily, gifts arrived at my door that would make my pregnancy easier or items I would need in the days to come. In casual conversation one afternoon, a rocking chair was mentioned. The following night, a beautiful bent-wood rocker showed up at my door, compliments of Madawi. The doorbell would ring and there would be Saleem, holding a plate of my favorite foods. "From princess," Saleem would say as he smiled and presented me with the latest gift. It went on and on.

A pregnant woman is revered in a way that is hard to express. Their culture truly understands that carrying the life of the future is a huge blessing and responsibility. Even the young adhere to this belief and act accordingly, which became apparent to me when I was five months pregnant.

Barely showing the signs of my condition and doing the things I normally did, I was working in our flower garden early one evening when I heard a huge rumbling sound in the distance. It was such an unusual sound that it immediately got my attention as it became louder and obviously closer. Curious, I headed into the villa to check out front and see what all the commotion was about. Just as I reached my front door, my doorbell rang. Surprised, I opened it to find Fahad standing in *thobe* and *guthra,* smiling from ear to ear. I could barely hear his words over the clamor of his brand new Ferrari, idling behind him. As he had predicted when I first started tutoring him, he had bought the car he wanted and he was there to take me for a ride. Before he put the car in gear, he paused and looked at me with such intent.

"Mrs. Teresa," he began, "we will go around the compound. I don't want to take a chance on hurting the baby."

"Fahad," I replied, "you aren't going to hurt the baby."

"But, Mrs. Teresa," he continued in a very concerned voice, "the streets are dangerous. I will take you on the street after the baby is here."

Sensing his immense concern and respecting him for it, I agreed that it was a deal, but only if he let me drive it in the secluded desert one day. He beamed again and drove me around the compound with the car's tee tops removed at a maximum speed of ten miles per hour!

With Madawi's help, special permission was granted for me to give birth at the airbase hospital, which is usually reserved strictly for royalty and Saudi military and is completely off limits to American expats.

The privilege would only include the last three months of the pregnancy and the birth; however, all other prenatal care would have to be obtained through local hospitals and doctors that expatriates were allowed to use. Doctor Badera, a British-trained Egyptian obstetrician at the Al-*Mana* hospital, was the first doctor recommended by our company doctor at the compound medical clinic, but a list of acceptable others was available.

I tried Dr. Badera, but the visits were frustrating beyond imagination. You were to make an appointment, yet you did not see the doctor at your appointed time. Rather, you showed up on the day of your appointment and were seen based on when your file came up. For those who had figured out the system, it was easy. One would simply send her driver to the hospital following the *Fajr* prayer on the day of the appointment. The driver would have her file pulled, subsequently placing the madame near the beginning of the stack of files for the doctor to see. Hence, by the time the lady would arrive at the hospital, she would be seen much quicker than those who waited until they arrived to have their file pulled.

Unaware of how things worked, David and I arrived at 9:30 a.m. for my first appointment and sat until the *Dohr* prayer around 11:30 a.m. I was then instructed to return after the *Asr* prayer around 4 p.m. because my file was still low in the stack. I finally saw Dr. Badera at 7:45 p.m. that evening. To top it all off, David and I could not wait together in the same waiting room due to the Kingdom's segregation policies. Naturally, he wanted to attend the doctor appointments with me, but he had to wait in the men's section while I waited in the women's until it was our time to see the doctor. You can imagine how frustrating this would be. So, in the name of convenience, we sought another doctor for my routine monthly prenatal visits. This was a mistake that makes me cringe to this very day.

We selected Doctor Sulleiman, a doctor on the clinic's referral list, because several women on the compound had recommended him. I was in my third month and doing beautifully when I called for my first appointment. I was full of energy and progressing normally, as far as I could tell. I saw Dr. Sulleiman for my third and fourth month visits and all was fine. At each appointment, he assured David and me that everything was going well. Feeling terrific on my fifth month's visit, the day before I was to take a two-week cruise on a yacht in the Ionian Sea off the coast of Greece, I was hit with the shock of my life.

Following what seemed like a routine ultrasound, Dr. Sulleiman proceeded to tell David and me some incredible news.

"It seems, Mrs. Teresa, that your cervix is open and the placenta is low," he paused. "It is clear," he continued, "you will lose the baby, perhaps sooner if you fly tomorrow."

Stunned by what we were hearing, he began to talk about scheduling an appointment to abort the baby! As I sat on the examining table, I heard his words, yet I could not break the surreal feeling that I felt. It took me a few minutes to digest what he was saying and snap back to reality. I then began to question.

"But," I stammered, "everything has been just fine, Dr. Sulleiman. I feel too good. How could things be this bad? You never said there could be a problem ... everything has been going so well." My eyes darted at David, seeking answers.

"I told you in previous visits that things were not progressing properly," Dr. Sulleiman defended.

"No, you never said anything," I retaliated as my temper began to rise. Again, announcing that he was correct, he left the room to "make preparations," and David and I just stared at each other for a moment. Then, almost simultaneously we agreed that this just could not be so. I felt too good, and I knew that he had never mentioned that there were any complications or even the possibility of such. Then, as has happened so many times in my life, that little voice, that little inner voice that is there when needed, kicked in, *"seek another opinion."* Perhaps a Saudi woman would never question this doctor, but I was not going to simply accept his diagnosis.

When he returned to the room, I demanded a copy of my file. Dr. Sulleiman was immediately defensive and spoke to me as if I were just an emotional female who did not understand the medical ramifications. I persisted, and David, sensing my feelings, stepped in to bolster the request. Under duress, Dr. Sulleiman spoke to his nurse in Arabic and she disappeared. As we waited, he continued to try and tell me that we were incorrect and that we were making a grave mistake.

Time passed, oh, so much time. It seemed like an hour before the nurse returned, when in reality, it was probably only 20 minutes or so. As we waited, my blood pressure continued to rise and my heart felt as if it would beat out of my chest! When the nurse returned, Dr. Sulleiman spoke to her again in Arabic. After her response, he then turned to us.

"It seems as if our copier is broken," he began as he handed me the folder. "The copies are not very clear."

I opened the folder, and down the middle of his previous diagnoses, a blank line was conveniently marking out the remarks he had made on each visit. Enraged, I stomped from his office, my *abaya* flying behind me like the wicked witch of the west, as David tried to keep up with me. By the time I reached the office building doors, I was ready to spit nails and then … cry. I hit the doors so hard that they bounced off the wall behind me, resounding throughout the building. The heat blasted me like I was stepping into a furnace, and all I wanted to do was run. Run from this place, run as fast as I possibly could. The entire way to the car, my voice became louder as the tears ran down my cheeks, and my determination grew stronger as I rambled to David about what to do next.

"Go to Al-*Mana* now. This can't be true. I know it's not. Who does he think he is?" As I slammed the car door, I exclaimed, "I will see Dr. Badera tonight!"

Despite my determination, a small part of me could not help but be scared, very scared. What if this quack was correct? What if I was going to lose my baby? My emotions swung between fear and anger, with the anger coming across a lot stronger. Without a word, David drove like a bat of hell to *Al-Mana,* and I offered no objection. He, too, was raging with emotion. The conversation halted as we stopped and started with each stop sign, speeding in between. Each of us was trying to process what we had heard, trying to get a handle on what we were feeling. Finally, at a traffic light when the car completely stopped for more than a moment, he grabbed my hand and broke the silence.

"It will be okay, honey," he encouraged. "We will see Dr. Badera."

Even though I knew in my heart, deep in my heart, that Dr. Sulleiman was wrong, I still needed to hear it from Dr. Badera.

In front of *Al-Mana*, the car came to a jolting stop as David parked in a partial parking space with the front of the car on the sidewalk. Although unusual to Americans, it is a common sight in the Kingdom. Without saying a word, he jumped out of the running car and left me behind. Discussion was not required. I knew he was going in to get me an appointment, have my file pulled, and he knew I would sit in the car. As I sat, I quivered in spite of the 100-degree heat.

"We have to come back after Asr," he said rather quietly as he got back in the car. He pulled from the space and began to drive. After a few blocks, the silence was broken.

"Do you want to go get some lunch?" he asked.

"No," I replied, "I want to go to Madawi."

He understood. Without saying a word, he whipped a U-turn and headed for the palace.

I found her as I often did in the afternoons in her leather recliner in the salon reading the newspaper.

Her face lit up as we entered at an unexpected time.

"Mrs. Teresa," she exclaimed as she stood, smiling to greet us.

We greeted, as we always did with traditional kisses. I then took off my *abaya* and folded it as is customary before I sat, while David and Madawi greeted. She was quite comfortable with David and never felt the need to veil in front of him. With David she acted as if he were a member of the family as well.

Before I could begin, Madawi did.

"Are you excited about your trip?" she inquired as she settled back into the recliner. "Are you packed?" she continued.

"Oh, Madawi!" I sputtered, not purposefully interrupting or ignoring her questions. "He says I am going to lose the baby!"

"Who? What?" she questioned, obviously confused as to the problem and shocked as well.

Then, as the mixed juices appeared as they always did on a silver platter in front of me, I took a deep breath, selected a glass of juice, and paused for a moment until the Filipino servant left, not wanting her to overhear. The Filipino servants and nannies seemed to hear everything and would pass the information on to willing ears. If I was ever curious or wanted to know more details about something, I would just ask one of the Filipinos. After taking a long sip of juice, which was refreshing after the heat and the emotional exhaustion that was starting to engulf me, I told her the events of the morning. She leaned forward and listened intently without saying a word until I was finished.

Then after a long pause, she firmly stated, "That is crazy, Mrs. Teresa, *kolasse.*" She pushed firmly back into her chair as she spoke. Her hands flying at lightning speed while she talked.

"It is crazy," she repeated. "You look too good to be sick. There is nothing wrong with the baby!" she stated in her matter-of-fact way, and the issue was concluded in her eyes. A long pause followed as we all sipped our juice. It was Madawi who continued the conversation.

"If it will make you feel better, you see Dr. Badera tonight, but there is no reason." She continued stating her point again, "The baby is fine."

As always, she had a way of making things okay for me. After all, she was a mother of six. I relaxed as much as possible under the circumstances, and we spent the remainder of the afternoon in the salon talking, drinking and, of course, eating. When Madawi excused herself to pray at the *Asr* prayer, we left for *Al-Mana.*

It was past 10:30 p.m. before the nurse called my name from the other side of the partition, the partition that separated the women. Before she could finish saying my name, David came from the men's waiting room and I from the ladies, and we were in front of her face ready to see the doctor. I had rehearsed a thousand times in my mind how I would approach Dr. Badera about this visit. He would know it was not a regular visit, but I did not want to let him know what we had been told. I wanted to hear his honest diagnosis.

As we entered, the nurse showed us to our chairs. Before I sat, she stepped in front of me and brushed my chair off, which was done for me every time I sat in a chair at the doctor's office when I was pregnant, out of respect, I assume. Dr. Badera stood and welcomed us in the sincere Arab way. "It is good to see you, Mrs. Teresa," he stated as he greeted me, and then turning to David, "and to see you, Mr. Davids."

Settling into his chair behind his desk, he continued, "and how can I help you this evening?"

I began trying to be as clear in English as I could while being vague so as not to skew his response. "I cannot tell you why, Dr. Badera, but I need to know … know tonight how the baby is doing."

With a somewhat questioning look on his face, he sat up more erect in his chair and placed his elbows on the desk. "So you want to know how the baby is?" he repeated.

I responded affirmatively and then smiled the best fake smile I could muster. "I can't tell you why I need to know right now," I paused, "I just need to know."

Sensing my distress, he jumped right to the point. "Okay," he replied curiously as he wrote an inter-hospital work order. Shortly, he handed the paper to me as he called to his nurse who was always standing right outside the door. He told her to take me to radiology and have an ultrasound done. He then instructed her to bring the results back immediately to him. We rose to follow the nurse and thanked him.

"I promise I will tell why I need to know," I said as we shook hands, which is customary to do when arriving and departing a room in Saudi, and we left.

It was well past midnight before we entered his office again, which is not uncommon in the Kingdom.

Taking the file from the nurse, he sat again behind his desk. As he mulled over the papers, David and I sat quietly, anxiously awaiting his diagnosis.

"Well, Mrs. Teresa," he began. "everything looks fine." He smiled and leaned back in his chair, obviously tired from a long evening. Still not reassured, my questions began.

"And my placenta?" I questioned.

"It is fine," he replied.

"You mean it is not low?" I inquired.

Taken back by the nature of my questions, he sat upright again. "Well, yes, it is a little low, Mrs. Teresa, but that is exactly where it should be at this point of your pregnancy," he replied. He then explained how the placenta starts low and moves up with the progression of the pregnancy, drawing a small diagram on some paper to illustrate. Satisfied with the response, my inquiry continued.

"And my cervix?" I questioned, "is it open?"

The curiosity on his face intensified. "Mrs. Teresa, your cervix is open, as it should be," he responded rather firmly. "Why such questions?" he continued obviously curious as to their origin. For one final piece of assurance I inquired again, relaxing just a little.

"And you are sure that the baby is fine?"

"Yes," he replied very firmly. "Everything is fine, Mrs. Teresa."

He continued, "Why do you ask such questions?"

Taking a deep breath and feeling very relieved, I shared the events of the day with him. He listened intently, his eyes piercing me as if looking for details, which is typical for Arabs when they are unsure.

"I assure you, Mrs. Teresa, you are just fine," he responded when my story was complete.

"And so it would be okay for me to fly to Greece tomorrow?" I asked.

"Do you want to fly to Greece tomorrow?" he asked, smiling.

"Well, yes," I hesitated. "But only if it is safe for the baby."

"Then, of course, you may fly." He paused, "The baby is just fine." And he smiled as he closed my folder.

After the scare of our lives was over, the next four months passed quickly. Finally, at my seventh month, I was allowed on the airbase to begin seeing Dr. Kurat, Madawi's obstetrician. Fortunately, from this point on it was not only the perfect setting to be pregnant but the perfect pregnancy as well.

During my eighth month prenatal appointment, Dr. Kurat wanted to have one final ultrasound done. He was a bit concerned about how big the baby was getting. Holding my inter-hospital order, as everything seems to require an enormous amount of paper in the Kingdom, David and I waited outside radiology. After a while, my name was called and in we went. As the British technician, Sharon, performed the ultrasound, we chit-chatted. When she homed in on the baby, she pointed out "the bum," as she put it, and then the baby's face appeared, clear as a bell. It was if I was looking at a photograph, and I gasped with amazement. I actually saw my child 20 days before he saw the world. Then, because my excitement was almost uncontrollable, I asked, "Is it a boy or a girl?"

"Oh now, hon, I can't give you that information today," Sharon replied in a heavy accent, "as we can't be sure. It could be her thumb, you know."

"I realize that it's not exact, I just want to have an idea," I replied.

"I understand you want to know, but I can't tell you because of what happened in *Riyadh*," she answered.

"What happened in *Riyadh?*" I questioned.

Sharon proceeded to share with David and me a story about a pregnant lady in *Riyadh* many years before, just after the hospital had purchased the ultrasound equipment. Believing that they were doing the right thing, the staff told this particular father-to-be that the baby still in the wife's womb was a boy. Unfortunately, it had been her thumb, and the woman gave birth to a baby girl instead. The story goes that the father then refused the baby girl because the medical staff had told him that he would get a boy. The baby girl, to him, was not his. The child was kept at the hospital for months and finally sent to an orphanage. Astounding!

"Oh, Sharon, I promise that if it is a boy or a girl, we'll take it home!" I declared.

Sharon laughed as she replied, "Oh, I know you will, but I would be on a plane to London if I told you." She chuckled again as she managed to sidestep my endless inquires.

The following Thursday, I saw Sharon shopping at the *souks* downtown on King Khalid Street. She recognized me first and she came running across the street, calling to me. She leaned close to me and said, "You know I think you have a boy there. But don't hold me to it!" She smiled as she left with her friends. I looked at David and our excitement shown through the smiles on our faces. As my due date approached, be it a boy or a girl, the anticipation began to swell.

To add to the exhilaration, my dear friends, Gay and Molly, decided to organize a baby shower for me. It would be a surprise shower on the compound with fifteen of my American friends invited ... and Madawi. Because not just anyone can call the palace and speak to the princess, David was assigned the task of inviting Madawi to the shower. Gay and Molly would do the rest. It was not until after the big surprise that I learned of the comical events that precipitated the shower.

I was under the impression that I was having a dinner party that particular evening. Madawi and the Colonel, my parents, Robert, Gay, Molly, and Don were invited. I was busy getting ready when the telephone rang, about 30 minutes before my guests were scheduled to arrive. It was Molly on the line, frantic and insisting that I come to the recreation center immediately to give my opinion on some artwork she was previewing to buy for the compound restaurant. Objecting because of my dinner party, I offered to help the following day. That excuse failed with Molly, and she insisted I come over immediately. Reluctantly, I agreed to run down quickly.

When I arrived, the room was filled with over 60 ladies to surprise me! It was a joyous and memorable occasion. The funny thing was, as I entered the room, I noticed many women there were women that I really did not associate with and was a touch surprised to see them. Afterward at dinner at our villa, David, Gay and Molly laughed deeply as they told me how the ladies on the compound who were not originally invited were calling and asking to be invited to the shower once they knew the princess would attend! All of them wanted to see the princess and be able to say that they had been to a shower with her. Above all, they wanted to see what she would give me as a present. Peyton Place at its extreme, no one wanted to be left out.

Fortunately, they got their wish. Madawi did attend, and she was quite excited to see what an American baby shower was all about. Her daughters joined in as well. Maha was a touch disappointed, however, because she thought that a baby shower meant that it would literally be raining babies, and she was curious as to how this could be! As I opened gifts and passed them around the room, everyone moved to the edge of their chairs as I reached for the small box Madawi had handed to me when she kissed me on her arrival. Inside I found the most exquisite 18K gold and diamond pin. In Arabic, written in diamonds across the top, it said *"bisme Allah."* From each end of the pin hung a smaller pin, one all diamonds set in 18K gold saying *"Allah,"* and the other a small "evil eye" pendant, also 18K gold and encircled in diamonds as well. All of these were meant to thank God for my new blessing and keep the evil eye, as the Arabs believe, away from the new baby, keeping him safe. It is a beautiful piece that one day my son will pass to his first born as a gift from his Saudi princess, his "auntie" Madawi.

Shortly before my due date, Madawi mentioned, in her way, one afternoon that I needed a nanny. For her, the idea of a child without an accompanying nanny just did not exist. Each of her children had their own nanny. A second "Mama somebody," as Madawi's children always referred to their nanny by name proceeded by "mama," to stay with them, care for their belongings, and fill in when Madawi was not present. Never were the girls alone, without the supervision of a caring nanny, preferably a Filipino one. I was truly touched by her offer, as I knew what it entailed. Only Saudis were in the Kingdom without a sponsor, and only Saudis could sponsor a *TCN* into the country. Even David and I were sponsored to be there by David's company. Hence, for Madawi to make this offer to me, she was actually offering to take full responsibility for this woman's actions while in the country, pay for her airline tickets, visas, medical expenses and her room and board. My only financial responsibility to this nanny was her monthly salary, a mere 1,000 SR (approximately $250) per month and any bonuses we chose to bestow. Therefore, an offer of this sort was more than just a suggestion. It was a commitment to me, to our friendship, and a tribute to her trust in me and how I would treat this woman.

Although honored by her offer, I had mixed emotions at first about the idea of a nanny. While it would be nice to have help, I did not want my baby thinking he had someone else as his mom. I explained to Madawi that the idea of a nanny did appeal to me, but I could not possibly want a nanny to care for my child, to provide those basic nurturing duties that come from the person we all know as "mom."

"I want to be the one to take care of the baby," I explained, "it is my way."

"I understand, Mrs. Teresa," she began. "You've seen my children when they are hurt or cry. They come to me if I am there, not to their nanny. They know who 'Mama' is." Placing her tea on the table, she added, "But it wouldn't hurt to have someone clean the house and do the wash." She continued, her hands gesturing along with her words, "And you spend all of your time with the baby." She glanced at me and paused ... a long pause as she resettled in her recliner.

"And you understand," she said with reluctance, "I don't arrange for others, even Saudis," she paused, "to get nannies into the country ..." She began to ramble a bit, clearly wanting to say something, but not wanting to say it directly. "I just can't do that because you never know." She hesitated again, "What goes on in someone's house."

I had heard numerous rumors of TCNs being abused by their employers in Kingdom, but I never witnessed it. However, from Madawi's response, I then knew that the rumors I had heard were likely true. Silence fell over us. Uncomfortably, we sat and sipped our tea. Conversation was not needed. We both understood how the other felt.

As always, after this kind of encounter with

Madawi, the doorbell rang three weeks later. This time it was our new nanny, Alice. It was all arranged. She would live at the palace with Madawi's Filipino nannies and servants; the driver would bring her to the villa every morning and come back to collect her in the evening. She was completely available for us, seven days a week, at our beck and call.

Soon it was Halloween, Trick-or-Treat night on the compound, and all of Madawi's kids and each of their nannies were at my villa as they were every year to join in the festivities with the American children. I am convinced that the nannies had as much or more fun than the kids at Mrs. Teresa's villa. When they would accompany the children to the compound, it was their opportunity to be in an environment more like their homeland. They were free, so to speak, free to be with other Christians, with Americans, in a world within a world that was more like that to which they were accustomed. To be sure her children contributed as well, Madawi had Mama Ginny, the oldest and most respected of her nannies, go to the store that morning to buy tons of candy for us to distribute with ours to the trick-or-treaters. The entire week had been consumed with costume preparation, sprinkled with a little English study along the way. The girls were so excited as we began the evening with pizza at my villa before the traditional door-to-door visits for candy.

The evening was a whirl, and I was exhausted by the time the festivities were complete. I closed the villa door after hugging and kissing each good-bye and fell against it in exhaustion. I looked at David as he was cleaning up the villa. With a deep breath, I smiled softly as the real excitement was about to begin.

"It's time to go, I guess," I said as I took another deep breath.

"Yeah," he agreed as he gave me a subtle smile.

I gathered my bag, and we were off to the hospital. I had seen Dr. Kurat that morning, and he had said that if labor did not begin by the evening, I was to come in anyway. For the entire three months that I had seen Dr. Kurat, he had never once referred to Islam. He was always the professional, religiously removed doctor; however, as soon as I went into labor, he revealed his beliefs. As he would look at the fetal monitor printout, under his breath he would repeat *"insha Allah"* and *"bisme Allah."* In an unusual way, this was comforting to me, particularly at this time. As labor progressed, the topic of medication arose. He made it clear that I would be fine, and that he was not comfortable with the doctor who would administer the epidural. As I had incredible trust in Dr. Kurat, it was enough for me to say no to the idea if he was not comfortable with it. Consequently, I endured the pain as he and David disappeared from the room.

In contrast to Madawi, I was any thing but royal in labor! Whereas she was calm, cool and collected, I was completely opposite in my demeanor and unaware of the grave situation that had developed. As I remained in the private labor room, I learned that David had been asked to accompany Dr. Kurat to his office. I had no idea why, and I was too exhausted to question further.

As the tea was served and idle conversation ensued,

the topic eventually turned to me.

"I feel we have a little problem, Mr. Davids" (Arabs always seem to add an "s" to David's name), Dr. Kurat began. Concerned, David listened intently.

"I feel we must take the baby out," he continued, "but I need your permission." Before David could answer, Dr. Kurat added, "Otherwise, I must wait ten more hours to do so without your word."

"If that is what is needed," David answered, "then get on with it. You can't leave her like that for ten more hours."

With that, the anesthesiologist was called and preparations were made. Almost symbolic or meaningful in some way, I heard the *Fajr* prayer call in the distance as the anesthesia mask came toward my face. *Mason David McCown* arrived by cesarean section at 4:08 a.m.

Curious about his conversation the night before, David asked a British nurse the following day why Dr. Kurat had made the comments he had made the night before. She explained cesarean birth is not viewed in the Saudi culture as a real birth; hence, men are reluctant to agree to such.

The room I awoke to was not nearly the suite Madawi had had, but it was nice and private. On my pillow, I found a small little box containing a surprise from David. It contained a new 24k gold bracelet, which is the traditional gift given to women after birth in the Kingdom. I was elated, and the pampering continued. Unlike the west, Saudi hospitals are in no hurry for you to leave after birth. I was pampered for five days, and the nurses met every need of my baby and me. In addition, my new Filipino nanny was on hand should the nurses not meet one.

As my five days passed, I saw several surprising aspects of Saudi family life — things I could not believe. As I walked down the hall, I saw many young girls there with their new babies. Although I understand babies and family are very important in the Saudi culture, it was surprising to see so many babies having babies. Many of the teenage moms did not seem very happy, and I knew why. For most of the more common Saudis, each new arrival did not automatically come with a nanny to help, as their budgets could not always afford the luxury of many servants. I knew that these young moms would not be able to rely on their husbands because Saudi men do not help like many American husbands do. I felt for these teenage moms because I knew they had lost their carefree childhood — prematurely forced into a marriage perhaps not of their choosing and to a man perhaps four times their age. I understood the hardship these teenagers would face as they went home with their new baby and possibly more children waiting for their care. The girl in the room next to mine was only 17 and birthing her third child. My favorite nurse from Scotland told me that one lady down the hall had just had her 12th child. Imagine the somber sunken black eyes of a young human birthing machine and you can envision some of the faces I saw.

Mason, not surprisingly, was the only Caucasian baby in the hospital; hence, they never needed to compare our hospital bracelets. As each new duty nurse would enter, she would comment as to how white he was. I could not help but chuckle.

Thirteen dark-haired, olive-skinned baby girls were Mason's nursery mates. Each night around 4 a.m., I would hear the wails of the many babies around the corner in the nursery. Shortly after the chorus would begin, one of the night nurses would roll Mason's bassinet into my room and silence would follow. Through the broken English explanations of the nurses' aides, I learned that they believed Mason was the culprit. David and I thought they were mistaken until his second night at home. He screamed all night, and it was obvious that the nurses were correct. He was the ringleader!

For the male side of the birth celebration, the men at the airbase remarked that they would have *kebsa* to celebrate: a whole goat for a boy and a half goat for a girl. Not really wanting to celebrate the birth of his first born with a goat, David kindly told the guys that a cake was more appropriate for our culture. Consequently, on the day following Mason's birth, David was met with a huge sheet cake at the office iced with *"Marhaba,* Mason," and everyone joined in to eat.

My desert home was a wonderful place to be pregnant, in spite of my brush with Dr. Sulleiman. The people were caring, respectful and joyous at the sight of a woman with child. They understand it is from the woman that a new generation comes, and in turn, revere the woman for the role that she plays.

ॐ *Chapter Thirteen* ॐ

Two for One

The mysterious Saudi powder was more effective than I could have ever imagined. When Mason was only ten months old, I learned that we had another angel on the way. Madawi was as surprised as me, and we laughed that I got "two for the price of one!" As before, my pregnancy proceeded beautifully; however, unlike before, I endured the long hours to see Dr. Badera at *Al-Mana* hospital for my prenatal care. Again, because of her concern, Madawi graciously arranged for me to see Dr. Kurat at the airbase hospital for the birth and final three months of my prenatal care, a privilege that I welcomed. The British technician, Sharon, who had told me Mason's sex at the *souks,* was more forthcoming with her prediction of the new baby's sex. However, she was unable to verbalize her opinion at the hospital, so she coyly handed me a small piece of paper when I left the ultrasound room. As she placed it in my hand, she smiled and wished us the best. When I was in the hall, I opened the tiny piece of paper and read her message.

"I believe it is a girl! Congrats!"

That afternoon at the palace, I shared the news with Madawi.

"Now you know, Mrs. Teresa," she started as we had our regular lunch, "only *Allah* knows."

"I know that it's not for sure, but it's still exciting," I replied. "And if it is so," I continued, "I would like to ask your permission about her name."

"My permission?" Madawi queried as she gave me a questioning look.

"If it is a girl, Madawi," I started, "I would like to name my little princess after my big princess." I looked at her intently to read her true feelings through her eyes. "Would you mind?"

Madawi stopped eating and looked at me, surprised. "You want to name her Madawi?" she asked.

"Yes, I would be honored." I replied.

"Of course, Mrs. Teresa!" Madawi exclaimed, "But it would be I who would be honored."

And so it was decided that if the baby were a little girl, her name would be *Michelle Madawi McCown*. My little princess named after my big princess to honor our friendship and to commemorate the time and place of her birth.

Only five weeks before my due date, the company surprised us all with a move. All company families would move the following week into the new DM 22 compound. With the first move, they had placed all families on one of two compounds. However, they believed that we could be better served and safer if we were all combined onto one large compound. DM 22 had all the amenities of DM 18 and more. It also had a medical clinic, a building built specifically as a preschool, and a made-to-order dance room complete with mirrors on the wall. The day the Colonel and Mashael took me to see the compound when it was finalized that my company would rent the facility, he beamed as he showed me the dance room. It was just what I wanted. Although we had known they were building a new compound for us, we had no idea that they would complete it so quickly. I never dreamed it would be so close to the birth of my daughter.

Between the excitement of my delivery and our move to the new compound, anticipation also grew about Madawi's cousin's wedding in *Riyadh*. Although invited, I unfortunately was unable to attend. We had discussed it, but it was just too close to my due date to go flying around the country. My mom — Mama Anne as the family had come to know her — was invited to go with Madawi and the girls, and I got to enjoy the excitement of it all through her.

Dress selection and the like, we had a ball getting my mom ready to party in *Riyadh*. Soon, Wednesday came and Saleem arrived at her villa around 3 p.m. We kissed and she was off for the weekend. I watched the car pull away from the doorstep, feeling hot, heavy and really pregnant in the summer heat of the desert. I went inside and decided that I needed to rest for a while. Reaching for the hot tea Ann had brought me, I settled down into my recliner and smiled because I knew the fun that Mama was about to experience.

The next morning, something unusual happened. Because I had never gone into labor with Mason, I had no idea what was happening. It was my water, leaking. Not really knowing what was going on, but knowing enough to seek help, David and I headed to the airbase to see Dr. Kurat. Sure enough, I was in labor two weeks before my due date. I called Daddy from the hospital. He immediately wanted to call Mom and have her fly back from *Riyadh* before the wedding that evening.

"No, Daddy," I protested, "I'm fine." Encouragingly, I said, "Plus, Dr. Kurat said that he's going to let nature take its course tonight, and if nothing happens, he will induce labor in the morning. Please don't call Mom and spoil her fun." To further bolster my plea, I added, "Really, nothing will happen tonight." Daddy reluctantly agreed.

At 4:28 a.m. during the *Fajr* prayer just like with her brother, *Michelle Madawi McCown* was born naturally. By 5:30 p.m. the following day, Mama, Madawi and the girls arrived at the airbase in *Dhahran* with guards snapping to attention as the entourage proceeded down the halls with *abayas* flying behind each of them as they headed to my room. Her birth had been a surprise to us all. After the traditional greetings, everyone settled in to speculate about what had happened to bring Michelle Madawi so early. After lengthy debate, we all agreed her early arrival was probably because I had overdone it in our move to DM 22, our new compound surrounded by the Arabian Gulf, the week prior.

Feeling assured that we had solved the mystery, we enjoyed tea in my hospital room as Madawi recounted the night before. Talking with her hands as usual, she laughed as she told us all about Mama.

"It was around 3:30 a.m. when Mama Anne came to me," she began. "I know it was 3:30 a.m. because I looked at my watch when I saw her coming across the floor, and I just knew that she was coming to tell me that she was ready to sleep. But when she got to me, she told me that you were having the baby!" Madawi exclaimed as we all listened intently. "I told her, yes, I knew you were having a baby, but she insisted that you were having the baby that very minute." Madawi broke with a laugh of amazement. "I told her no way because you were not due for two weeks." Madawi continued to tell the story, getting more excited with each detail. "She wouldn't listen to me!" Madawi uttered with the utmost enthusiasm as she looked at me to convince me that what she was saying was true to the letter. Throughout the story, Mama interjected periodically to collaborate the events. Madawi continued.

"Mama Anne insisted that you were having the baby right then, and I told her she was just nervous because she was away from you. I then told her to go to the house with the younger girls to sleep." Madawi's energy was heightened as she continued, "And then she came to my room this morning, just after I had gone to bed, and told me that Baba Don, my father, had called and that you had the baby!" Madawi's surprise about Mama just knowing was evident in her body language as she concluded the story. We were all amazed how she just knew. Then we drank more tea and laughed some more.

"Next time," Madawi began and then sipped some tea. "Next time Mama Anne tells me something is happening," she interjected, "I'm going to believe her!" We all laughed at the passion in her statement and agreed to always listen to Mama Anne!

Because Michelle Madawi was early, she was jaundiced and had to be in an incubator for several days. After Mason's birth, I needed time to recuperate and enjoyed the days of rest. However, with Michelle Madawi, things were different. Because of her early arrival, the nursery at our villa was not complete. I had no clothes that would fit her because she was premature and small. With all of this raging in my head, I became extremely anxious, cooped up in that hospital room. I was driving everyone crazy walking the halls, checking the monitoring records in neonatal intensive care, double-checking her feedings and vital signs. By the second day, the nursing staff had had enough of me and obviously told Dr. Kurat. As he entered my room that evening, he explained that he understood that I felt good and was anxious. Looking at David, he offered a wonderful suggestion.

"Why don't you take Teresa out for a while?" he suggested. "Perhaps have a nice dinner and let her do some things that she feels she needs to do."

David was surprised and questioned, "You mean I can take her and then bring her back while she is still admitted as a patient?"

Dr. Kurat agreed somewhat emphatically, looking at each of us with a sneaky smile. "As far as anyone is concerned, you're only out and about in the hospital."

Who would ever imagine that a doctor would just let a patient disappear for a few hours! Quickly, I jumped out of bed, put my *abaya* over my pajamas, and slipped on my tennis shoes.

"Let's go!" I exclaimed, and David agreed. Stopping

first by the nursery to check on Michelle Madawi, we were off for an evening of dinner and shopping. The evening really lifted my spirits and gave the nursing staff a much-needed break from me. Dr. Kurat was so intuitive and knew exactly the right medicine for me.

After the seemingly endless five-day period, Dr. Kurat came to my room to discuss Michelle Madawi.

"She is doing much better," he began. "We will take her out of the incubator today." "However," he continued, "she is still small at only 2.1 kg (approximately 4-1/2 lbs.), and I usually do not let babies go home until they weigh over 2.5 kg." Seeing the disappointment on my face, he did not even pause before continuing. "However, since you and David are Western and this is not your first baby, I will release the two of you tonight."

Grateful and relieved, I thanked him profusely for all that he had done for us. Before he left, he turned to me again and added, "Call me on my mobile if you have any questions or need me for any reason."

That evening we took our Michelle Madawi to her new home to meet her big brother. Two evenings later, allowing me time to rest, Madawi stopped by to see Michelle Madawi and me. She wanted to hold the baby since she could not when she had visited in the hospital. We all enjoyed the evening snuggling the baby and playing with Mason. Before she left, she stopped abruptly on her way to the door.

"Oh!" she exclaimed, "I almost forgot." She reached in her handbag and gave me a small gift bag.

"For Madawi," she said as she smiled a beaming smile.

I opened the small package and found a beautiful hair barrette, about one and a half karats of diamonds set in 18-karat gold. I could hardly find the words, as I was completely stunned.

"Oh, Madawi," I stammered, "it is absolutely beautiful. Thank you!"

"And it will beautiful on little Madawi," she added. "You're welcome."

I reached up and gave her a big hug.

"Thank you so much," I whispered in her ear.

"*Afwan*, Mrs. Teresa, *ashufee baden, insha Allah*," she said most sincerely, and out the door she went.

When Michelle Madawi was only seven months old, another round with obstetricians in the Kingdom came my way. This time it was not a happy occasion as before. It was *Ramadan,* and I had a horrible pain in my lower abdomen that started with what I believed was my monthly menstruation. Two days passed, and the pain became more localized in my right lower side. Unable to bear the pain any longer, I sought help at our compound clinic. Believing it to be an ovarian cyst, the compound doctor, Dr. Neal, wanted me to see Dr. Wahib at the Saad Medical Clinic, a newer clinic that had very reputable physicians. Because it was the weekend, if Dr. Neal referred me on this particular night, I would have to go to the local on-call emergency room, which was not Saad Clinic.

My situation was grave. If I possibly could, Dr. Neal wanted me to hang on until Saturday, the first day of the work week for Saudis. If it had not been for him, I would have never made it through the next 36 hours. I was in excruciating pain, and I could not move. Dr. Neal tapped a private stock of class three drugs to give me powerful painkillers, which were strictly forbidden in the Kingdom. Luckily, the company had received a small amount for our clinic to use in such emergencies. He came by the villa every two hours, even through the nights, for the entire 36 hours to check my blood pressure, make sure that I was okay, and administer more medicine when necessary.

Finally, Saturday morning came. Dr. Neal called, and David drove me to Saad the moment their doors opened. Seeing that I was in so much pain, the nurses fortunately put David and me in a private room to wait, allowing us to be together. As David read, I lay on a stretch of hard, interlocking hospital chairs until we saw Dr. Wahib around 4:30 p.m. that afternoon. He also felt I had an ovarian cyst, but he could not see anything clearly on the ultrasound. Consequently, he decided to perform a labrinscopy that evening. Not really wanting what I assumed was optional surgery in a third world country, I protested.

"Mrs. Teresa, we do not have a choice," Dr. Wahib began. "You will be fine. This is only a surgery to see what is wrong. Two stitches only, promise."

Still concerned, I agreed because my little inner voice wasn't screaming, I was in excruciating pain, and I saw his British degree on the wall in his office. He had attended the same medical school as Dr. Kurat. I noted this to him, and he said that he knew Dr. Kurat. This made me feel better, but only a little.

Because it was *Ramadan*, normal daily routines are

completely reversed. The days are like nights and the nights like days. I was to report to *Al-Thomairy* hospital around 8 p.m., and Dr. Wahib would do the surgery around 11:30 p.m. Because everything happened so suddenly, not even Madawi could get me into the airbase hospital. Permission to go there takes time to process, even for a princess.

David and I reported to the hospital as Dr. Wahib had instructed, but nothing is fast in the Kingdom. It took David over an hour to have me admitted while I sat in pain. Around 9:30 p.m., I was finally in my assigned room. Nervous, I paced with a limp due to the pain while David checked out all the features of the room. As we talked and I hobbled, a small-framed Indian nurse's aide came into the room with a small stack of white towels, offering them to me in broken English. Having already showered at home, I shook my head, meaning that I did not need any towels right now. Assuming that she would put them in the bath, David and I continued talking. About 30 minutes later, the same little nurse's aide came in a second time. Again, she had a stack of towels in her hands, only this time they were blue, but I did not take much notice at the time. I shook my head "no," indicating that I did not need any towels right then, and I tried to tell her through body language that I had already showered. She stared at me for a few moments, looked at David and then left. I simply could not understand why she wanted me to take a shower so badly. Another hour passed, and she came in yet again. This time she had a large stack of peach-colored towels, nice fluffy ones that looked as if they were new. She offered them with a most desperate look on her face. Then it clicked. She thought I had been refusing her towels each time, and she had brought more appealing towels for the "demanding American woman." I looked at David and could tell that he got the same impression. As he turned his back to us to chuckle, I smiled and immediately responded.

"Oh," I began, taking the stack of towels from her, "thank you, thank you, *Shukran, Shukran*," I repeated, hoping she knew Arabic since she did not seem to know English.

Within a moment she had the most unbelievable look of relief on her face, as if she were thinking, "Finally." After she left, we laughed deeply — only in Saudi Arabia! The humor was just what I needed to break the tension of my situation.

It was not long before they came to take me to surgery. I was a nervous wreck. The idea of surgery in the Kingdom, unlike the idea of childbirth, was frightening to me. I never had a problem with the idea of giving birth in this distant, third world country because it is a natural, everyday occurrence. Women do it every day! Surgery, however, was a different story.

As she had done with both of my pregnancies, Mom spent the morning contacting people on the compound she knew had my blood type, A negative, to ask if they would be on standby that evening should I need blood. The idea of obtaining blood from the local blood bank was not an option for me. All Westerners working in the Kingdom must go through screening for AIDS;

hence, all Westerners have been cleared of HIV or they would not be in Kingdom. Locals, on the other hand, were a different story and more at risk for tainted blood. In Saudi Arabia, anyone can give blood at the blood bank. Because of the huge demand due to excessive car accidents, a person donating would be paid 500SR (approximately $125) for one pint, which is more than a month's salary for most of the TCNs.

As my gurney entered the operating room, I was quivering from both the chill of the room and fear. I was chattering with endless and sometimes asinine questions as they moved me onto the operating table. Once again, I saw the anesthesia mask come toward my face in slow motion, with bright, strong lights behind it. I passed into the realm of unconsciousness.

The next morning I slowly opened my eyes, attempting to focus, wanting to know where I was. Naturally, I tried to move but there was a tight, pulling feeling on my abdomen. Still groggy, I ran my hand across my abdomen only to find a huge bandage stretching from one hip to the other. That got my attention, and I snapped to consciousness quickly. As I tried even harder to get up, I sensed the presence of someone in my room. I looked up, and there at the end of my bed was the little Indian nurse's aide from the night before.

"What happened?" I demanded. In her broken English, she tried to explain.

"Tubes," she said as she motioned to her abdomen with her hands. "Take out, not good." It truly was not the word *tube* that got me; it was the fact she used the plural — tubes.

"Tubes!" I shouted, and she jumped at the tone of my voice. I struggled to sit up and immediately drew on my past experience with a cesarean to turn to my side and then push up. As I moved, the nurse's aide protested.

"No, no, madame," she chattered as she tried to get me to lie back in the bed, "Sleep ... rest," she insisted.

Ignoring her protests, I reached for the phone. My hands shook as I tried to dial the compound. I had to speak to Dr. Neal. *"Sterilize the infidels,"* is all that I could hear in my head, vividly remembering my experience with Dr. Sulleiman, as I dialed. *"These crazy fundamentalists would love to sterilize all the infidels, the Christians."* By the time Dr. Neal was on the other end of the line, I was in an outrage.

"WHY weren't you here to make sure this did not happen?" I screamed into the receiver. "WHY the hell did you let them do this to me?"

He attempted to gain information from me and find out what had happened. Because I was not listening, his questioning was fruitless.

"I'll literally have your head for this, and I'll see you at 'chop-chop' square," I shouted, referring to the form of capital punishment used in the Kingdom and to the place where the punishment was carried out. After threatening him with his job and shouting more at the top of my lungs, I slammed down the receiver.

Immediately, I dialed the palace. Poor Abdulla. The palace operator was so frightened by the tone of my voice; he must have said something to Madawi as she answered the phone quicker than usual.

"What is wrong, Mrs. Teresa?" she questioned with urgency.

"Oh Madawi," I panted through the pain and the emotional upheaval, "the doctor sterilized me ... he removed my fallopian tubes!"

"What?" she demanded without expecting an answer. After a moment, she responded calmly.

"You must calm down," she continued. "I will find out what has happened, but you must calm down." Then she inquired, "What room are you in?"

"230," I said breathless, "*Al-Thomairy*." I responded and then took a deep breath as if beaten. "I'm in *Al-Thomairy* Hospital," I quietly repeated.

"I will be in touch," she responded abruptly and then hung up the phone. This time, I slowly returned the receiver to the cradle. I was exhausted and hurting. As I was climbing back into the bed, Dr. Wahib, David and the little Indian aide came running into the room. All three tried to help me back into the bed. As Dr. Wahib touched my arm, I yanked it away.

"Damn you," I spat, "damn you for doing this to me." And my threatening rage continued. "I work for a princess, you know, and I'll have your head by Friday," which is the Islamic Holy day and the day executions are performed.

"Please, Mrs. Teresa," Dr. Wahib replied calmly. "Please get into the bed, and I will explain." I started to protest and shout again when I felt David's hand lovingly grip my shoulder.

"Now, Teresa," David said. He never calls me Teresa unless it is serious. Then lovingly, yet firmly, he said,

"Listen to what the doctor has to say." After a moment of silence on everyone's part, I asked more quietly and rationally.

"What happened?" I stammered somewhat sarcastically. Pulling a chair up beside my bed and reaching for his clipboard, Dr. Wahib began to explain.

"There was a baby," he started. "You were about six weeks pregnant, but the baby was in your right fallopian tube."

"You mean it wasn't a cyst?" I questioned.

"No," he continued, firmly but caringly. "And it wasn't your monthly menstruation that was the cause of the blood. You were hemorrhaging."

I looked at David and then back at Dr. Wahib. He continued as he began to draw a diagram for me. "The baby was here, and I had to remove this tube," he explained. "You still have the left tube, and you can still have more children, only you will have to be careful when you conceive."

"Hemor...rhaging?" I stammered. Perhaps due to the residual effects of the anesthesia or my emotional outrage, I was somewhat foggy and a bit behind his explanation. "Back to the hemorrhaging," I requested.

"Basically, Mrs. Teresa, if we had not gone in last night and found this, you would probably be dead now." Boy, did those words snap me back.

"What?" I questioned. I couldn't believe what I was hearing.

"Yes," Dr. Wahib continued, "I saw it the minute I went in with the labrinscopy. There was no reason to bring you out of anesthesia just to put you back under," he explained, looking to David for support. "I had to do it," he stated, defending his actions. "I spoke with David, and we both decided not to wake you to tell you."

How stupid I felt. How appreciative I was for Dr. Wahib and how awful I felt about the way I had acted. I began to apologize, but Dr. Wahib stopped me.

"I understand how you must have felt," he interjected. "It is okay." He then stood to leave, "I'll check on you on my afternoon rounds."

"Thank you, doctor," David and I said in unison as he left.

It is amazing how human emotions work. I immediately felt a huge loss for a baby I did not even know I had carried. Feeling ashamed of my behavior, I telephoned Madawi and then Dr. Neal to apologize and explain what had happened. Exhausted from the surgery and my outburst, I soon slept only to be awakened at 9 p.m. by children running up and down the hallway of the hospital wing. *Ramadan*, I immediately thought with a sigh of exasperation, I had forgotten that it was *Ramadan*.

Baby or not, I still got the "five-day hospitalization plan" in spite of my protests. Being in any hospital is bad enough, but to be hospitalized due to losing a child while in an Islamic foreign country during *Ramadan* was unbearable. Dead silence fell over the corridors of the hospital during the daylight hours, the hours when I was awake, followed by excessive noise from numerous visitors into the wee hours of the night. During regular months, the hospital ended visiting hours around 10 p.m., but during *Ramadan*, it was open until 3 a.m.

I could not get any rest. All I could do was toss and turn and look at the arrow on my ceiling, seething about my confinement. In all hospitals in the Kingdom, each room has an arrow on the ceiling indicating the direction of *Mekkah*, the Islamic Holy city, so that the sick or their visitors know which way to face for their five required daily prayers. By the end of the five days, I hated that arrow. I hated that I had to be there. I hated that I could not be home to cuddle my beautiful children as I mourned the loss of the third.

To brighten my spirits, Madawi sent gifts daily, along with my favorite foods from the palace kitchen for lunch and dinner. David would come and sit with me during his lunch and bring the children by in the afternoon. I wanted to see them, to kiss them and hug them, but we did not want them there too much. We did not want them to catch whatever germs might be flying around. By day, my American compound friends came bearing gifts and the latest compound news, and by night my Arab friends arrived also bearing gifts. The outpouring of concern and love truly touched me in spite of my loss, and soon I was in my villa again with my two little angels and all was right with the world.

It was almost a year later before I heard the name of that awful Dr. Sulleiman again. At a dinner party one evening, Gay asked me if I would like to help her take dinner the following evening to another lady on the compound, a customary thing we would do for each other if someone was sick.

"Dinner, for who?" I began. "What happened?"

"You know, Sue in 1411," Gay said as she leaned forward the way she always did to fill me in on the scoop. "She lost her baby," Gay explained.

"What do you mean, Gay? I didn't know anything was wrong," I interjected as we sipped our after dinner coffee.

"Oh, yes, just yesterday," Gay continued. "It seems that something was wrong so she had to have an abortion."

My head jerked in Gay's direction as I was putting my coffee cup back on the coffee table. The word "abortion" alone sent cringes down my back after our experience, and I could not get my question out fast enough.

"Who was her doctor?" I asked rapidly.

"Oh," Gay paused thinking how to enunciate his name, "a Dr. Sulleiman, " she said. "His office is off of King Khalid Street."

At the sound of his name, my heart dropped, and that night ... I cried. To this day, I am not sure if he was out to get rid of the infidels, non-believers/Christians as they are known by the radical Muslims, or if he was simply a quack. But either way, my heart went out to Sue and to all the other women who may have been his victim along the way. David and I talked extensively about what had happened to Sue. I wanted to call her, but David stopped me.

"Let her believe what she believes," he paused mournfully. "What's done is done." He continued rationally, "To tell her your suspicions would only hurt her. Right or wrong, what you say would not bring her baby back." He was right, of course, and I never mentioned anything to Sue.

ॐ *Chapter Fourteen* ॐ

Daily Life

One would assume that the daily rigors, the routine of life, would be simple, particularly in such lavish accommodations as the compound. Wrong! Simple daily existence for a Westerner in the Kingdom of Saudi Arabia is a challenge at best. This is not to say that tasks cannot be accomplished, only that to do so is extremely different from what Westerners are accustomed. In such, a true sense of "us" and "them" develops within the expatriate community, with "us" including whites, blacks, Asians, Britons, Americans — anyone who is not Arab. Although I had a deep closeness and sentiment in the Arab world through Madawi and my other Arab friends, when it came to daily life, my heart and my understanding of what was normal still fell in the "us" group.

Periodically during my ten years in the Kingdom, a unique list would pass through the expat community. I first saw the list in the early 1990s and was amused by its contents. Yet I did not have a full understanding of its true meaning until I had lived daily life in the desert for ten years. Each time I saw the list, additional entries were included by new expats who found it and added some of their own sentiments before passing it along. The authors of this list are unknown, but its ability to convey the essence of understanding daily life in the Kingdom from a Western point of view is powerful in a comical way. Appropriately, this special list is entitled, *"You Know You Have Lived In Saudi Arabia Too Long When..."* (Appendix D). It is through this list that I share some of the experiences we faced as we passed our days in the desert sun of this completely different world.

"You Know You Have Lived In Saudi Arabia Too Long When ... you think 500 SR (approximately $125) is a good price," or *"... you own more than one Rolex."*

Contrary to popular belief, expatriates in Saudi Arabia do not make a lot of money. Salaries are not exorbitant. In reality, they are fairly comparable to those in the states; the difference lies in the expenses. In the United States, mortgages, power bills, car payments, various insurances and garbage collection must be paid. For the expat in Saudi, these necessities are part of the compensation package; hence, expendable cash is available for the expat to enjoy in other ways.

Couple the dispensable cash with the fact that Saudi money has a surreal feeling for the expat, lavish spending then comes easily. It almost felt like we were conducting our daily lives with "monopoly money," psychologically not holding the same weight as the American greenback. When I would take the children with me to the market on Thursdays, I bought them a little surprise. Most little surprises worth having were 50 SR, and I thought nothing of it. However, it would be inconceivable for me to allow them to spend $13 (approximately 50 SR) each on a little shopping day surprise stateside. And the same was true on a larger scale for the parents. For a new pair of stateside-styled trousers or an umbrella for your garden table, the price would be 500 SR (approximately $125) which was usually seen as a good price, particularly because you did not have to hassle with buying it stateside, paying almost double the price to ship it to the Kingdom, and risking its removal in customs after all the trouble.

"You Know You Have Lived In Saudi Arabia Too Long When ... you have more carpets than floor space."

Becoming consumed with fine Persian carpets is a habit that expats fall into as a direct result of the expendable cash that they enjoy. Not only are the Persian carpets found in the Kingdom the finest carpets produced on earth, as an expat in Saudi Arabia, you are where you can buy them at prices far below any other offered in the world, with the exception of Iran. Because expats do not own their villas in Kingdom, the idea of spending money on them is rather silly; hence, expats look to other things to change the look of their home and invest their cash. Thus begins the obsession with expensive carpets. When we left the country for the final time, we shipped home 28 Persian carpets.

"You Know You Have Lived In Saudi Arabia Too Long When ... you think carpets belong on the wall."

Many Persian carpets take an Iranian family years to weave. Made from pure silk with over 700 knots per square inch, these pieces are exquisite works of art. Perhaps because money is not an issue with the Saudis who own this caliber of carpet, or perhaps because these carpets are virtually indestructible, Saudis have no trouble placing them on the floor to be walked upon. Westerners, on the other hand, view these carpets as an investment and as something that should be kept on the wall, safe from feet.

It is amazing how the unique carpets of the region also offer the expat a venue of expression, focus and entertainment. With very little recreational entertainment available, to learn about these unique pieces becomes a passion and an expensive pastime. Not only it is fun to read and learn about Persian carpets, it is even better to poke around various carpet stores, locate a particularly unique piece and enjoy the event of buying it.

For the Persian carpet connoisseur, another form of entertainment comes into play. Once you have done a lot of business with a particular carpet dealer, it is not unusual to invite him into your home for a private carpet showing. For this event, you invite several of your carpet-loving friends over, provide snacks, tea and coffee, and then the fun begins. The carpet dealer will arrive with a truckload of carpets, his TCN will unload and reload the unpurchased carpets, and an evening is spent viewing his wares. The first home showing I attended was astonishing. After the initial conversations and refreshments, everyone became quiet, and the showing began. With the first pass of the carpets, the TCN would open them one by one and lay them on top of each other in the middle of the floor, creating a small mound of carpets. Then, at a slower pace, the carpet dealer would go through the stack again from top to bottom. As at an auction, individuals would indicate their interest in a piece either through a nod or a small hand gesture. If no movement was made on a particular piece, the TCN would fold it back up and put it back in the truck parked outside. By the time the bottom of the mound was reached, ten or twelve had usually been pulled aside, based on the number of serious carpet buyers present. It was at this point that the individuals who had not seen a carpet that captured their interest would leave. Then serious looking began. The remaining guests would end up on the floor on their hands and knees analyzing the piece or pieces of their choice. They would fold over the corner to check the knot count, count the number of colors in the weave, and generally size up the piece as to how much they would be willing to pay. More tea was served, and the conversations would begin as the carpet dealer meandered from individual to individual, answering questions and sizing up his expected sales. The tea continued to flow and the bartering continued, usually ending with a request for a tip for the TCN on top of the agreed price. It was always a fascinating event to observe.

"You Know You Have Lived In Saudi Arabia Too Long When … you think every major sale is preceded by cups of tea."

When the shopkeeper notices your interest in an item, he approaches to work the sale. As he talks to you about the item, another TCN will show up with a tray, usually silver, carrying cups of tea, small spoons and a bowl of sugar cubes. It is not only customary, but expected, that you take the tea. To refuse the tea would be an offense to the shopkeeper, and he would probably not negotiate to a price you would pay as a result. Following their ritual of buying is expected, and you are expected to participate, even if the event takes all evening. Discussion of family, weather and general conversation must also be included. As the conversation continues, the topic will eventually get around to the asking price of the item. The shopkeeper will give you a price, knowing full well that you will not take it. Subsequently, a little fuss must be made as to how expensive the quoted price is. More tea and casual conversation follows. Then it is the purchaser's turn to offer a price. My general rule of thumb was to counter-offer 50 percent of the asking price, which would always lead to a dramatic, lengthy refusal by the shopkeeper. Then, more tea. The ritual continues until either a price is met and the item purchased or someone walks away because the sale cannot be agreed upon. It is taboo to enter into negotiations if you do not have any intention of purchasing, no matter the price. If you are just looking and do not plan to buy, you should refuse the tea at first.

"You Know You Have Lived In Saudi Arabia Too Long When ... you can't buy anything without asking for a discount."

Not to participate in the bartering ritual is offensive, even for smaller purchases, and can actually throw the shopkeeper off balance. One evening as the mosques wailed the *Maghrib* prayer, I just had to have a pack of gum. David pulled to the side of the road for me to quickly run up to the "chuck and puke" to buy one single pack of chewing gum. "Chuck and pukes," as the Westerners called them, are small stands found all over the Kingdom, particularly on the roadside, with items such as sandwiches, sodas, gum and cheap toys. These stands obtained their name from the many who had eaten at such establishments, only to be sick later in the day. Saudi Arabia does not have a board of health, as Americans know it, to monitor food sales, and they do not have "*Quik Trips™*" or "*7-11s™*" on every corner. As I ran up to the window, the shopkeeper was closing his curtain in respect of the prayer. I stopped him, protesting that it would only take one minute. In broken Arabic, I requested one pack of gum. The gentleman plopped two packs of gum down and declared, "one *riyal*." Seeing the two packs of gum and only wanting one, I reiterated, "*la, wahid.*" Exasperated, he plopped two more packs of gum on the counter and repeated, "one *riyal*." Frustrated, I tried again to buy only one pack of gum and tried to express this verbally and nonverbally. Even more exasperated, the shopkeeper turned, mumbled something under his breath and plopped down two more packs of gum and stated firmly, "one *riyal, kolasse*." At this my eyes widened, my eyebrows went up and a look of surprise flooded my face, "*tieeb, kolasse,*" I responded, grinning from ear to ear, and ran back to the car with six packs of gum for 25 cents! We laughed all the way home.

Another time that I was privy to the unusual response of breaking the bartering rule was when a fellow company employee, Sam, was visiting and wanted to buy a machine-made carpet he saw a vendor selling on the roadside. We were on our way back to the compound from the airbase and had to stop at the traffic light. Sam saw the old man on the side of the road with his carpets for sale laid out on the sand. Although not the quality of carpets we preferred, Sam was adamant that he liked a particular one he saw. So, when the light turned green, David made a U-turn to come around to the intersection again so that Sam could inquire as to the price. At the light again, Sam quickly hopped out and ran to the man and back. As he jumped in the car, the light turned green and David took the same path again in case Sam wanted to continue with his roadside shopping. David did not risk pulling off the road in fear of being stuck in the soft sand, and parking on the shoulder is extremely dangerous in Kingdom. So for safety's sake, we kept moving and around we went again.

"What did he say?" I asked as we whirled under the underpass.

"I offered 500 SR and he said 400 SR," Sam answered. Clearly, confusion was brewing.

"400 SR!" David declared. "That's too expensive for a machine-made."

David and I suggested he offer 200 SR. Not understanding the way things worked, Sam refuted because he really wanted the carpet and felt that 200 SR was too low. Again at the light, Sam ran to the man, as David and I endured the endless horn honking from the drivers behind us when the light turned green.

When it was obvious that we could hold our position no longer, David made the path again, leaving Sam on the side of the road. When we returned to the light, Sam jumped in and around we went yet again.

"Well, what did he say?" David asked.

"I offered 400 SR," Sam sputtered out of breath from all the running back and forth in the heat, "and he said 300 SR."

"What?" David exclaimed in amazement. "Go again and tell him only 250 SR."

Still thoroughly confused as to what was going on, Sam jumped out again and ran to the little man while David and I made the loop laughing. Never had we experienced bartering over a large purchase where the shopkeeper went lower than we had offered! Again at the light, Sam hopped in and we, very curious by now, inquired in unison, "Well?"

"I said 250 SR and he said 150 SR!" Sam shouted.

"Oh, for Christ sake!" David responded, extremely tired of driving in circles by now. "Go give the man the money and let's get going."

So Sam jumped out and ran across the sand again. As we made the loop again, we saw Sam heave the carpet onto his shoulder and head to the intersection. When we stopped, he shoved the carpet in first and then followed. As the light turned green and we headed for the compound rather than the loop, David asked, "Well, what did ya pay?"

"100 SR," Sam said breathlessly.

Many times when shopping, you never could expect what would happen, particularly when the participants speak different languages. We all laughed as we rocked down the highway bound for the compound.

"You Know You Have Lived In Saudi Arabia Too Long When … you think that the further you inch into the middle of the intersection, the faster the light will turn green."

For such a patient society in most areas of life, the highways of Saudi Arabia are devoid of calm forbearance. It is amazing to see these docile people get behind the wheel of a car and make a 180° turn in temperament. As you wait for the light to turn green, Arabs, if first in line, will inch little by little into the intersection on a red light. Hence, when it does turn green, the driver is almost through the intersection. If an expatriate is at the front of the line at a red light and unwilling to inch forward, one of two things will happen: the driver behind you will back up a little, pass you into the intersection and then back up in front of you; or he will honk his horn relentlessly to encourage you to inch into the intersection!

"You Know You Have Lived In Saudi Arabia Too Long When … you think a red light means 'run it.' "

It was common practice for David to pause and count to ten before entering any intersection on a green light. Without fail, the other direction of traffic would always run at least five to eight cars through the red light before someone would finally stop and allow the other direction to honor its green light. Unlike in America, each direction of traffic at most intersections gets its turn for the traffic light. Consequently, the light rotates to all four directions independently. The theory is that three sides stop while the fourth has right-of-way. The government actually tried to run the lights as they are in the states, with two lanes going simultaneously, and then the other two. However, too many people were killed in traffic accidents.

Only a year before our departure from Kingdom, the new *Dhahran* airport opened, a project that took many years to complete. Inclusive of all of the latest technology and beauty that Saudi tends to bestow on its new buildings, the airport did have one major drawback that became obvious on opening day. To approach the airport, one must cross an expansive amount of barren land. The designers of the airport incorporated a system often used in the west to accommodate various levels of traffic flow. Over the three-lane highway were signal lights: green arrows and red Xs. The idea was that if traffic volume were heavy into the airport at a particular time, two inbound lanes would have green arrows and one outbound would have a red X, with the reverse being true if the outbound traffic were heavier. On opening day it became obvious that this system would not work. Many people were killed in numerous accidents because no one followed the arrows or the Xs properly. The situation was so bad that many people rescheduled their departure flights for several days until the route to the airport could be safely adjusted.

Driving in Saudi Arabia is a challenge even for the strong at heart. With the exception of Turkey, I have never experienced such chaos on the roads that I did in Saudi Arabia. The first week I was in the Kingdom,

I rode with my head in my lap! The second week, I at least would look out the window, but David told me, "Don't look at them or you will give them the right-of-way." He was correct. Thank God women cannot drive in Saudi Arabia because I do not think I would have had the nerve to even try!

At all times, the driver must be on full alert and ready for the unexpected. Reverse lights have a whole new meaning in the Kingdom. It is quite common to look up and see someone backing down the highway because they missed their exit, or for a driver who wishes to go the other way to just turn across the median at any point in time.

The published list of punishments for traffic violations is severe, including jail time and flogging for various infringements. Yet, even though traffic laws exist, they are rarely enforced with non-Westerners, almost never enforced with Westerners, and never with royals. As a result, anything imaginable is possible on the roads in Saudi Arabia. It is utter chaos.

David drove a huge Suburban, a GMC, enunciated "gymse" by the Saudis that housed a powerful engine. With his theory being "if they can't catch us, they can't hit us," our average driving speed on the highway was about 100 miles per hour, and we would be routinely passed by faster cars. He essentially did all that was necessary to avoid an accident: use speed, go over sidewalks, and run into the sand, whatever was required to avoid the collision.

If involved in an accident, the two drivers would be taken immediately to jail until fault was determined.

This determination would, accordingly, be decided because of two underlying factors. With regard to American drivers, the fundamental way of thinking of the Saudis is: if the American were not there, the accident would not have occurred. Another important note in understanding the process is to know that most Americans carried automobile insurance and most locals did not. Consequently, the American was usually found to be at fault because he was there and had insurance that would cover the repair of the local's car.

"You Know You Have Lived In Saudi Arabia Too Long When ... you make left hand turns from the far right lane."

Only the very bold or long-time expat would attempt this maneuver. Tricky at best to turn left at great speeds while crossing four or five lanes of traffic from the far right hand lane, it was done on a regular basis by the locals. Marked lanes do exist on the roads in the Kingdom, but the majority of the driving population rarely adheres to them. On a three-lane road, it was not uncommon to have five or six rows of cars across because they fit onto the pavement!

One time in *Dammam*, David and I were thoroughly entertained by this phenomenon. The traffic light was not functioning, and a Saudi police officer was in the middle of the intersection attempting to direct traffic. With very few people even acknowledging his existence, it was a free-for-all. Our direction of traffic, however, was stopped and waiting to see what would occur. As we watched, the cars on either side of us, unable to stay out of the excitement any longer, began to inch quietly and slowly into the intersection behind the officer. Not wanting to be pushed from the rear, David began to inch forward as well, keeping up with the other five cars on our front row. Slowly, our line of massive vehicles moved forward as the officer swung his arms and blew his whistle at the other three directions of traffic. Then, just as our line of cars was only a foot behind this man, he turned and jumped at the sight of our line of traffic upon him. With his look of surprise, the entire line of cars zoomed past him, honking as if chastising his being there.

"You Know You Have Lived In Saudi Arabia Too Long When ... you think all gas stations are made of marble."

Obviously, gasoline in the largest oil-producing country in the world is not very expensive. Not so obvious is that it is dispensed from lavishly designed stations that always offered full service. Self-service was not an option. Many of the stations are made of marble and decorated in extremely unique ways. The price of gasoline was approximately $.60 per gallon, as compared to $4 per gallon for water in the Kingdom.

Despite the elaborate design of the gas stations, we were amazed to find their antiquated emergency fire set-up: red buckets filled with sand labeled "fire" and hanging on the pillars of the elaborate décor. As an extra bonus, any driver who would fill his tank would receive a box of tissues, compliments of the station. The Saudis loved to display their free tissues in the rear window of their cars.

"You Know You Have Lived In Saudi Arabia Too Long When … you invite friends for a cookout on Saturday, but they show up on Thursday, and you are ready for them!"

Because Friday is the Holy day for Muslims in Saudi Arabia and throughout the Middle East, Thursdays and Fridays are the weekend. The work week runs from Saturday through Wednesday. Now this seems easy enough, but it is not. As Americans, we associate the weekend, the days of play, as Saturday and Sunday, and it is surprising how this fact becomes ingrained over the years. Subconsciously, it is hard to get used to referring to the days off from work as Thursday or Friday. Unknowingly, Americans will invite friends over for Thursday, but say Saturday in their verbal invitation because of our upbringing.

To complicate the situation, the first two workdays of the Saudi workweek, Saturday and Sunday, are days off for stateside employees. Hence, little communication or work is done between the Kingdom and the states on these days. By the time stateside employees return to work on Monday, the work week is half over for Kingdom employees, essentially leaving only Monday through Wednesday to get any work accomplished between the two. As a result, the weekdays seem to fly when you are in the Kingdom.

"You Know You Have Lived In Saudi Arabia Too Long When … you think a picnic means pulling over to the side of the road with a TV, a carpet and a water pipe."

The Saudis are a nomadic, desert people by tradition. In spite of their enormous economic and structural leap during the twentieth century, they still tend to revert to their nomadic heritage. Drive the *Corniche* on a Thursday afternoon and you will find row after row of tents along the side of the road, Saudis picnicking and rekindling a connection with their roots. They picnic, however, with all the pleasures of the modern world. On the roadside, you see most of the *Bedouin* tents sporting a television, a satellite dish and several new model Mercedes outside in the sand. Inside, the people sit on Persian carpets laid on the sand and lean on pillows for support while enjoying a traditional *sheesha* pipe. With 200 or more yards of sand before the refreshing waters of the gulf, the Saudis tend to put their tents as close to the highway as possible, avoiding close contact with the water. As Americans, we never could determine why they would shy away from the water that always lured us so.

"You Know You Have Lived In Saudi Arabia Too Long When ... you enjoy camping in the sand."

A favorite pastime both expats and Saudis enjoy is camping. As Americans, most of us associate camping with woods and streams, not sand and bottled water. However, the desert is the only option for camping in the Kingdom, and it is wonderful.

It was in the winter, February, when our entire family, including our nanny, was privileged to be included in a week-long desert camping trip with Madawi, the Colonel and the girls. Our base camp was set in the Northern Province near *Tabuk*. Because service is the only way of life in the Kingdom, our camp was set up by numerous servants from the palace and was ready when we arrived. It was easy to become accustomed to this form of camping: all the fun but none of the work!

To reach the campsite, we drove more than three hours north from *Dhahran*, further and further into the sand. The last hour of our trek covered the most remote part of the northern desert. The landscape was empty except for the road and camel herds. Because camels are such large animals, it can be extremely dangerous, if not fatal, to hit one of these beasts on the highway. With no city lights and only the headlights of the Suburban to guide us, we were extremely cautious the entire journey. Following the palace driver who was sent to guide us, we made our way down the meandering highway through the sand dunes in the black of the night. Periodically, we would see small lights in the distance, removed and almost surreal. It was other Saudis seeking their *Bedouin* roots by camping in the remote desert sand. An hour or so past the last village, the driver signaled for us to turn right off the paved road and onto the desert. Placing the Suburban into four-wheel drive, we followed up and over sand dunes for another ten minutes or so, wondering the entire time where in the world we were going and praying that Mohammed knew the way.

As we topped the final dune, an expansive camp lay before us, encircled with strings of light bulbs marking the territory. At least 25 tents formed two circles, each with its own open center area and small passageway into the center. To the right of the second more distant circle of tents, a herd of goats and camels meandered, which were to be our dinner rations for the week. To the right of the first circle of tents were three 18-wheel trailers completing the circle of the first encampment. Soon we learned that the first encampment was the family area and the second circle of tents was for the men. We were segregated by gender even in the remote desert while camping!

As we approached the family camp, the driver motioned for us to enter, and he continued to the men's camp, as he was not allowed in the family camp. David, on the other hand, was extremely privileged to be included in a Saudi family camp as he was a Western man with his family. Honking as we entered the open area, everyone ran out to meet us as they had been there for a week already. Cold wind hit us as we stepped from the Suburban, but none of us seemed to care. We were on another adventure.

After the greetings were complete, Madawi led us to the communal tent, basically our salon for the week where everyone would gather if they were not out in the desert or in their sleeping tent. It was a large, traditional *Bedouin* tent, perhaps 35 yards long and 20 yards wide. The ground was covered with numerous Persian carpets that served as our floor. In the center of one side of the tent were a big-screen TV and VCR, connected to the huge satellite dish outside by long cables. Spaced everywhere were what I call "floor chairs," which are much like what Americans use at the beach. The seat is on the floor, yet it has a padded back for comfortable seating. To the far end of the tent was a big fire pit encircled by more floor chairs. To complete the luxury was an expensive stereo system with large speakers to facilitate the evening music and dancing.

As we sat in the communal tent, we drank tea, listened to Arabic music, and caught up on everything that had happened since we had last seen each other. As we talked, the children ran and played, giggling with joy to be together again. After a while, I felt the need to find the ladies room, so I asked Madawi where I should go. "Just across the center," she said, and off I went. In the cold misty rain, I stood outside the tent looking around the encampment.

"Across the center," I thought to myself, "but where across the center?" As I continued to survey the area, up walked Susan, Nora's nanny, and I asked her the way.

"There, Mrs. Teresa," she said as she pointed at one of the 18-wheelers.

"There?" I clarified.

"Yes," she repeated with a smile, "it will do."

With a destination in focus, I ran across the courtyard and up the stairs of the truck. When I entered, my mouth literally fell open. There in the middle of the desert, inside an 18-wheel trailer, was a beautiful two-room marble bath! The first room was equipped with two lavatories topped with brass fixtures and a beautiful mirror. The second room housed the toilet, a full-size bathtub and another lavatory and mirror. A bath fit for royalty, literally! I said to myself as I chuckled, "Boy, we are really roughin' it on this camping trip."

Since David and I were married, we got our own *Bedouin* tent as our sleeping quarters. Again, we found carpeted floors, a mattress complete with linens, folding chairs and a propane heater, all filled and attended to daily by unseen hands. In the other tents of the camp were various nannies, with several to a tent. Our children, on the other hand, slept in one of the 18-wheel trailers with Madawi's children. Madawi and the Colonel occupied the third. Although I did not go into Madawi's trailer, which would not have been appropriate with the Colonel present, I did enter the children's. Inside it was like being at home, complete with mattresses, nice linens, a bath, closets and, of course, a TV and VCR.

Next to the communal tent was a slightly smaller tent used as the eating area and an additional lounge. As Saudis traditionally eat on the ground, this experience was extremely educational. Long sheets of plastic "table cloths" were placed on top of the carpets, and food was displayed on massive platters from one end of the tent to the other. At mealtime, shoes would be removed and everyone would find a spot around the plastic and eat until they could eat no more.

It is the Saudi custom to graciously offer their guests anything they want. If a particular food or item were not available in the eating tent, or the camp for that matter, Madawi would have a driver drive all night to *Al-Khobar* and back to bring the item to you. Nightly, Abdullah would go around to everyone before his midnight runs to the city to see what you wanted him to bring you the next morning. One night I had a craving for Pringles™, and they were delivered by a servant to my tent flap the next morning.

For entertainment, we rode all-terrain vehicles across the dessert, ran around and played on the never-ending sand dunes, and played with the camels and goats that would soon be a meal. Camel, slaughtered I am told in a special way, is common meat eaten by Saudis. Usually hung by the hoofs in the meat markets in town, the shopper may purchase a portion that is cut off by the meat vendor. Fortunately, my children never knew that they ate their new furry friends before the week's end, and they thoroughly enjoyed the camel's milk along the way.

Most interesting to me was our foremost form of amusement, looking for *fagah* in the sand. *Fagah* is a vegetable that grows wild under the desert sand. To search for *fagah*, you walk along slowly and look for small mounds that have pushed up the encrusted sand. As we walked and looked for miles, Madawi explained to me that, "the better the rain during the rainy season, the more abundant the *fagah*." She also told me of how the nomads of the desert would rely on *fagah* to survive a desert journey. At the end of the day, the servants would clean and prepare the afternoon *fagah* harvest over the open fire pit in the communal tent. Peeled, quartered and covered with butter, *fagah* is delicious, tasting somewhat like a potato. As the *fagah* cooked, the children ran around outside in the setting sun chasing *jamboorah*. The child that caught the most would receive enormous cheers from the adults.

The highlight of our week was our day in the desert, exploring away from base camp. Around 9 a.m. one morning, which is early for most Saudis, everyone mounted a desert vehicle to begin our adventure. Because females cannot drive in the Kingdom, the isolated desert provided a perfect opportunity for Nora to practice the driving skills she had learned while stateside without being discovered. This was no problem for her father since he was so westernized. Clad in *guthra* and *igal*, to hide her female identity, Nora was allowed to drive her jeep, which was only driven by her driver everywhere else in the Kingdom. Our caravan was comprised of 22 desert vehicles. As the vehicles lined up, the Colonel instructed David to follow close behind Nora in her Jeep, as he would be in front of her. David took this instruction to mean more than a simple line order; he knew he was to keep careful watch over Nora from the rear and watch for potential trouble.

Farah and Bandari joined our Suburban for the adventure. The girls wanted to be with Mason and Michelle and knew that they would have fun with Mrs. Teresa. Over the rolling dunes we began, enjoying the meandering camel herds along the way. After over an hour's drive, we came to a stop at beautiful escarpments, some towering over 500 feet in the air. The desert, because of the January rains, was dotted with brush, lush vegetation and small flowering plants. The sun shone bright and the cool breeze nipped at our noses as we wandered around the area looking for *fagah* and enjoying the numerous earthen colors the desert painted for us. After a while, the Colonel announced that he knew a special place that he wanted to take us for lunch. So we all mounted our vehicles and set out across the dunes again. More camel herds dotted our route, and everyone enjoyed the simple act of getting to our next destination. As one vehicle would see a special camel herd, unique escarpment or anything else that they wanted to share, they would honk their horn, hang out their window and gesture to the point of interest. It was fun as we yelled "yee-ha" over each of the larger dunes, rocking to Arabic music in between.

As the leader of our caravan, the Colonel and Madawi's SUV topped one of the never-ending dunes. Simultaneously, Madawi leaned out her window pointing to a beautiful meadow in the East, indicating the desired destination for lunch. It was absolutely breathtaking. The area was made up of about a football field's width of lush, deep grass surrounded by desert sand as far as the eye could see in every direction. Having planned the event, the Colonel had sent servants ahead to have carpets and floor chairs strewn all across the area for our resting pleasure. Also, there was a truck and several servants already prepared to serve us tea and a delightful spread for lunch. Unbeknownst to me as I was busy running and playing with Madawi and the children, the Colonel disappeared only to reappear riding a Bedouin camel! We heard a screeching sound, and over the desert he came, riding as his forefathers had done in centuries past. We all clapped and chuckled at the sight of the Colonel, the prince, on top of this semi-wild camel! What fun we had together enjoying the nice cool weather, the beautiful landscape and our friendship.

"You Know You Have Lived In Saudi Arabia Too Long When ... you buy a falcon hood for your gear shift."

Although we never did this (we didn't have a gearshift in our Suburban), many Americans purchased the abundantly available falcon hoods to place on the head of their gearshift because it would get so hot in the vehicle due to the extreme desert heat. Falcon hoods are plentiful because Saudis revere falcons for their sporting and hunting abilities. Many of these birds are worth thousands of dollars. Also, a number of Saudis own falcons for enjoyment and will do anything to protect their investment.

One bizarre incident regarding an expensive falcon stands out in my mind. A Westerner in Riyadh was in his kitchen one morning enjoying his coffee when he noticed a bird on his grill outside, picking at the remains of the previous night's barbecue. A little amazed and not recognizing the bird as a falcon, Henry proceeded to approach the bird, which readily came to him. He knew that this must be someone's bird because it was so tame and in such good physical condition. Being an animal lover himself, Henry decided to locate the owner of this immaculate bird and placed an advertisement in *The Arab News*. The very day of the advertisement's publication, an Arab man came to Henry's door inquiring about the bird. Happy to return the bird to its rightful owner, Henry refused the man's attempted thank you gift. The next day, Henry awoke to a loud knock on his door and found a brand new Mercedes in his driveway! Just a small "thank you" from the prince whose bird he had returned.

*"You Know You Have Lived In Saudi Arabia Too
Long When ... your ideal vacation is anywhere you can
eat a pig."*

Saudi Arabia maintains tight control over its population and the expatriates within its borders. Anything
that is seen as against the teachings of *Islam* is prohibited within the Kingdom to everyone, not just Muslims. Ham, bacon, pork chops and hot dogs are commonly a large part of a Westerner's diet, and it is difficult for Westerners to accept the idea that these items
are not obtainable on the local market in Saudi. But
that is not to say you cannot get pig, as we referred to
pork in Kingdom. A lot of pork is sold on the black market, within the expatriate community, but a high price
is paid. A friend of mine paid 500 SR (approximately
$125) for a 12-pound ham smuggled into the Kingdom
across the causeway from the country of Bahrain. David
and I were never so brave as to try and smuggle pork
into the country because we felt like the price of de-
portation if caught was too high to risk trying.

On one occasion, a friend of ours drove to the UAE
(United Arab Emirates) to the south of Saudi for a long
weekend holiday. The UAE is also a Muslim country,
but it is much more tolerant to Western ways than
Saudi Arabia. Our friends purchased various pork
items to bring with them across the *empty quarter* of
the Kingdom, believing they would not pass a customs
patrol on this route. However, just to be sure, they did
take the time to carve the various hams they had purchased to look like a chicken or a turkey, only a little
pinker. They placed their contraband in coolers, and

across the desert back to Saudi Arabia they came. Unexpectedly, Saudi officials had established a make-shift roadblock on the road. The checkpoint had not been there the previous Wednesday when our friends had traveled to the UAE. Frightened, the women sat in the back seat with their feet on the coolers as the men confronted the custom officials. Obviously not believing the men's persuasions that they did not have anything illegal, the officials decided they wanted to look inside the car to be sure. Everything packed in the car was unloaded on the side of the road. Suitcases, pillows, coolers, everything was spread onto the sand. When the officials looked inside the cooler, they asked our friends what it was. They responded straight-faced and nonchalantly, "chicken." Satisfied, the customs officials sent them on their way.

When you were privileged to get some "short nose beef," another term for pork on the compound, you treasured it, saved it for holidays, and never told your neighbor you had it because they would want to eat some! Whenever I would dream of a shredded barbecue pork sandwich, I knew it was time for a vacation.

"You Know You Have Lived In Saudi Arabia Too Long When ... you drink Listerine™ over ice."

As with pork, alcohol is strictly forbidden in the Kingdom. However, it seems that it is only forbidden to Westerners. I personally saw many bars hidden in Saudi homes that would rival any bar I have ever seen in the states. Because Westerners could not obtain alcohol legally, we were left with two choices. Either you made it or you bought it on the black market.

Many expats made the homemade brew, basically "Bathtub gin" or "white lightning" as my mother would call it. After this art was mastered, many expats renamed this bathtub gin "*sideeke*," which is the Arabic word for "friend." The problem with *sideeke* is that its potency could never be determined. You could get one bottle, drink the entire thing, and not even feel tipsy. But your next bottle could be 180 proof!

If making the homemade brew or consuming it was not your forte, you could, if you had the right connections and enough money, purchase commercially produced alcohol on the black market. One fifth of Jack Daniels™ could cost as much as $100. Some on the compound indulged, yet most just learned to like *sideeke*!

The company was aware of what went on regarding the consumption, purchase and making of homemade alcohol, but it turned its head. They did make it clear, however, that they would not stand behind anyone caught bootlegging *sideeke* and that employee would suffer the fullest extent of Saudi law if caught.

"You Know You Have Lived In Saudi Arabia Too Long When ... you think the uncut version of 'Little House on the Prairie' is provocative."

As with the pork and alcohol, Western films were not tolerated. Sex and questionable subject matter were never seen on Saudi TV or were benign commercials until the last two years of our stay. We could get movies on the local economy; however, they would be edited for content. The strange thing to me was what they chose to edit. Foul language was not a problem and not omitted, as I suppose they had no meanings associated to the words. However, any physical contact between a man and a woman was cut. If it were a quick peck of a kiss, there would just be a simple tape edit. If the kissing or physical touch went on any longer, they would edit the scene by overlaying alternate video, somewhat like a screensaver, that showed a little robot impatiently tapping his hands as if waiting.

Royal or affluent Saudis, on the other hand, had another option of obtaining recent releases from the states that most Westerners were not privy. David and I were lucky in this respect as Fahad always had the latest Hollywood flicks and would let us borrow them. However, when Fahad left the country to attend a U.S. college, we had to turn to alternate sources for our video entertainment.

On the local black market, we could buy more recent American movies that had been duplicated in Bahrain and smuggled over the bridge connecting the two countries. However, this method of obtaining new movies had its drawbacks. The manufacturers of these videos did not copy the movie from existing video. Rather, they had gone to the theater and videotaped the movie while sitting in the audience. We could always tell a Bahrain tape, you could see people's heads bob throughout the movie and hear their laughter and conversations!

Also on the black market, but with much more success and better video quality, was a compound business that opened — *"The Video Guys."* The endeavor was the brainchild of one of the residents and proved to be extremely lucrative. The *"Video Guys"* would have DVDs shipped in through secret sources, copy them, sell them, and even deliver them to your home. Our little compound video store soon incorporated membership points and bonuses! They made a small fortune, and we had great movies at our disposal.

Numerous times I attempted to take American videos into the country via my luggage; however, they were always children's videos. I never attempted to bring others, particularly R rated movies, into the Kingdom. Most times, the customs official would see the children and understand the videos were for them. On only one occasion did a customs official decide that I was trying to hide something, and he confiscated my copies of "Winnie the Pooh," "Cinderella" and "House of Mouse." After three weeks of careful review, the officials returned the tapes to us, for which we were thankful because items taken are rarely returned to their rightful owner. When we were packing our household belongings to leave the Kingdom for the final time, we were told by many to double-check our video library for anything questionable. Little did we know that shipments are checked upon departure as well as arrival. A bare breast in an R rated video could have caused us trouble and levied a hefty fine of 1,000 SR ($250) or more. To be caught with an X-rated video could bring a fine as high as 10,000 SR ($2,666).

Print media was not excluded from the extreme censoring of the Saudi government. Envelopes containing department store flyers from the United States would be opened, and the advertisements for underwear and lingerie would be removed before you ever saw the statement. *Yachting*™ magazines would arrive with either the people in swimsuits cut out of the magazine, or the bare body parts colored over with a black magic marker. To say the least, reading a stateside magazine could be a holey experience at best. It is amazing to think of how many TCNs must sit in a room somewhere in the employment of the Saudi government, coloring ladies' bare legs and arms in magazines and on product boxes. Some of these men were somewhat lazy with their censoring effort, simply scribbling black marker across the bare parts. Others, however, seemed to possess finer motor skills and creativity by taking the time to actually cover the restricted parts by coloring outfits on the pictures!

"You Know You Have Lived In Saudi Arabia Too Long When ... you think being liberated means sitting in the 'family section.' "

As I have mentioned previously, Saudi Arabia is a gender-segregated society. Yet it goes further than special events or gatherings. It pervades every aspect of their society.

It is females with females and males with males. All eating or recreational establishments offer a "men's section," which is strictly for men, or a "family section," which is for women, children and men who accompany their wives. There were times I thought I could sidestep this custom under the guise of saving time or because I was an American. Each time I was confronted with an enormous protest of *"la, la, la"* as the shopkeeper chased me from the men's section.

Even in the family section of an establishment, further segregation was imposed. It was extremely common to be in the "family section" of a restaurant and have the Saudi families' booths or tables partitioned from the rest of the room with rolling wood partitions so the Saudi women could comfortably unveil to eat. Hence, even in the liberated family section, Saudi women still hid, or their husband's hid them, behind the partition, not to be seen by other Arab or Western men in the area.

"You Know You Have Lived In Saudi Arabia Too Long When ... you think only men should hold hands in public."

In the Saudi culture, it is very natural to see two men walking down the street holding hands. However, as a Westerner, harboring Western values and sense of normality, it is a hard thing to look at and not impose the values we hold toward the act. Saudis, we were told, felt men holding hands was as an act of friendship, not a sexual one. Yet, it must be considered that the men in the Kingdom are not allowed to date women or to have contact with the opposite sex. At times, I questioned if all of the hand-holding I saw was merely a sign of non-sexual friendship.

Because of their employment contract, foreign men from third-world countries (TCNs) working in the Kingdom are not allowed to return to their home country, perhaps to their girlfriends or wives, for a least two years, if not longer. The availability of single women for these workers within the country is minimal, if not inconsequential, because dating is forbidden even if one had the opportunity to meet an available woman.

Conversely, David and I were not allowed to hold hands in public. No public display of affection between husband and wife is permitted. He could, however, hold my arm to help me in some way. For example, when I was pregnant, he could help me out of the car or up the stairs if necessary, but once the assistance was complete, the contact ceased. We could never just stroll along the *Corniche* or down the sidewalk enjoying the beautiful weather holding hands. It was forbidden.

"You Know You Have Lived In Saudi Arabia Too Long When ... you measure time by the number of prayer calls."

The second pillar of faith in Islam is to observe prayer. Muslims pray five times a day: just before sunrise (*Fajr* prayer), at midday (*Dohr* prayer), in the late afternoon (*Asr* prayer), again at sunset (*Maghrib* prayer), and lastly at nightfall (*Isha* prayer). All Muslim countries observe these prayer times, yet most do not shut everything down in observance. Saudi Arabia is different. Everything, and I mean everything, rolls up its gates and closes for each and every prayer time every day of the week. No matter where you are, no matter what you are doing, everything comes to a screeching halt at prayer. You can be in the grocery store and if prayer call begins, you must stop your shopping, leave the store, sit on the curb or in your car, and wait patiently (either 20 to 40 minutes depending on the prayer) to continue with life. Hence, your time is not yours, not dictated by individual wills or wishes, which can be extremely inconvenient and frustrating to the Western Christian shopper.

Prayer times dictate everything. Because they change constantly with the rise of the sun and the moon, everyone carried a copy of the prayer schedule to make sure we sat on the curb as little as possible. All outings from the compound were determined by what we could get done between prayers and where we needed to be by the start of the next call to either sneak in a friendly restaurant or be back on the compound.

This is not to say that you cannot do activities during prayer. Remember, contradiction and change are epitomized in the Kingdom of Saudi Arabia. Many of the TCNs realized that prayer times are a religious-based Saudi custom and would allow the Westerner leeway. All of us knew which restaurants in town were more lenient and would allow us to break the rules a little.

One Chinese restaurant near the popular shopping mall would place a worker outside the kitchen door when the prayer call began. If Westerners approached, they would look both ways down the street, like something out of a movie, and if no religious police or Saudis were in sight, they would kick the door open for us to enter through the kitchen. Once inside, we were not allowed to order our meal until the prayer was complete; however, we could at least sit down, enjoy any water we had in our bags, and browse the menu to pass the time.

Early one spring a new, delightful Lebanese restaurant opened on the Corniche. Manicured landscaping intermingled with three- and four-tiered mushroom-shaped water fountains surrounded the stairway entrance. The restaurant was designed to incorporate private, outdoor wood-benched seating overlooking the Arabian Gulf, air-conditioned indoor seating to escape the heat, and amusement park rides throughout to entertain the younger patrons. At this new establishment, the family section got the best view of the gulf on the left, and the men's section was on the right of the indoor structure. As excited as everyone else about a new place in town, we made plans with friends to give it a try on Thursday night.

We entered and were graciously seated indoors as construction was not complete on the outdoor seating. It had been our experience that if we had our food when prayer time began, we would be allowed to sit and eat; however, the service staff would leave and the lights would be turned off, leaving us to enjoy our meal in darkness. Knowing this, we dismissed the pre-order conversation and ordered our selections quickly. Shortly after our entrees arrived, the call of the prayer was heard and the lights went down. Expecting this, we continued to enjoy our meal and talk with our friends when, suddenly, there was a loud slam of a door and a man began to yell in Arabic, *"Salat, Yellah,"* as he clapped his hands. Behind our partition, we were near the commotion but not sure what was occurring. He continued to shout, and loud noises of something hitting tables could be heard. We sat quietly in our cubicle, waiting and holding our breaths as we listened to the chaos. Within a matter of minutes, the uproar ceased and all went quiet, really quiet. Waiting a few moments to be sure the coast was clear, David peeked out from behind the partition. Outside the glass front doors, he saw the back of a *muthawen* obviously still yelling and demanding people go to pray, as people scurried toward the nearby mosque. Relieved yet shaken, we sat for a while to make sure it was okay for us to leave and not be seen by the *muthawen*. To say the least, we lost our appetites, so we left enough money on the table to cover our bill and left as soon as we could.

"You Know You Have Lived In Saudi Arabia Too Long When ... you send friends a map instead of your address."

Tucked into each birthday invitation the children ever gave to non-compound friends was a map. No one has an address in Saudi Arabia; hence, no yellow pages are available and no one even has an address listed on their business card. When you do get a business card or a shopping bag from a particular store, the cross streets are the closest ones to be listed, rather than a numbered street address. To receive mail, everyone has a post office box. This is not a problem when visiting or inviting friends to a party; mainly it is just an inconvenience. However, one can imagine the problems that arise should there be an emergency and help is needed. How can the fire truck or the ambulance find you if there is no address?

"You Know You Have Lived In Saudi Arabia Too Long When ... you expect gold for every birthday and holiday."

In spite of the things we had to sacrifice as Westerners in the confines of the Kingdom, there definitely were benefits. Because of the expendable cash afforded us, gold was the item of choice among the women who liked to jump on the shopping bus on Saturdays, Mondays and Wednesdays to spend cash in an effort to brush away the blues. Gold, purchased by weight based on the exchange rate of the day, was everywhere, literally dripping from the ceiling in the gold *souks*.

At first, I told myself the gold was not real to keep from wanting every beautiful piece I saw. Soon, I, too, was in the stores quite often checking out the latest styles and wanting a new piece whenever any occasion arose. Birthdays, Christmas, Valentine's Day, and even Groundhog Day brought forth a little piece of gold. However, its luster soon dwindled. In an unconscious way, the gold soon represented the invisible prison, the lack of personal freedom, in which I existed. Many times when one of the company employees would consider completing their contract and returning stateside, they would weigh their finances against their lack of freedom and decide to remain in the Kingdom for another two years. This happened so frequently that a term was coined, the "golden handcuffs," which referred to the imaginary shackles of money, wealth and the good life that kept everyone there. In time, the incredible sight of abundant gold did not turn my head, and I avoided the gold *souks* like the plague unless I had a gift to purchase.

"You Know You Have Lived in Saudi Arabia Too Long When... you need a sweater and it's 80 degrees Fahrenheit," or *"... you wear a jacket inside and take it off when you go out."*

While Saudi Arabia is one of the driest countries in

the world, there is a great variety in climate, temperature and humidity from one region to another.

During the summer months in the coastal area of
the Eastern Province, temperatures are known to rise
above 120 degrees with humidity often registering 100
percent. Consequently, expats become acclimated to the
heat after their first year in Kingdom and 80 degrees
began to feel a bit chilly.

In contrast to the extreme summer heat, eight
months out of the year in *Dhahran*, the weather was
absolutely delightful, sunny with balmy breezes. With
relatively little cloud cover, it always seemed as if it
were another pretty day. Because humans need change,
I used to dream of sleeping to the pitter patter of rain
and the clap of booming thunderstorms, and I even
begged David on several occasions to go outside and
spray the window with the water hose so I could take
a nap.

One April afternoon, I was riding my bicycle to the
compound grocery store, dressed in jeans and a long-
sleeve blouse, greatly enjoying the beautiful cool and
spring-like weather. Once inside the store, I ran into a
friend who commented that it was actually 93 degrees
outside! I could always tell a new arrival because she
would only wear a sweater in the winter their first
year. Yet, by the second year, she would be bundled up
like me when it was only in the '60s.

Because of the extreme summer heat, most compound residents kept their air conditioners set on 75 or
80 degrees, which was comfortable, yet 30 degrees cooler
than the outside temperature of 120 degrees. In such, it

was always handy to take a sweater to a dinner party to wear inside after walking over.

Although not insurmountable, the rigors of daily life in the Kingdom were challenging. In the beginning, I struggled through each day to accomplish even the most minuscule of tasks. Yet as time passed, I became more understanding of the way things worked and learned to laugh at situations and myself. I learned patience. I learned to prioritize and not always assume things should be the way I thought they should be. I learned to expect less, which allowed me to avoid frustration more often. Only three months into our stay, David and I developed our "expectation theory," which we believe helped us to remain in this unusual environment for as long as we did. Our theory, developed from a simple experience, proved to teach us an invaluable lesson for living within the boundaries of Saudi Arabia.

After moving into DM 18, it became obvious that we needed a filing cabinet. We only required a small two-drawer cabinet so that we could file minor household information and other documents we wanted to keep. After two unsuccessful weeks of searching from store to store, David finally asked some of the Saudis at work where we could locate one. They explained to him that we could find what we wanted in warehouses in *Dammam*, so we decided to go searching the following Thursday morning. Through haphazard parking lots and sand, we drove to find the correct warehouse. After about a half an hour, we found it. Inside there were two gentlemen minding the store, and we expressed to them our desire to find a filing cabinet. Surprisingly, they knew what we wanted without a lot of theatrics. Bobbing his head from side to side and smiling, the Indian man led us to a huge stockpile of filing cabinets. Stacked from floor to ceiling, there were hundreds of them. After the great debate over color and the number of drawers we needed, we selected one and the man indicated that he would have it brought to our vehicle. Negotiating what seemed like a fair price of 250 SR ($67), particularly since we had wanted one for some time, we paid the man and left. Our simple expectation was seemingly met.

Excited to have finally found our filing cabinet, we unloaded it as soon as we returned to our villa only to find that no handles were included! How silly of us to expect handles with our filing cabinet. Had we not expected the handles, we would not have been disappointed with their absence. Thus, our "expectation theory" surfaced. It was then that we learned not to expect anything and question everything about daily life in the Kingdom.

ॐ *Chapter Fifteen* ॐ
The Girls' School

My adventures began quickly after my initial employment with the family. Only one week after I started, Madawi ask me to attend the girls' school party. It was through this conversation that I learned Madawi owned two private schools: one for boys and one for girls named *Al-Hamdi Boys' Private School*, and naturally, *Al-Hamdi Girls' Private School*. Through her excitement of sharing this information and her mannerisms while sharing, her passion for education and her value of its importance was evident from the very beginning. Only time would show me just how deep she held to this value.

Contrary to popular belief, females in the Kingdom are educated, yet the curriculum is strictly monitored by the Ministry of Education to ensure adherence to Islamic principles. In addition to the traditional studies of mathematics, reading, science, physical education and social studies, the Saudi girls' curriculum also includes languages, usually Arabic, English, and French. Fifty percent, however, of their academic time is spent studying Islam. The daily schedule is rigorous with the girls starting at 6:30 a.m. and finishing the day at 2 p.m. The students change classes every 25 minutes to include all of the required courses.

During an afternoon chitchat in the salon with Madawi, the details were set for me to go to the girls' party the following evening. Saleem would arrive at my villa around 6 p.m. to drive me. Excited about the invitation and curious as well, I inquired further so I would know how to dress.

"It's a graduation party," she replied nonchalantly as she snacked. Graduation party? I thought. But it's only April and the girls do not get out of school until mid-June. How could this be a graduation party? How could they graduate when they have not finished the coursework yet? I would soon have answers.

The following evening Saleem arrived as planned and took me to the palace. I was shown into the salon, offered tea, and there I sat and sat and sat, another custom which over the years became all too familiar to me. Another rule of thumb passed to me by Mom that holds true in this desert world is "hurry up and wait." Almost an hour and a half later, Madawi appeared around the corner dressed in a long skirt and tunic blouse, obviously Italian, with her *abaya* flying behind her, adjusting the veil on her head as she headed for the door.

"*Yellah,* Mrs. Teresa," she called as she continued to walk, "it's time." Quickly, I gathered my *abaya* and my handbag and followed her in a trot to the door. As I'm only 5'5" tall and Madawi is well over six feet, I always seemed to run to keep up with her elegant, stately gait.

Once outside, I was shocked. Several cars, a few BMWs and Cadillacs, all new models and adorned with curtains, lined up to gather all the females from the palace who would attend the party. The evening's entourage included Madawi, her five daughters and all of their nannies, and me. In retrospect, I assume that I was the honored guest that night as I was instructed to sit with Madawi in the backseat of the extended BMW 750SL. With Madawi's car in the lead, the line of cars left the walled world of the palace and headed for the school, with Madawi draping, not wrapping, her scarf over her face the minute we left the inner sanctuary of the palace walls.

Had I not been told, I would have never guessed that a school was harbored behind the towering, plain walls I saw. Only four men, all dressed in traditional attire, were outside the wall. No women or children were in sight. As we approached, the men snapped to attention, raising their shoulders in a more formal posture, and then the huge gates opened for our car to drive inside. Upon passing through the gates, Madawi's headscarf came off as if she wanted it on no longer than was absolutely necessary.

After observing Madawi's behavior with her scarf, I looked out to see what lie ahead; and there, right in front of me, was a most elaborate temporary stage in the school courtyard, complete with a fantastically painted backdrop under the shelter of the beautiful twinkling desert night sky. Surrounding the courtyard were eight buildings, identical in color and shape, which comprised all of the school's classrooms and offices.

Between the stage and our car were rows and rows of chairs. Normally, it would not be unusual to see rows of chairs in front of a stage. However, in this culture, it was definitely different and held an underlying meaning. The various types of chairs mark each lady's place in the societal hierarchy. The first row consisted of huge overstuffed fabric chairs that you would find in a living room, complete with Persian carpets and coffee tables elaborately decorated with flowers, expensive chocolates and tissues. These chairs were reserved for Madawi, other royal attendees and honored guests. Behind the first row were four rows of nice upholstered chairs much like dining room chairs. These rows were reserved for women of second tier importance, honored non-royal guests. Behind these rows were numerous rows of metal folding chairs reserved for the regular moms of the students. Since the Saudi society is segregated in all aspects of life, fathers were not allowed to see their daughters' graduation from high school. This particular year, my first of ten *Al-Hamdi Girls' School* graduation parties, I was seated in an overstuffed chair next to Madawi.

Everywhere there were ladies dressed to the hilt in the latest Italian styles, greeting each other in the traditional Saudi way of kissing on the cheeks, simultaneously shaking hands, and usually uttering the standard "hellos" in Arabic. It was obvious that everyone wanted their chance to greet the princess because she never had to mingle or move around the crowd. Everyone came to her and smiled the entire time they spoke with her. I stood quietly to her side and observed while they conversed in Arabic, speaking only when I was introduced to someone. I smiled continuously until my cheeks hurt.

Soon the dim lights around the stage shown bright and everyone took their seats as music filled the air. The performance began with lengthy introductions to reflect the names of the royal attendees. Special words of thanks were given to the headmistress and other honored female guests from the Ministry of Education who were there to observe, critique and report any deviance from what is considered acceptable by the Ministry. A respectful, solemn reading from the *Quran* followed. Then we all stood as the Saudi Arabian National Anthem was played. Over the years, I heard the anthem played numerous times, but I am not sure if it has words to accompany the tune. I never heard anyone sing it.

With the formalities complete, the party began. It was not like what Americans would call a graduation. I equate it more to a play or dance recital. Each class/grade level performed a play, a dance or a reading, depending on what they had learned that year, each with its own elaborate backgrounds and costumes for each segment. The evening was delightful, even though I could only understand the English portion of the presentations. However, I could not help but notice the strong American influence reflected in the show.

During the intermission, Madawi leaned toward me seeking my opinion of the show so far, that is, from a Westerner's point of view. In that our relationship was in its infancy and this was my first graduation party, we were both feeling the other out as to our individual beliefs, opinions and general views of mutual things in our world. As our conversation about the different performances of the show continued, I could not help but still wonder why the graduation was being held in late April rather than at the end of the school year. I soon formulated the words to ask her, without offending her. She immediately replied that it was important for the girls to have their fun now, which would allow them to be more focused when the final examinations would begin at the end of May. I cordially agreed that this made sense.

Madawi then added, "Plus," she hesitated, glancing towards the ministry of education ladies in the overstuffed chairs, "no one will expect it now."

I later learned that she was referring to the *Muthawen*, commonly referred to as the religious police, who watch everything done in Kingdom to make sure that the teachings of Islam are upheld. Girls dancing and women gathering in large crowds is not allowed in the Kingdom, which explains the lack of activity outside the wall of the school when the evening began. The event was being held in secret — when no one would suspect.

The show included two unique factors that made this first graduation stand out in my mind. Each factor is radically different from what a Westerner would expect at an event such as this. Throughout the entire performance, the audience talked. I found it amazing that it did not distract the girls from performing more than it did. The ladies either talked with each other or shouted loud comments regarding the show. As a Westerner, I perceived this to be very rude, but no one else seemed to even take notice of the noise level. The other thing that intrigued me was the food. Throughout the evening, not solely during the intermission, the audience was served refreshments by Filipino and African servants while the children performed. I was constantly offered sweets, tea, juice, small sandwiches, little pizzas and expensive chocolates. By the end of the four-hour performance, I was as overstuffed as my chair.

Through a whirl of goodbyes, our entourage made its way to the pre-cooled vehicles that suddenly appeared before us. This time, I did not ride with Madawi; rather, I was given another car with another driver to take me solely to my compound, which was in the opposite direction of the palace. I made no attempt to converse with the driver, and I smiled quietly all the way home as the Arabic music played and the car swayed. I felt very honored to have been included in what seemed to be such a special event. I was impressed with the level of performance by the girls, the style of the costumes, and the complexity of the sets. It was truly a first-rate school program. As the years passed, I was privileged to be invited to nine more of *Al-Hamdi's* graduation parties, most of which were essentially the same. However, the second year, the year Nora graduated, and the last two graduations I attended stand out in my memory.

During my first year with Madawi, she learned of my experience with dance and choreography. Consequently, she decided she wanted to include dances that

I could choreograph in their next graduation party. Also during that year, the new boys' school she had built was finished, including an underground auditorium with Bose™ sound system, elevated stage and curtains. As a result, the second graduation party I attended was indoors at the boys' school and contained even more pro-American elements than the first.

To help out for my second graduation, I choreographed a cute dance to *"Rockin' Robin"* for Fatma's class. Beginning one month prior to the graduation party, the driver took me to practice with the girls every afternoon for an hour or more to teach and rehearse the dance. I believe they truly enjoyed our time together, and I know that I did. They were very attentive and anxious to learn. Before long, all the girls knew me, perhaps because they enjoyed our dancing so much or perhaps because I was the only Western women there. As I walked in the courtyard or through the halls, the girls would call out "Ello, Mrs. Teresa," as I made my way through their private, secluded world.

To attend the second graduation, I was not privy to ride with Madawi, as it was no longer necessary for me to go to the palace first and then be treated as a guest. Our relationship over the year had developed to the point that she considered me part of the family. Madawi did, however, send an invitation to me via the driver that would allow me to enter the gate without her. Beautifully engraved with gold Arabic writing, the invitation was impressive.

As I arrived at the gate of the boys' school for the party, it was as it had been the year before. Yet, when I

entered the gate this time, I did so on my feet. Only
Madawi's car was ever allowed to drive in. As I approached the men in my *abaya* (they knew me because they had seen me at the practices), they greeted
me as it seemed everyone in *Dhahran* did, "Ello, Mrs.
Teresa." I returned the greeting and basic good wishes
in Arabic, and without breaking my stride, I headed
for the door as I had done every day for the past two
weeks. However, just as I started to enter, they stopped
me, even though they knew me, and requested my
invitation.

"We must, Mrs. Teresa," they replied with a smile
to my look of surprise, trying their best to be as respectful as they could be as they did their job.

Everyone who entered the party, even Mrs. Teresa,
had to produce an invitation or she could not enter. At
the end of the evening, the invitations would be counted
and matched to the number of ladies inside. Although
graduating per se is not illegal in Kingdom, a large
crowd of women gathering and dancing is. It was very
important to know if someone came that should not
have been there, important to know that the *Muthawen*
had not sent a lady in to spy and to report of such
things.

The night began as all nine graduations did with
lengthy introductions, thank yous, respectful readings
from the *Quran,* and the Saudi National Anthem. However, this year as the lights rose for the performance to
begin, I did not get an overstuffed chair on the front
row; rather, I was in the second, dining room chair row.
At first thought, this chair change could be seen as a

demotion, when in reality, it was a promotion. After a year with Madawi and the girls, I was seen as part of the family, and they felt no need to impress me. The front row, on the other hand, was needed for attending royals and honored guests, not family. As everyone settled in for the four-hour performance, the food rolled in, and the party began.

This graduation party was just as beautiful and well coordinated as the previous year. I beamed with pride as the girls performed *"Rockin' Robin."* They did a terrific job! They wore Capri pants made from a wild floral print and coordinating pastel tee shirts of four alternating colors, black sunglasses and tennis shoes. The girls brought down the house. The mothers went wild with their performance, and the auditorium shook for at least five minutes afterward from the cheers and traditional shrieks.

The 1997–1998 school year was a special year for me and my affiliation with *Al-Hamdi.* Looking back, I believe it was the peak of my career with the Saudis for many reasons. This was the year of the biggest graduation party ever held for the *Al-Hamdi* graduating seniors. It was special because it was the year that Madawi's oldest daughter, Nora, graduated, which was an accomplishment that Madawi had not had the opportunity to achieve, as women had not always had the opportunity to learn in Kingdom. The year also brought the first public speaking contest for females in the Eastern Province. This was a remarkable achievement and step towards equality. And it was also an unexpected triumph for the *Al-Hamdi* team to boot.

With the anticipation of Nora's big day, Madawi approached me in January to seek my help. Not just to help with a little choreography as before, but she requested that I provide extensive assistance with the festivities. She wanted me to completely organize a graduation party for Nora to be held the weekend prior to the school's party.

"You know, Mrs. Teresa," she began, "that this is the year Nofie graduates."

"And I am sure you are very proud," I said, smiling to show my understanding.

"I would like for you to do a party for Nora," she continued. "I want it to be special since she is first."

Realizing that this conversation needed more attention, I stopped what I was doing and joined her on the sofa. "Sure," I answered without realizing what I was agreeing to at the time.

"I want you to work with Nora for ideas and make it very special," she instructed and questioned, "and what will you charge?"

In my mind, I was a little taken back. I was already on her payroll, and I did not expect her to pay me to do a party as well. "I don't know," I stammered, not sure where the conversation was going.

"Does 5,000 sound fair?" she questioned.

"Okay, that sounds fine to me," I paused, assuming *riyal,* "it's a deal."

The next day Madawi called and let me know that they were considering the Al-Nimron Hotel for the party. The driver would pick me up that afternoon and take me to the hotel where I would meet Madawi and

Nora. We all thought it was a good idea to see the facility, start brainstorming for theme ideas, and decide if it would work.

With about 500 on the invitation list for the celebration, the Al-Nimron ballroom facility seemed adequate. The main ballroom encompassed about 12,000 square feet of space with a huge marble staircase on one end and a small stage on the other. Adjacent to the ballroom was a 2,000-square-foot room that could be partitioned off from the main ballroom and serve nicely as the buffet area for breakfast. Not wanting to stop there, Madawi decided it would be a good idea to incorporate the hotel's dining room for the dinner and the hallway that connected the two as well.

After walking the entire lower level of the hotel with Madawi and Nora, carefully noting each detail of the facility, my mind began racing. Suddenly, an idea came to me, and the decorating ideas began to flow.

"What about the Orient?" I exclaimed with enthusiasm, searching for a response. Madawi and Nora's faces revealed interest, but I could see that some convincing was necessary. To illustrate my vision and share my enthusiasm, I began to pitch decorating ideas as I moved, which encouraged them to move around the facility with me.

On the end with the large marble staircase, I suggested a big dragon coming down the stairs through a huge poppy-red Oriental god gate, as I call it. The dragon would have red-lit eyes, breathe smoke via a smoke machine inside, and be made like a float with chicken wire and multi-colored paper. To pull the theme down onto the main floor, I envisioned a large pond with floating colored lights, a 12-foot high wooden pagoda painted gold and surrounded with trees and shrubbery as if you were in an Oriental garden. I actually got a little carried away with ideas and suggested real goldfish for the pond, but Madawi and Nora laughed and exclaimed that I would kill the fish! The thought of those poor little dead gold fish floating on the pond and horrifying the guests sank the idea.

At the other end of the ballroom, I pitched an idea for an Oriental screen effect with backlighting. This would reveal shadows of Oriental shapes such as dragons and other Oriental symbols that we would make out of wood. It would also serve nicely as the backdrop for the stage, which would hold the all-female band for the evening. To top off the ballroom, I suggested draping large pieces of satin fabric from the ceiling, banners about two feet wide in strong Oriental colors to give the room a festive touch.

I recommended another poppy-red god gate to mark the entrance to the buffet room adjoining the ballroom, which would accommodate the numerous buffet tables and seating for guests who wish to sit and visit away from the sound of the band. Staying with the theme, I suggested decorating the buffet tables with Oriental umbrellas, a wooden dragon image lit with spots in the center, and various Oriental centerpieces and decorations spaced periodically on the buffet and sitting tables.

Noting some signs of acceptance, I continued through the hotel, the ideas flowing as I went. Down the marble staircase from the ballroom to the hallway,

I envisioned another god gate and a huge brass gong hanging on a poppy-red stand, little white lights on the stair rail, and a guest book on a podium at the bottom. To the right of the staircase in the marble entryway, I recommended an *abaya* check-in with another pond, a small one with floating lights and lots of shrubbery. A smile began to emerge from Madawi, but Nora was still contemplating my ideas.

"And we can have Oriental outfits made for Ramel and another driver so they can greet guests outside as they open the doors for the ladies to enter," I continued, becoming more consumed with the plans as I went. To the left of the staircase in the hallway to the dinning room, I suggested a small bridge covered with vines and Oriental flowers to carry the theme through the hall to the other end of the hotel. Realizing that the hotel would not allow very much decorating in their main restaurant, I simply visualized a dragon ice sculpture for the dinner buffet and small Oriental lanterns on the tables.

Out of breath, I stopped in front of the restaurant buffet, sighed from the excessive amount of energy just spent, and looked at Madawi and Nora. With her hand to her chin, Madawi's eyes moved around the room, and there was a long pause of silence.

"Yes," she exclaimed, "I like it!"

We both then turned to Nora for her opinion. After all, it was her graduating party we were planning. She, too, paused, looking down as she finally spoke.

"Okay, Mrs. Teresa," she said somewhat hesitantly. I do not believe she could really visualize all that had poured out of my mouth. Sensing this, I offered to do some sketches and bring them to the palace. With that, a large smile came over Nora's face.

"Okay, Mrs. Teresa," she stated again, much more enthusiastically.

As promised, I went to the palace the next evening with sketches for Nora and Madawi to see. Cross-legged on the salon floor, my energy returned as I described each sketch, noting additional details and decorating touches that had come to me since the day before. Four hours and numerous cups of tea and juice later, they both broke into huge smiles and accepted the proposal. Work would begin immediately, and Madawi and Nora offered to help. Before it was all said and done, both families, Madawi's and mine, pitched in to help with countless hours of work at the palace building the dragon, painting the god gates and finishing other details. Up until the wee hours of the night, even on Mother's Day, we all labored and produced the most wonderful graduation party that the social elite of *Dhahran* had ever seen. When I accepted this responsibility, I never expected that the next six weeks of my life would be consumed with this production that ended up costing over $13,000 in decorations alone!

From the start, the school year swirled with excitement and new challenges. In the midst of Nora's party preparations, the invitation arrived. *King Faisal University of Petroleum and Minerals (KFUPM) Girls' School* was hosting their "first annual public speaking competition" in the Eastern Province. Naturally, the phone call followed. It was Madawi, and she wanted to see me her in office the following morning.

"Mrs. Teresa," she began as she stood from her chair and proudly handed me the invitation, "will you coordinate our team?"

Amazed that the competition was even happening given the cultural restraints placed on females, I immediately accepted the chance to be a part of this historic event.

"I would love to," I replied, "and we'll do great!"

"To win," Madawi hesitated, "is not important. I am just happy that the girls can participate." She paused thoughtfully, "It's a big step."

I did not need to ask for clarification; I knew what she meant. Little by little, girls were achieving more recognition and more opportunities than ever before in this gender-biased society.

As expected, I attended the planning meeting at KFUPM to register our participation and learn the rules and requirements of the upcoming competition. We were only allowed to have three representatives, so I held interschool tryouts two weeks later for the interested students. Each girl who wanted to be a member of the team had to write a two-minute speech and present it to a panel of judges on why she felt she should be selected to represent *Al-Hamdi* in the public speaking contest. Content and organization of the speech did not concern me because I knew that I could teach the team these things. In order to do well at this event, I knew I had to find the girls with the best command of the English language. If the student had this quality, the rest would fall into place.

To make the critical decision, I asked Madawi, the headmistress; Mrs. Fawzia, the vice headmistress; Sultana; and the school's English teachers, Beverly and Maha, to assist me with judging the interschool competition. Excitement filled the air on team selection day, as nothing like this had ever occurred within the walls of this secluded private school. Actually, nothing like this had ever happened to any female students anywhere in the Kingdom. We had 11 eager, nervous students from the tenth, eleventh, and twelfth grades try out for a position on the team. Unexpectedly, the competition was stiff. I had prepared evaluation sheets for the judges, and when the scores were tallied, they were extremely close. Yet, three prevailed, and, ironically, one from each of the grade levels: Safa from the senior class; Sylvana from the junior class; and Fatma, Madawi's second daughter, from the sophomore class.

Excited and eager to begin, the girls selected their topics from the assigned list provided by the organizers of the contest. Safa chose to write on *Diabetes*, Sylvana selected *The Role of Women in Islam*, and Fatma wanted the remaining topic of *Rainforest Deforestation*. Long hours of research, revisions and practices began. Not only were my afternoons at the school consumed with speeches, my nights fell prey as well. Because their society is nocturnal, it was not uncommon for my phone to ring after midnight beginning with, "Ello, Mrs. Teresa, I have a question about ..."

In addition to the three required topics for the first round of speeches set forth by the competition planning committee, a plan was set for a second round to determine placement of the top five speakers of the first round. The second round would consist of impromptu speeches from 50 pre-set topics, rather than polished prepared speeches like in the first round. Knowing that the judges would look for organization, not look for substantial content in impromptu speeches, I drilled my team once their first round speeches were complete.

"Attention getter, tie to audience, preview, thesis, one or two points, and conclusion!" I would shout as we practiced pulling topics from the selected list. "It really doesn't matter what you say," I would reiterate, "even if you feel funny. The most important thing is organization, organization, organization!"

The night of the contest finally arrived. Held in the university auditorium, a huge cheering section turned out from *Al-Hamdi* to encourage our team. Naturally, only females were allowed to attend. After the *abayas* were discarded, an hour of socializing followed among the students and ladies attending. As the start time drew near, my team became even more anxious. I encouraged them by letting them know I was proud of them no matter what the outcome. Then with one final thumbs-up to the girls, I took my seat with my stopwatch in hand. The lights dimmed and KFUPM's competitor in the *Role of Women in Islam* speech took the stage. With applause and cheers following the first competitor's conclusion, one by one the other girls stepped up to follow. The competition had begun. Soon Sylvana, a touch nervous, took the stage to represent *Al-Hamdi*. She did a good job and

University Girls' School

مدارس الجامعة

FIRST ANNUAL INVITATIONAL
PUBLIC SPEAKING TOURNAMENT

PROGRAM GUIDE

was under her five-minute limit, but she did not stand out from the other five participants in her topic.

Still encouraged that we were holding our own, we watched as the competition moved forward to the *Rainforest Deforestation* speeches. Fatma, with her boyish gate, stepped up to the podium. With a deep breath she began.

"Close your eyes and imagine. Imagine a world without butterflies, a world without ..." she continued, and the audience was mesmerized.

Unlike any other Saudi ladies' gathering I had attended before or after, there was utter silence in the audience. Studying and good grades were never Fatma's forte; however, brains and theatrics were. Much too soon, the yellow card appeared indicating that she had one minute remaining. A touch flustered, Fatma cut short her final point and jumped to her conclusion.

"So," she paused very theatrically, "open your eyes and know that the beauty can remain if we seek to eliminate the tragedy of rainforest deforestation." The crowd erupted! She was phenomenal in her presentation. I beamed with pride, as I just knew she had won. Adrenaline still pumping, we listened to the three remaining speeches on deforestation. In our minds, however, none compared to Fatma, and our chatter at intermission reflected the feeling.

Safa was the first to present on diabetes, and the *Al-Hamdi* group cheered as she approached the podium. It was as if magic dust had been sprinkled on my girls that evening; Safa took the place by storm. Clear, focused, organized and dramatic, her speech stood out and brought down the house yet again. We could hardly control ourselves as we jumped for joy upon her completion; however, we had to regain our composure and endure the final five prepared speeches of the evening.

A second intermission followed, and our excitement was uncontainable. As we enjoyed the refreshments provided, we talked, analyzed all of the presentations and decided that our girls would be in the second round. Finally the judges returned with the final five names, and the crowd was called to order.

Silence fell over the auditorium as the KFUPM competition coordinator approached the microphone to announce the second round participants. As she did, my heart raced, and everything on my body that could be crossed was.

"First, I would like to congratulate all of the girls on their achievements here tonight." She continued, "Everyone did an outstanding job and moved us forward in our plight." The crowd applauded reflecting their agreement. The emcee continued.

"From *King Faisal University of Petroleum and Minerals (KFUPM) Girls' School*," she hesitated to enhance the suspense, "Maha Al-Sharook." Applause shook the room as Maha's friends cheered.

Her voice resonated the second finalist, "Rowena Al-Nabie also from *King Faisal University of Petroleum and Minerals Girls' School*." More applause followed.

"And from *Dammam Girls' School*, Faten Al-Subahie." Again, the cheers of excitement pervaded the room as our group sat on the end of their chairs. The anticipation was killing me, particularly since there were only two spots left.

"Safa Al-Bab…" she began over the microphone, and our group went wild before she could even finish Safa's name.

"And finally," she hesitated yet again, "Fatma Al-Saud from *Al-Hamdi Girls' Private School*."

"Yes!" I shouted as I jumped from my seat, while everyone from *Al-Hamdi* jumped up, screaming with delight.

After a few moments to let the victors revel in their accomplishment, the emcee called the audience to order to explain the rules and progression of the second and final round: the impromptu speeches. Five folding chairs were placed in a semi-circle in the center of the stage, and the girls took their seats. Tension and the unexpected silence drifted over the audience. The solemn voice of the emcee pervaded the arena, calling the first participant to approach the basket and withdraw a topic, "Maha Al-Sharook." Maha took her topic and stepped to the podium for her allotted one-minute preparation time. The impatient crowd sat with quiet anticipation. With a nod to the judges, Maha began. Thirty seconds later she concluded, and I knew we had it in the bag. No organization and much rambling pervaded Maha's impromptu speech. Fatma was next. She stepped to the basket to pull her topic, and took her one-minute preparation time. No one in the audience made a sound. With a deep breath, she, too, nodded at the judges and stepped behind the podium. Clear, succinct and organized phrases followed, with a touch of Fatma's natural theatrics as she proceeded just as we had practiced. Again, the crowd went wild when she finished. Next came Rowena and Faten, and neither held a candle to Fatma's presentation style and organization. Finally, Safa approached the podium as the final competitor. Like Fatma, Safa's speech was well organized and concise, and we all shouted with glee upon Safa's completion. Our cheering section talked quietly as we anticipated the final outcome. Thankfully, our long hours of hard work and preparation paid off. Fatma took second place and Safa took first! *Al-Hamdi* had prevailed.

Still riding high from the speaking competition, I opened the door to my villa a week prior to Nora's graduation to find the palace driver unexpectedly on my doorstep. He exclaimed, "From princess," and

handed the unanticipated garment bag to me. I knew
Madawi and Nora had gone to Italy after the speaking competition to find outfits for the graduation party,
but I had no idea that they would shop for me as well.
I was ecstatic with the unexpected gift. Quickly opening the bag, I found the most beautiful deep-orange
silk chemise in typical Oriental style with a round-
top neckline and covered buttons. The ensemble was
accented with embroidered flowers dotted everywhere
in bold colors. By *Ventilo* of Italy, it also had a matching long silk skirt with an extended slit up the side. It
was just like Madawi to find the perfect color and the
perfect fit. She knew me and knew me well.

The celebration of Nora's graduation went off without a hitch. The evening was beautiful, and the room
was filled with a mystic air. The night was dreamlike
with low lights, Arabic music resonating over the continual chit-chat of hundreds of women, all dressed to
the hilt and all proud to have been included in the event
of the season. This time, I made it to the sunglasses in
my evening bag. I danced and partied with the women
until 8:30 a.m., leaving them still going as I left.

The following Sunday evening Madawi came to my
villa for a casual cookout on the patio. She came alone
wearing blue jeans and a tunic blouse, ready to kick
back and relax after the big night. When I met her at
the door, she was holding a basket filled with two dozen
white roses for David and me to thank us for all that
we had done to make Nora's party a success. Tucked
inside the roses was an envelope, one that I did not open
until the evening was over. We enjoyed an evening of

> *To: The Dearest Friend David and Teresa*
>
> *From the bottom of my heart, I thank you very much for helping me to design and present this wonderful evening for my daughter, Nora. Without you couldn't be possible especially your love touch with spread all over the material, and I hope I'll be there for your little children in their graduation So I can truly pay you back. With my deepest appreciation.*
>
> *Love,*
> *Princess Madawi*
>
> May 1998

Replication of thank-you note given following Nora's graduation celebration.

peacefully swinging on the patio swing as we relived the party, noting all the details. As the evening drew to a close, Madawi made her way to leave, thanking us again for a job well done. Once she was gone, David mentioned the envelope and handed it to me to open. Expecting the 5,000 SR (approximately $1,300) that we had agreed on for me to do the party, I was surprised to find $7,000 American dollars instead! She obviously was pleased.

The night of Nora's actual graduation began as previous ones. However, this particular year I did not get a chair. Rather, I was on a riser in the back of the room running the 2,000-watt spotlight that I had purchased from the states the previous summer for my compound dancing business. It was my idea to incorporate the spot in order to enhance the presentation of the performances, and it worked out well.

As the formal introductions preceded the thank yous and acknowledgment of honored guests, the crowd sat restlessly. Then, unlike previous years, Madawi stepped to the podium and began in Arabic. Knowing that it was unusual for Madawi to speak before the *Quran* reading and national anthem, my senses perked up and I tried to determine what was going on. I sat patiently as I struggled to decipher the Arabic. Then, beaming, Fatma and Safa approached the podium, and an extended stream of applause and cheers followed. Again, Madawi spoke as Beverly and Maha, the school's English teachers, approached the podium with more applause. Although I was not sure, I believed that they had just been congratulated on *my* accomplishment with the girls' public speaking team. A touch annoyed for being overlooked, I sat back on my stool to perform the duty of running the spotlight for the evening.

Nora's graduation also was permeated by American influence. Numerous performances incorporated American songs and more English speaking presentations were included than ever before. Unlike American graduation ceremonies, *pomp and circumstance* is not played as the graduating class enters and receives their diplomas. Rather, each class selects a song that is meaningful to them. Nora's class selected the theme song from *Titanic*. The song coupled with the spotlight created a special atmosphere, and the room swirled with magic as the girls entered in their flowing gradu-ation robes. Because *Al-Hamdi* really does not have school colors so to speak, each year the graduating class designed the robes they wore.

Once on the stage, the graduating seniors formed a semi-circle to accept their much anticipated high school diploma. As Mrs. Fawzia called each girl's name, Madawi presented each with her diploma, a kiss on the cheek, and a small gift: an 18-karat gold necklace to mark the occasion. The room was jubilant with the girls' achievement, and everyone shrieked with delight as each senior was recognized. Soon, the entire room began to dance the night away following the official graduation conclusion.

I personally ended the evening with anger. After four hours of contemplation behind the spotlight, I was certain that I had been overlooked. I did not under-stand how they could ignore my role in the girls' suc-cess at the speaking competition. I was deeply hurt and copiously angry. Without saying a word to anyone, I broke down my spotlight and had the servants carry it to the waiting car.

I avoided Madawi and did not speak to her for the week that followed. Sensing my change in behavior, Madawi called and requested that I come to her office at the school the following Saturday.

"Mrs. Teresa," she began, smiling as she moved from behind her desk to the sofa in her office, "we missed you after the party." She paused delicately because I believe she knew why I did not stay and celebrate. "Why didn't you stay and dance with us?"

"I just wasn't up to it," I replied, less peppy than usual.

She sat in silence as if encouraging me to continue. Being the way that I am and feeling that I was speaking to a friend, not just an employer, I finally spoke.

"Honestly, Madawi," I began, "I was hurt."

"Hurt?" she questioned, "Why?"

"Well," I hesitated, "I was hurt that I wasn't mentioned for my efforts with the speaking team." I stopped to collect my thoughts before I just let my mouth run. Madawi threw her head back and chuckled, but not in her usual way. It was more like she was chuckling to cover her true feelings, chuckling to not reveal something for which she herself was ashamed.

"But, Mrs. Teresa," she began, "we all know that you are the reason our girls did so well." She paused before continuing, "But we couldn't say your name." My look conveyed my thoughts and she continued, "Because you are not one of us. The ministry could not see you getting an award for something our school did."

With that, no further discussion was required. Neither of us really wanted to acknowledge the reality of her explanation. Because I was not Muslim or a teacher at the school in the eyes of the Ministry of Education, I essentially did not exist. My efforts with the speaking contest were known as the efforts of someone else to the outside world. I was still rather annoyed, but I reassured her that I understood, as I knew it was not her fault or her rules.

Several weeks passed and the situation was not mentioned. Then, one afternoon, I received a call from the princess, requesting my presence at the school. My curiosity raised, I agreed to meet her the next day.

I always wore my scarf on my head with my *abaya* to enter the girls' school. I used this tactic so that a casual passerby or watchful observer would not know that a Westerner, a non-Muslim, was entering. Once inside the towering walls, I removed the scarf as my *abaya* flew behind me when I made my way through the halls, greeting the individual staff members along my way to Madawi.

Stepping quicker than usual, I cut short the lengthy hellos and headed up the stairs to Madawi's private office. As usual, the driver had arrived after one o'clock, and, for some reason, I felt the need to hurry. Out of breath, I peeked into Madawi's office to see if she was alone. Sitting behind her desk reading, she sensed my presence and raised her head. Once our eyes met, her face broke into a huge smile.

"Come in, Mrs. Teresa," she exclaimed as she stood to greet me.

We kissed in the traditional greeting, and I began to chatter as I removed and folded my *abaya*. Casual conversation ensued as we sat on her sofa to have some tea; yet, the noise level outside increased as we continued to talk. Soon the noise became too loud not to notice.

"Come, Mrs. Teresa," she suddenly announced as she bounced up from the sofa. "Come with me," she reiterated, and I followed.

The door to the next room was closed, yet I could hear giggles leaking through. Proudly, Madawi opened the door for me to enter, and I found the room packed with students, Mrs. Fawzia, Sultana, Beverly and Maha. I entered to cheering before an explanation was given.

"We love you, Mrs. Teresa!" the girls shouted as they backed away from a cake on a table in the middle of the room. My eyes popped with surprise, only to be filled with tears of happiness.

"For me?" I questioned, looking at Madawi for answers.

Nodding encouragement, she insisted that I sit on a chair provided. As the flutter of compliments continued, Mrs. Fawzia called the girls to attention.

"Girls, *yellah*," she called in a raised voice. "Please," she paused, "please be seated." Once the room was somewhat quiet, Fawzia began again.

"Mrs. Teresa, you are very special to us. We want you to know how much we appreciate all that you have done for *Al-Hamdi*," she continued as she handed me a small package. "Please accept this as a sign of our love for you and our appreciation for what you do for us."

Completely taken by surprise, I could not stop the steady flow of tears down my face. I stood and hugged Fawzia.

"*Shukran*," I exclaimed as I turned to face the girls. "Thank you all so very much." I wiped a tear and continued, "This is so thoughtful, but it was not necessary."

At that, the girls could contain themselves no longer, and they all rushed to hug me before they departed to their next class. The "we love yous" and the "thank yous" swirled as the girls ran out. More hugs and well wishes followed as each teacher made her way to leave. It truly touched me that they had gone to this trouble for me. Organized surprise parties with thank you gifts are not their traditional way of thanking someone. When the majority of the crowd had departed, Madawi and Fawzia encouraged me to open the package. Inside I found an 18-karat gold necklace with a built-in swirl pendant crossed with parallel lines of small diamonds. It was unique and very pretty.

"You shouldn't have done this," I said, looking directly at Madawi.

"I didn't," she immediately replied lively. "It was Fawzia and the girls," she smiled proudly as she glanced in Fawzia's direction.

"We wanted to thank you before," Fawzia began and hesitated. "But we couldn't ..." She abruptly ended without completing her sentence and then paused again. Looking down and then up to me again, she concluded, "What is important is that we love you."

Understanding, we all dropped the subject of why I couldn't be acknowledged earlier at the graduation party. It was as Fawzia had said. What was important was that I knew they cared. Madawi had always understood what I had to offer would be beneficial to the girls, but it was not until after the speaking contest that she could find a way to make it work for me to be in the school to actually teach.

Later in the month, Madawi took her desire for me to teach in the school a step further. She asked me to teach the sophomore and junior classes a weekly course on human communication. After a persuasive presentation to the mothers explaining the benefits of my teaching the class, Madawi asked me to set up a program to encompass basic communication skills for the girls. My portion of the program was a segment of a larger wellness program she wanted to implement in the coming fall. At her request, I developed a program designed to teach the sophomores and juniors basic communication concepts, and Shideh, an Iranian educator, taught the seniors the basics of etiquette to compliment my efforts. Finally, after six years with Madawi, I was inside the walls of *Al-Hamdi* to really teach, not just choreograph and teach dances and other fun, frivolous things.

Every Tuesday afternoon for the next two years, I would go with my scarf and *abaya* to *Al-Hamdi* to share the radical concepts of human communication and introduce the girls to foreign ideas that had never before pervaded the walls of the school. On my first day, I went to Madawi's office. She seemed so energized about the course beginning, as was I. After a flood of discussion and excitement, Madawi showed me which classroom would be mine: the room upstairs next to her office. In retrospect, I find two reasons why I was assigned this particular classroom, the only classroom in that building. Either she wanted me close to observe, or she wanted me close to protect, perhaps both.

To mark the first day of classes, Madawi introduced me to the girls in Arabic, explaining, I assume, the purpose of my class with them and what they would achieve. She wanted so much for the girls to understand their potential, to understand that they could be whatever they wanted to be if they worked hard and wanted it badly enough. For my benefit, after a few minutes, she converted to English.

"So, girls," she turned to me, "this is Mrs. Teresa." The girls all expressed their joy in my presence, as most of them already knew me from when I taught dances for the graduations.

"Thank you, Madawi," I responded to the warm greeting. And without further adieu, Madawi left us to begin.

A bit nervous, I stepped in front of the teacher's desk provided. As I did, the girls clamored through their backpacks for paper and pencils.

"Okay, girls. May I have your attention?"

As requested, each girl turned to face me, opened her copy book on her desk, and sat ready with pencil in hand to write down what I had to say so that she could regurgitate the information on a test at a later date. I paused at this observation and thought for a moment as they stared at me eager to learn. Then it hit me. "This is all they know," I thought. By the virtue of their society and by the virtue of their religion, they are taught to learn and accept, not question. I had to explain.

"Oh, no, girls," I smiled. "You may put your paper and pencils away." Each revealed a questioning look at my comment.

"My class is different!" I exclaimed. "In this class we are not going to take notes," I encouraged, hoping to convey my enthusiasm. "In this class," I paused to raise anticipation, "we are going to talk."

With that statement, the Arabic chatter began. I believe they were either amazed or thought they had just entered a playtime class headed by this huge sucker, much like a substitute teacher. Allowing them a few moments to digest this new idea, I soon called the class to order again.

"Now that is not to say we are not going to work in here," I said rather loudly to regain their attention. "It means we are going to discuss and learn things about ourselves and about our friends," I said, emphasizing the word "discuss." With this the girls smiled broadly, indicating their approval. Then we began, interactively learning what communication and non-verbal communication is, we studied communication in relationships and perceptions, how to be a better listener, how to present prepared speeches, and many other aspects of the discipline. The class truly gained confidence, self-worth and understanding. In time, I realized that they did not see me as the sucker substitute, as I assumed my first day of class; rather, they respected me and gained, I believe, invaluable information that will help them in their personal lives for years to come.

The centennial year for the Kingdom of Saudi Arabia fell between 1999 and 2000 on the Western calendar. It was a glorious year marking the 100th year of the country under the rule of the House of Saud. Celebrations were everywhere, all year long. The Eastern Province marked this momentous occasion by erecting symbolic wood *dhows*, banners and other representative icons of their heritage throughout the city. Special gold coins encircled in silver were minted to mark the year as well. Everyone was joyous and celebratory of the country's progress, and this excitement pervaded every occasion that year at *Al-Hamdi*.

The ninth graduation party I attended exhibited a different tone and homage than previous years. Whereas Western and basically American themes had dominated previous ceremonies, the Kingdom's centennial brought about a subtle, yet fundamental change in the attitudes of the teachers, the students and Madawi. Sparking a sense of nationalism and pride, this historic year yielded change in what was important to them all. Subsequently, I was not asked to help with this graduation. I only provided my spotlight that evening, and showed one of the nannies how to use it so I could enjoy the show.

The evening began as usual, and again, I was in the second row, dining room chair. In spite of the usual events marking the beginning of the graduation, there was a very different feel to the night. At the time, I did not see these differences as negative; rather, I saw them as a positive step toward acknowledging and praising their heritage. Since my first visit to *Hofhuf* when I saw how the Saudis had shoved their roots to the wayside in exchange for Western ways, I had encouraged healthy nationalism. I was proud for them and proud that they were finally taking pride in themselves, their country and their heritage.

With the exception of the English class presentation in which it was necessary to speak English, all performances that evening were completely Saudi. The performance was not anti-American, just pro Saudi. Throughout the evening, the girls exalted the beginnings of the country through traditional dances, songs and attire. The students symbolically revealed how the House of Saud came to power, how they united the divided tribes, and then illustrated the good things that were felt by the people after the change of regime. The food flowed, as did the Saudi pride. Even though I was a Westerner looking in and not truly a part of their world, I felt pride as well. Little did I know, little did I see that things were changing for me. I missed how this was a sign of what was to come. I never expected what would happen at the final *Al-Hamdi* graduation I would witness.

The late fall of 2000 brought another speaking competition our way. KFUPM had not held the second annual public speaking contest in the 1999-2000 school year. We laughed, attributing the oversight to their not doing so well in the first. The logistics of our participation in the second competition followed the same pattern as in 1998. Yet, this particular year *Al-Hamdi* did not fare as well. The selected girls worked very hard, but unfortunately, I did not have the same level of natural speakers, fluent in English, as I did for our team in the first competition.

However, our lack of placement success is not what is important with regard to the second speaking competition. It was the global events at the time, which marked the beginning of the anti-American, pro-Islamic sentiment that are so important to note. Two events immediately preceding the second competition set the tone for the speech topics and subsequent events at *Al-Hamdi*.

In September of 2000, Ariel Sharon, now prime minister of Israel, entered the Islamic Holy sites of the Dome of the Rock and the Al-Aqsa Mosque on Al-Haram al Sharif in Jerusalem with thousands of Israeli police, bodyguards, and supporters. Intended as a provocative demonstration of Israeli sovereignty over Jerusalem, his presence in the Holy sites infuriated the Muslim community worldwide. Behind *Mekkah* and *Medina*, the Al-Aqsa Mosque is considered the third Holiest site in Islam.

Only three weeks later, on October 16, 2000, Israeli police fortunately turned back members of the Temple Mount and Land of Israeli Faithful Movement, supported by Sharon, from entering the same sites. Had their infiltration not been halted, I believe a holy war of incalculable magnitude would have erupted. These events were seen by the Muslims as an incursion on their Holy places, and in my opinion, are what triggered the current Middle East insurgence.

The sentiment of the Muslim outrage was reflected in the girls' assigned speech topics during the second public speaking competition. There was no discussion of solving global issues like *Rainforest Deforestation* or informing the audience on *Diabetes* as before. Rather, the evening encompassed pro-Islamic reaction and encouragement to stand against the invaders of their Holy ground.

It was my last graduation, the graduation in May of 2001 that truly revealed how life in the Kingdom had changed, how the sands were shifting. Unlike previous years, I got my own driver to take me to the graduation. Unlike previous years, the hellos when I entered were somewhat cold. They were not rude, just robotic. In retrospect, I can see that anti-Western sentiment existed, subtly just below the surface. I did not get the overstuffed chair or even the dining room chair. I had to fight to even get a chair. I finally sat in a regular folding chair that was stuck in the row over by the wall, placed there by a caring servant who still had feelings for me and continued to treat me as before. As the evening began, the tone was set by the very first act, an extremely pro-Islam and anti-West display that continued throughout the evening. As a result of global events, a sense of supremacy filled the ceremony as they exalted Islam and its beliefs.

Ironically, the treatment I felt with my ten graduations parallels the road I followed as a Westerner in the Kingdom for ten years. In the beginning, the West and its ways were praised following the Gulf war. By the end of our stay in Saudi Arabia, being relegated to the metal chair by the wall was symbolic of how pro-Islamic sentiment grew and began to marginalize Western influence in their culture.

ॐ Chapter Sixteen ॐ

Islam and the Holy Times

A basic principle Westerners must recognize about the Kingdom of Saudi Arabia to truly understand its people and their ways is that it is an Islamic state, dictated by *Sharia* law, with no division between the sacred and secular aspects of life. Their devotion to Islam guides every aspect of daily life. In fact, *"Islam"* literally means *"submission to the will of God."* One of the first Arabic terms a Westerner learns within the boundaries of this land, because it is heard at least once in almost every conversation with a Muslim, is *"Insha Allah,"* which means "God willing."

Although it was never a major topic of conversation or confrontation, Madawi revealed various beliefs of Islam to me over the years on different occasions. In retrospect, I believe that she purposefully concealed anything she thought I would see as negative against Islam. Additionally, she masked aspects of her religion that would indicate that I was bad in the eyes of Islam. She never pushed me to accept Islam and outwardly respected my beliefs, in spite of the fact that her religion told her not to befriend me. The *Quran* states:

"O Believers! Take not the Jews and the Christians as friends and helpers. They are but friends to one another. And if any among you takes them as friends and allies, then surely he is one of them. Verily, Allah does not guide the wrongdoers." [Al-Maa'idah (5):51]

I witnessed how Madawi truly lived her religion; it was part of her. She consistently and deeply followed the principles of Islam because it was her choice to do so, not to impress anyone or make a show of what she did. She taught by example, and it was through her words and actions that I came to understand Islam as I do.

Islam strongly emphasizes each follower's direct relationship with God and His will. Muslims accept much of the Bible's Old Testament and recognize many of the Biblical patriarchs and prophets, including Jesus Christ. It was fascinating to me that when a particular situation or conversation would arise and turn to religion, our understanding and acceptance of the Bible's Old Testament was essentially similar. Many Muslims know Christian parables and some parables of their own reflect similar principles. However, in retrospect, I believe Madawi only revealed the similarities to me, shying away from the differences. Perhaps she knew my Bible better than I.

One time while talking in the salon, somehow the conversation turned to religion, and I learned that they reference "Ibrahim" who is my "Abraham;" they reference "Jabril" who is my angel "Gabriel." Many of the teachings and philosophies she shared with me parallel ones that I learned through my Christian upbringing. However, they believe that God's last and greatest prophet was Muhammad (PBUH) who lived in the seventh century A.D. They do not worship Muhammad, as many in the West assume. They worship God, one God, whom they call *Allah* in their language and revere Muhammad as his messenger.

Whereas Christians have their Bible, Muslims believe that God revealed to Muhammad (PBUH) in the Saudi city of *Mekkah* the Holy *Quran*, which is seen as the expression of His will. The *Quran* revealed in Arabic is considered by many to be untranslatable; however, translation to English has recently been permitted with the stipulation that the Arabic text must also appear.

Muslims see the cities of *Mekkah* and *Madinah* as the two Holiest cities of Islam with Jerusalem being the third. *Mekkah* is the site of the *Kaaba*, or Shrine of the Rock, and it is the most revered earthly place in Islam. The black stone set in a silver frame embraces the only relic of the first mosque built by Ibrahim. This is not to say that they believe Ibrahim (Abraham) was a Muslim, only that they revere him as a prophet from the time before Muhammad (PBUH). Annually, the *Kaaba* is covered with a black cloth (embroidered in genuine gold thread) decorated with verses from the *Quran*. Madawi once told me to die while on pilgrimage to *Mekkah* would be the epitome for a Muslim, as that person would go straight to heaven.

Madinah, on the other hand, was the home of the Prophet Muhammad (PBUH) after he fled *Mekkah,* and it is where he is buried. In addition to its importance with the Prophet, *Madinah* is the site of a major mosque and is a center for Islamic scholarship and learning. When you approach the two Holy cities on the highway from Jeddah, the interstate splits. Two huge signs over the road indicate the driver's options: one highway for believers into the cities, and a second for non-believers, which goes around the cities. Non-Muslims are strictly forbidden to enter. Consequently, I was always fascinated to watch when the *Hajj* was televised so I could get a glimpse of this forbidden world.

As an expression of devotion and their direct relationship with God, Muslims adhere to five primary duties in their life. These duties are referred to as the *"Five Pillars of Faith,"* and Madawi explained that they are comprehensively described in the *Quran*.

The first pillar of Islam is the profession of faith (*Shahada*). To become a follower of Islam one must profess, *"There is no god but God (Allah) and Muhammad is the messenger of God."* This is considered to be the "creed of Islam," and the strong tie to this important pillar of faith felt by the Saudis is reflected in their national flag, which holds an inscription of this declaration of faith. Under the inscription there is an unsheathed sword which symbolizes the "prosperity that comes only through justice."

Five times daily in prayer, all Muslims turn towards the *Kaaba* in the Holy city of *Mekkah* to fulfill the second pillar of the Islamic faith (*Salat*). The call to prayer is made from the top of the minaret at each mosque and rings from every corner of the Kingdom. Before each prayer, it is required that Muslims perform the cleansing ritual of washing away all sins before entering God's presence. There is no priest at the mosque; rather, an *Imam* leads the prayer. On Fridays, the Islamic Holy day (much like Sundays to Christians), there is a midday prayer at the mosque followed by a sermon. During the daily prayer times all commercial establishments close, and Westerners must quickly learn the meaning of patience. With the possible exception of Iran, no other Muslim country besides Saudi Arabia completely stops everything five times a day in observances of the daily prayers. Because the Kingdom follows the Hegira or lunar calendar, prayer times fluctuate throughout the year. Hence, it is extremely helpful to the expatriate to have a copy of the published prayer schedule. David always took the time to reduce and laminate my copy so that I could have it at all times. It was a constant help.

The Muslim year is divided into twelve months of twenty-nine or thirty days, ten to eleven days shorter than the Gregorian, solar calendar used in the West. The years are also numbered differently, starting in 633 A.D., the year of the Hegira when Muhammad (PBUH) fled to *Madinah* to escape his enemies. Since the Hegira calendar is shorter than the solar calendar, Holy holidays such as *Ramadan* rotate through different seasons of the year and never fall on the same day from one year to the next.

The third pillar of faith is achieved by the giving of alms or *Zakat* paid through a religious tax. This is

PRAYER SCHEDULE

Friday, 1 May 1998	3:34	5:02	11:37	15:08	18:12	19:42
Friday, 8 May 1998	3:26	4:57	11:36	15:06	18:21	19:46
Friday, 15 May 1998	3:22	4:53	11:36	15:05	18:20	19:50
Friday, 22 May 1998	3:18	4:50	11:36	15:05	18:24	19:54
Friday, 29 May 1998	3:13	4:47	11:37	15:05	18:28	19:58
Friday, 5 Jun 1998	3:11	4:46	11:38	15:05	18:31	20:01
Friday, 12 Jun 1998	3:10	4:46	11:39	15:06	18:34	20:04
Friday, 19 Jun 1998	3:10	4:47	11:41	15:07	18:36	20:06
Friday, 26 Jun 1998	3:12	4:48	11:42	15:08	18:37	20:07
Friday, 3 Jul 1998	3:14	4:51	11:44	15:10	18:37	20:07
Friday, 10 Jul 1998	3:18	4:54	11:45	15:12	18:37	20:07
Friday, 17 Jul 1998	3:23	4:57	11:46	15:14	18:35	20:05
Friday, 24 Jul 1998	3:28	5:00	11:46	15:15	18:32	20:02
Friday, 31 Jul 1998	3:33	5:04	11:46	15:16	18:29	19:59
Friday, 7 Aug 1998	3:38	5:08	11:45	15:16	18:24	19:54
Friday, 14 Aug 1998	3:43	5:11	11:44	15:15	18:18	19:48
Friday, 21 Aug 1998	3:48	5:14	11:43	15:14	18:12	19:42
Friday, 28 Aug 1998	3:53	5:17	11:41	15:12	18:05	19:35
Friday, 4 Sep 1998	3:57	5:20	11:39	15:09	17:58	19:28
Friday, 11 Sep 1998	4:01	5:23	11:36	15:06	17:50	19:20
Friday, 18 Sep 1998	4:04	5:26	11:34	15:02	17:42	19:12
Friday, 25 Sep 1998	4:08	5:29	11:31	14:57	17:34	19:04
Friday, 2 Oct 1998	4:11	5:32	11:29	14:53	17:26	18:56
Friday, 9 Oct 1998	4:14	5:35	11:27	14:48	17:19	18:49
Friday, 16 Oct 1998	4:17	5:39	11:25	14:43	17:12	18:42
Friday, 23 Oct 1998	4:21	5:43	11:24	14:39	17:06	18:36
Friday, 30 Oct 1998	4:25	5:47	11:23	14:35	17:00	18:30
Friday, 6 Nov 1998	4:28	5:52	11:23	14:32	16:55	18:25
Friday, 13 Nov 1998	4:32	5:57	11:24	14:29	16:52	18:22
Friday, 20 Nov 1998	4:37	6:02	11:25	14:27	16:49	18:19
Friday, 27 Nov 1998	4:41	6:07	11:27	14:27	16:48	18:18
Friday, 4 Dec 1998	4:46	6:12	11:30	14:27	16:48	18:18
Friday, 11 Dec 1998	4:50	6:17	11:33	14:29	16:49	18:19
Friday, 18 Dec 1998	4:54	6:21	11:36	14:31	16:52	18:22
Friday, 25 Dec 1998	4:58	6:25	11:39	14:35	16:55	18:25
Friday, 1 Jan 1999	5:00	6:27	11:43	14:39	16:59	18:29
Friday, 8 Jan 1999	5:02	6:29	11:46	14:44	17:04	18:04
Friday, 15 Jan 1999	5:03	6:29	11:49	14:49	17:10	19:10
Friday, 22 Jan 1999	5:03	6:29	11:51	14:53	17:15	18:45
Friday, 29 Jan 1999	5:02	6:26	11:53	14:56	17:20	18:50
Friday, 5 Feb 1999	4:59	6:22	11:53	15:02	17:26	18:56
Friday, 12 Feb 1999	4:55	6:18	11:54	15:06	17:31	19:01
Friday, 19 Feb 1999	4:51	6:13	11:53	15:09	17:35	19:05
Friday, 26 Feb 1999	4:45	6:07	11:52	15:11	17:40	19:10
Friday, 5 Mar 1999	4:39	6:00	11:51	15:13	17:44	19:14
Friday, 12 Mar 1999	4:32	5:53	11:49	15:14	17:47	19:17
Friday, 19 Mar 1999	4:24	5:45	11:47	15:14	17:51	19:21
Friday, 26 Mar 1999	4:16	5:38	11:45	15:14	17:54	19:24
Friday, 2 Apr 1999	4:08	5:30	11:43	15:13	17:58	19:28
Friday, 9 Apr 1999	3:59	5:23	11:41	15:12	18:01	19:31
Friday, 16 Apr 1999	3:51	5:16	11:39	15:11	18:05	19:35

ALL TIMES ARE IN THE 24 HOUR FORMAT AND ARE FOR THE DAMMAM AREA.
(THE SUNRISE TIME IS NOT A PRAYER TIME)

an annual payment of a certain percentage of a Muslim's property, which is distributed among the poor or other rightful beneficiaries. Many Saudis simply donate the construction of a new mosque to fulfill this pillar. As a result, many beautiful extravagant structures are found on virtually every corner in the Kingdom.

The fourth pillar of faith (*Saum*) is fasting during the Holy month of *Ramadan*, which is the ninth month of the Islamic calendar and celebrates God's gift of the *Quran*. At this time, the holiday begins and ends with the setting sun when "you can no longer tell a white thread from a black one." This is an analogy the Saudis use to mean "at sunset," when your eyes cannot distinguish the two; hence, *Ramadan* begins. At that point, cannons are heard throughout the Kingdom to mark the event.

During *Ramadan*, Muslims must abstain from smoking, eating, drinking fluids of any kind, and sexual relations between the hours of sunrise and sunset. During these hours, "nothing should cross the lips." Even for non-Muslims it is prohibited to eat, drink, chew gum, or smoke in public in Saudi Arabia during this time. Traditionally, preceding the evening meal with grape juice and dates breaks the fast for the Saudis. I was told that the dates would soften the digestive system enabling it to receive such a big meal following the time without food.

Ramadan concludes with *Eid Al Fitr*, which is a three-day holiday to celebrate the breaking of the fast. Whereas it is customary to greet a Muslim at the beginning of *Ramadan* with "*Ramadan Mubarak*," it is customary to greet them during the *Eid* with "*Eid Mubarak*," which basically congratulates them and offers good wishes for the event. The *Eid* is a celebratory time in the Kingdom, much like Christmas day in the states. Gifts are given, special foods are prepared, and everyone makes it a point to visit or call all family and friends to wish them well.

It is the month of *Ramadan* that was problematic for many Westerners in Kingdom. Many Westerners struggled with the concept that we, as Americans and perhaps Christians, had to abstain during the day as well and saw this as a major inconvenience. A fasting room was provided at work for non-Muslim men to eat lunch where they could be separated from the Muslim population. Water fountains in the workplace were shut down, and the tea boys had the month off. The guys used to laugh as they told how more pencils fell on the floor at work during *Ramadan* so one could take a sip from the water bottle he had hid under his desk. If seen by a Saudi smoking or drinking in the car, you would be chastised from a distance or perhaps pulled over and reprimanded in person. The question and comment always arose among the expatriates as to "Why only in Saudi Arabia?" Other Muslim countries do not require fasting by non-Muslims.

Although I spent ten *Ramadans* with my royal family, one vivid memory in particular comes to mind with regard to fasting during the Holy time. The cannons had sounded throughout the Kingdom the night before, marking the beginning of the Holy month. The next day, I went to the palace to tutor and found Madawi in the salon; however, this time she was not eating, just watching TV. Without thinking, I mentioned lunch, as I was accustomed to eating at that time of the day. Suddenly realizing my *faux pas*, I apologized.

"Oh, Madawi," I began, "I forgot." After a short pause, I continued. "I do apologize."

"Mrs. Teresa," she quickly replied in such a wise, soothing voice, "I fast because it is my religion," emphasizing "my." "It is not your religion to fast," she explained. "For me, it is something I do because of faith, and your eating will not tempt me because God gives me strength." Then she smiled and encouraged me to go ahead, motioning to the children's kitchen, "So go, eat."

I was so amazed at her response and touched by her devotion. Madawi was definitely in the minority of Saudis I knew. She understood and had a handle on the big picture of things. She did not believe that I, or anyone else eating in front of her, would be at fault should she decide to break the fast.

It always seemed so hypocritical to me how, on the whole, people in the Kingdom approached the Holy month of *Ramadan*. I believe that Muhammad (PBUH) meant for this month to be about sacrifice, sacrifice for God, a hardship to endure, and a pillar to fulfill. However, I observed Saudis somewhat bending the rules, making days like nights and nights like days in order to ease the fasting requirement. Typically during the fast, most people go to work later in the morning and sleep a lot during the day, significantly shortening their waking, fasting hours. Whereas stores during the other 11 months in the year would normally close around ten o'clock in the evening, during *Ramadan* they stay open until two or three a.m. The common people who are not affluent enough to sleep all day feel somewhat of a hardship, but most do not experience a sacrifice to the extent that I believe was originally intended.

One comical event occurred when Fatma was just at the age when she could perhaps begin fasting. Children, the sick, or menstruating women do not have to fast, as fasting could cause physical harm. (However, after menstruation, women are required to make up the fasting days they miss before the following *Ramadan*). One afternoon I arrived at the palace to find the Colonel in the salon rather than Madawi. While I waited for her, we visited when suddenly Fatma came bouncing in from the girls' salon. The Colonel welcomed her, happy to see her that afternoon, and she plopped down on the ottoman in front of him. Soon our discussion turned to food, as it always seemed to do when Fatma was about. Fatma ask her *Baba* if she could have a piece of cake. Taking this opportunity seriously, the Colonel began to explain to Fatma the meaning of the fast during this time and its importance to their religion. Fatma's big dark eyes were wide as she listened intently to her father, taking in every word as he spoke. To conclude his five-minute explanation, the Colonel put the choice to Fatma about eating the cake, expecting her to make the right decision. He further added that she could eat the cake, yet God would see her eating it during *Ramadan*. Seeming to understand, Fatma agreed with the Colonel, hopped up from the ottoman and kissed him on the cheek before skipping back to the girls' salon. Congratulating the Colonel on a job well done of explaining such a complicated concept to a child, I excused myself to go and study with the girls, stating that I would catch Madawi later. As I entered the girls' salon, there Fatma was stuffing her face with a huge piece of chocolate cake, and she appeared to enjoy every single bite!

"Fatma, what about what *Baba* just said?" I questioned almost chastising. "What about God?"

With chocolate morsels lining her mouth, she replied so innocently, "It's okay, Mrs. Teresa, God sees me eat every day!" Obviously missing the concept that the Colonel had tried so painstakingly to explain, she finished the cake and went back for a second piece.

The fifth pillar of faith to a Muslim is *Hajj*, the pilgrimage to *Mekkah*. *Hajj* is in part in memory of the trials and tribulations of the prophet Abraham, his wife Hagar and his eldest son, prophet Ishmael. Every Muslim who can afford it is required to make a pilgrimage at least once in his or her lifetime. At a specific time during the year, Muslims migrate from all over the world to perform the rituals of the *Hajj*, and the Saudi government bears a tremendous financial burden each year to accommodate the millions of *Hajjis* that make their way to the desert land to fulfill this pillar.

Hajjis, as the pilgrims are called, wear special cloths, the *Ihram*, which is comprised of two white cloths for men. One is wrapped around the man's waist and the other across his chest, and sometimes the men decide to shave their head. Women, contrary to popular Western belief, are not allowed by Islam to wear their veils while at the *Kaaba* in *Mekkah*. The veil, the covering of faces, is not a part of Islam, as Madawi and the Colonel explained to me one afternoon.

"The veil," began the Colonel as he paused in his military way before discussing something of importance, "is not a part of Islam."

"I always thought it was," I responded, somewhat surprised to hear this information.

"Oh, no, the veil," he repeated in his commanding voice, "the veil ... comes from our heritage." He settled back into his recliner to tell the tale.

"Many years ago, the sultan from the Ottoman Empire would come to Arabia and take the women he thought were pretty." Then he gave his signature look as he always did when he was shedding light on a subject and knew he had an attentive ear.

"To stop this, the women would cover their faces so that the sultan would not take them from their families to be a part of his harem." He concluded with a smile, indicating the cleverness of his forefathers against the sultan.

"I will definitely let others know this," I exclaimed as I had enjoyed his storytelling so much. "I always thought that it was something to do with religion."

"No," he replied emphatically and then smiled, again showing his pride in enlightening me on this matter. "As a matter of fact," he continued, wanting to educate me further, "women," he paused for effect, "in the old days, women fought side by side with the men," he said as he furrowed his brow and raised his fist to elaborate on their strength and courage. I could see that he was proud of this aspect of his history, and his future encouragement of the endeavors of the Learning Center showed exactly how deeply he felt about it.

Whereas *Ramadan* concludes with the *Eid* of Sacrifice (*Eid Al Fitr*), the *Hajj* is brought to a close with *Eid Al Hada*, which also lasts for three days and commemorates the annual pilgrimage, and it is in remembrance of the anticipated sacrifice by the prophet Abraham of his son. Well wishes of *"Eid Mubarak"* are given as well, and the Kingdom revels in the celebration.

In addition to the *Quran*, another important Islamic religious document is the *Sunnah*, the example or model of the Prophet. The *Sunnah* gives examples from Prophet Muhammad's (PBUH) own life, his conduct in private, things he said, and his instructions. The *Quran,* coupled with the *Sunnah,* are the basis of *Sharia* or Islamic law and are strictly adhered to in the Kingdom.

Yet another special time, sitting with Madawi and the Colonel in the salon, the topic of daily life and marital relationships arose.

"And that, Mrs. Teresa, is why Islam is better," the Colonel declared as the conversation took a turn. "The *Quran* tells us how to act, what to do," he continued, giving a side smile and raising a brow as he spoke. "It shows us the right path."

"Well, I can definitely see your point, Colonel," I replied diplomatically, wisely not wanting to open a confrontation by defending my beliefs. However, I could not help but push the topic a bit further. Reaching to the furthest depth of my imagination, I came up with a hypothetical scenario to see how he would respond.

"What if Madawi was in the hospital, dying, and your mother was in the hospital dying as well?" I questioned, pausing to increase suspense and severity of the scenario I offered.

"What would you do?" I queried, raising an eyebrow for emphasis. Without a blink of hesitation, he responded.

"I would go to my mother," he said in a final, commanding voice.

"You mean if Madawi was on death's door, about to die at any minute, you would go to your mother?" I reiterated, unbelieving as to the answer he had given.

"Yes."

Wanting to validate the Colonel's response, Madawi said, "And I would be angry if he did not."

"What?" I truly could not comprehend her view, particularly since my society advocates that a man stand with his wife. My religion taught me that a husband and wife should cling to each other, not their families. To think that the Colonel would choose to go to his mother, and to hear his wife insist that he do so, was hard for me to understand.

"You mean," I continued as I leaned forward more emphatically, "you mean you would go to your mother and leave Madawi to die alone if they were both dying at the same time?

"Yes." He restated his view, quite pleased with his response.

"And I would expect him to," Madawi added adamantly. "Just as I would in turn expect Fahad to come to me," she concluded softly, revealing categorically their concept of family lineage and respect of elders. For them, blood relation comes before anything else, even spouses.

Although I believe Madawi and the Colonel would have been open to hearing my views on religion, I survived ten years by not approaching the issue in a defensive manner. Because of the power the royal family wields, a word out of turn could have meant immediate expulsion from the country at best. Our company, as well as the U.S. Embassy, always told Christian expatriates to avoid the topic of religion with a Saudi. What little dialogue I had with the family about religion over the years came when they instigated the conversation. I would listen and learn, questioning things only when I thought it was appropriate and non-confrontational, yet never refuting with my own beliefs.

When I reference the Holy times in Kingdom, I not only refer to the Islamic Holy times of *Ramadan* and *Hajj*, but I also refer to the Christian Holy times of Christmas and Easter. Saudi Arabia does not tolerate any other religion to be practiced within the borders of its domain. As a Christian, you may not wear a cross, import a Bible, or meet with others to worship. Any of these actions, if a Saudi desired, could get you deported. Subsequently, there are no churches or synagogues in the Kingdom of Saudi Arabia, only mosques.

As a result, celebrating Christmas and Easter are done only behind the privacy walls of the compound. However, expatriates do all they can to make these times as much like home as possible. We even got to the point that it became comical to purchase items that were related to Christianity, almost like we were undercover agents on a mission. To get Christmas music, you would enter the music store and ask if they had any seasonal music. The shopkeeper, possibly Christian or at least open to the cause, would peer around to make sure no *muthawen* were near and either pull a selection from under the counter or escort you to a back room where the items were kept.

Christian holiday items were rare but could be found if you were willing to pay for such a privilege. Christmas wrapping paper could cost as much as $10 per roll if you were lucky enough to find it. One store in particular, a craft store frequented by Westerners, must have paid a lot of *baksheesh* or had friends in high places, because they always had Christmas decorations and wrapping paper behind the counter. Another establishment, a party supply store, opened in the late 1990s and got a little carried away with their offerings to their Christian consumers. They had the entire upstairs laden with Christmas and other Christian holiday items, brazenly open for any people to view. Unfortunately, and for no apparent reason, the store burned one night. Amazingly, the fire did not touch any other store that adjoined it. One wonders.

Madawi, however, understood and never seemed to have a problem with me practicing my beliefs as long as it was done in private. She allowed the girls to come to my villa and help me decorate my Christmas tree and bake holiday cookies. It became a tradition we perpetuated until the girls were teenagers and too old to be interested in such things any longer. She knew that I would not try to convert them to Christianity, only let them have fun and learn in a safe way about another culture. She and the Colonel even attended several Christmas parties I held.

"Well, he was a good prophet," the Colonel would always say upon my annual invitation, "so I don't mind celebrating the day of his birth."

The level of their understanding and open-mindedness is extremely commendable and unlike most Saudis.

Madawi always allowed me time off from work to celebrate the holidays and even helped me ship some decorations into the Kingdom in her shipments since they are never searched, and definitely nothing is ever confiscated. One December, I went with her to a women's conference in *Dubai,* which gave us the opportunity to learn new ideas for our business together (see Chapter Eighteen). This offered us a great chance to see Nora, who was then in her first year at the American University of *Sharja*.

Unlike Saudi Arabia, the United Arab Emirates (UAE) allows other religions to practice their faith. Although limited as compared to the states, the UAE does have stores that openly sell Christmas items to Christian citizens. I went wild in the store when I found the items, and Madawi stood back and watched me shop for almost an hour as if she were happy just to see me so happy. I walked out of the store with two box loads of decorations. So excited to have found the items, I beamed as we got into the Mercedes and the driver loaded my goodies into the trunk. After thanking Madawi again for bringing me by the store, it then hit me as to how I was going to get all of the stuff I had bought back into the Kingdom.

"You bought some cute things, Mrs. Teresa," she began as we got into the car.

"I know, Madawi," I replied enthusiastically, "and at such good prices." Then I paused, deciding how to approach the topic of my dilemma.

"But," I paused again trying to formulate the right words, "how will I get these home?" I questioned.

As always, Madawi had the perfect solution.

"Do not worry, Mrs. Teresa," she said in her calm, stately way. "I will ship them for you."

"Really?" I questioned with surprise and then responded with joy. "I would be so grateful."

"*Mofie mushkala*," she replied with that special raised eyebrow and side smile of hers. "*Yellah*," she said to the driver and we were off.

Because Madawi wanted to spend some extra time with Nora, I flew back to *Dhahran* before she did. Two days after my return, a knock came on my villa door. It was Romelo, delivering the two boxes from *Dubai*. As promised, Madawi came through for me yet again.

Whereas Madawi always made it a point to allow me to celebrate my Christian holidays, most Saudis are just the opposite. With the Kingdom having strict rules regarding importation of certain items, it was not uncommon to have such items removed from a shipment. If these items were on the prohibited list (Appendix B), the Saudi officials were correct to remove them. However, there were many times where items that were not prohibited were removed, perhaps because the custom official thought he needed it more than the owner. In any case, it happened and became an accepted fact to expatriates.

One year it seemed as if the delay of a large ship-ment to the compound was intentional, perhaps meant to disrupt our Christmas celebration. One hundred and seventy-two boxes full of gifts from stateside families and toys for under the tree were in customs by the 20th of December, awaiting clearance. Our mail direc-tor checked daily to see if the shipment was ready for release; yet each day he was given an excuse as to why the shipment was not ready. December 24th arrived, and it became obvious that the shipment was not go-ing to be released. Hence, numerous parents were out until the wee hours of the night to make sure all was ready for the following morning. Conveniently, the ship-ment arrived on the compound the morning of the 26th. I have no proof to my allegation; however, we all felt that the delay was intentional and the customs offi-cials probably got a good laugh out of believing that they ruined our Christmas. Little did they know that gifts are not what it is all about.

ॐ *Chapter Seventeen* ॐ
Miranda Who?

$\mathbf{B}$ecause it is such a foreign concept for Americans to comprehend, I must reiterate. Because the Kingdom of Saudi Arabia is an Islamic state, all aspects of life are dictated by *Sharia* law. There are no divisions between the sacred and secular aspects of life. The concept of separation of Church and State, as Americans understand it, does not exist. Religion and government are one in the same. It is also important to note that all nationalities are subject to Saudi law when they live and work in the Kingdom of Saudi Arabia. There are no exceptions. When accused of a crime, you are assumed guilty until proven innocent; thus, the American "Miranda law" does not exist in this desert land.

One man on our compound obviously did not believe this fact and made a huge mistake. While on holiday in Turkey, he decided to mail hashish to his post office box in Kingdom so it would be there when he returned. Through the subsequent search of our mail by Saudi authorities, he was imprisoned.

The government of Saudi Arabia is ruled by a hereditary monarch from the House of Saud who is also the principal religious leader and known as "the keeper of the two Holy Mosques." His court is the highest court of appeal. The King has the power to pardon, and he enacts regulations through his appointed Council of Ministers. However, the King must act in accordance with *Sharia* law and have the approval of the *Ulema*, the Royal family, the Council of Ministers, and the Consultative Council to implement these regulations.

Upon the completion of the new *Riyadh International Airport*, an article was placed in the local newspaper with the front page headline reading that "the new airport was open and the King encouraged all citizens to come and see *their* new airport," with the key word in the article being "*their*." As soon as the paper was distributed, Saudis from all over drove their white Toyota pick-ups to the airport and began to take "*their*" property. Benches, garbage cans, plants, carpets and everything that was not nailed down was taken out by the truckloads before the King could issue a proclamation not to take anything. As a result, the government had to replace the items and refurbish the new airport after its initial unveiling. The second article that appeared to declare the airport's re-opening read, "Come and see the *Kingdom's* new airport!"

To the foreigner, this situation may seem contradictory. If, in fact, they strictly adhere to their laws, why would the above story not be seen as stealing, thus resulting in the loss of many left hands? The understanding comes by looking at this situation from the Saudi viewpoint. The removal of the items from the airport was not seen as stealing because the King *gave* the items to them by advertising for them to come the *their* airport.

Theoretically, the Saudi regime assures equality for all people under the law. The protection of property and rights to privacy and happiness, as set forth in Islam through the *Quran* and the traditions of Muhammad (PBUH), are basic rights to all Saudis. Islamic law also provides a system of private law, civil and penal codes, laws regulating war and relations with non-Muslims. It is up to the *Shariah* and the *Ulema* to interpret the laws of the Kingdom; yet the *Qadis* hold the realm of civil justice.

Any individual has the right to petition the King at his open court or *majlis*, which is held every week. The country is divided into provinces, each headed by a Governor who is appointed by the King and advised by Provincial Council. These appointed Governors, all members of the Royal family, also hold weekly *majlis* for the citizens of their province. Colonel (now General) Awad held his *majlis* every Tuesday evening at the palace. It was during this time that anyone, Saudi or not, could go and speak with him about any issue. Should two people have a dispute, they can go together to a *majlis* and have the issue resolved.

For a non-Saudi or Westerner to enter or live in the Kingdom, a Saudi or an organization must sponsor the person, and only the spouse and immediate biological family members can live there or visit the employee. Tourism, for the most part, is non-existent. One time, a company employee, Bob, wanted to have his stepson visit the Kingdom for summer vacation; however, this was not allowed because he was not the biological father of the child. After being denied his request through the company and all other venues, Bob decided to go to the King's *majlis* in *Riyadh* to plead his case. Upon seeing the King, Bob's request was denied because it went against regulations. Disappointed and frustrated, Bob decided to return to the *majlis* the following week to ask yet again. This time, aggravated with Bob's persistence and lack of acceptance of the rules, the King told Bob that the answer to his request was definitely no. Further, if he returned another time to the *majlis,* he would be thrown in jail. Unrelenting, mainly due to his wife's pressure at home, Bob returned to the King for a third time. As promised, the King threw him in jail where he remained for several weeks. After his release, Bob was still determined to have his stepson visit. Yet again he went to speak to the King. Amazed with Bob's persistence (and clearly seeing that he was a committed family man), the King granted Bob his request by waiving the regulation this one particular time.

The Saudi Arabian legal system is based on *Sharia* law. In Saudi, the most orthodox of all Muslim societies, the law is strictly and swiftly enforced and violators are punished immediately. Murder and use or possession of illegal drugs are punishable by beheading. Theft, on the other hand, will result in the loss of the violator's left hand. Every city in the Kingdom has one particular mosque where punishments are carried out, usually the central mosque that has two minarets rather than just one. "Chop, Chop Squares," as the

Westerners knew them, were mosques you wanted to avoid on Fridays, the Holy day in which punishments would be implemented. Typically, all executions would be announced in the daily newspaper before the event, which was actually very helpful. This is not an event one would want to stumble upon.

A fellow expatriate on the compound, who was also a six-foot-two decorated Vietnam veteran, decided that he wanted to witness a beheading. I am not sure whether he doubted that it really happened or if he was just curious, but he watched the paper until he saw one scheduled. The entire compound became interested about the outcome of his adventure. Finally, an announcement was found in the *Arab News*: a beheading would occur the following Friday. I cringed as Steve recounted the event at the compound swimming pool three weeks later.

It actually took this hardened Vietnam Vet three weeks before he could even talk about what he had seen. As directed in the paper, he arrived at the square at the scheduled time for the beheading. He said the outdoor space was full of several thousand Arabs to witness justice. After what seemed like endless talking from the minaret, the accused was brought out from the mosque, appearing to be drugged in some way. Steve said the man was escorted onto a platform and made to bend on his knees. As the man came forward, the Arabs started pushing Steve to the front so that he would have a better view of the consequence for violating their laws. Ironically, Steve said it was not necessary for him to be pushed to the front to see because as soon as the criminal knelt, the entire crowd went to its knees, to pray, Steve explained. This left him as the only human being standing and offered a perfectly clear view of the events that followed. The executioner, wielding a long scimitar, took the man's head off in one fell swoop and the head rolled. Steve said he immediately felt nauseated and wanted to throw up. He emphasized over and over that he had never seen anything like it, even in Vietnam. With this story resonating in my mind, I made it a point to never be near Chop, Chop Square on a Friday.

The Saudis firmly and literally adhere to the concept of "an eye for an eye." Should someone in your family be murdered, the oldest male in the victim's family has the right to perform the execution if he desires. Otherwise, the executioner can carry out the punishment.

Shortly after David's arrival, before I arrived, a lady was punished at the double-minaret mosque for adultery. As punishment for her crime, she was placed in a black bag, thrown from the top of the minaret and then stoned to death by the women in attendance. We never heard anything about the man or if he was punished. There was no mention of him in the paper.

The Committee for Public Morality, known as the *Muthawen*, seeks to uphold the laws of Islam and govern standards of social conduct in Saudi Arabia. The *muthawen* essentially roam the streets of the Kingdom to confirm that everyone is in compliance. For the first few years, I did not even know they existed, perhaps because I did not do anything to draw their attention. It was not until my first minor encounter that I learned how to recognize them.

It was *Ramadan,* and I was out shopping with a friend since the holiday fell close to Christmas that particular year. Not wanting to be offensive, we both wore our *abayas* as we shopped. After looking through several stores, we headed for the car and had no idea that a gentleman was following us. His *thobe* was short, about eight inches off the ground, he did not wear an *igal* on his *guthra,* and he had a long beard tinted in red, all identifying traits of a *muthawen.* Before we could enter the vehicle, the man, in a rather loud voice, shouted at us in Arabic. At first, we did not realize he was speaking to us. It soon became obvious that we were the focus of his uproar. We stopped and turned to him as Saleem exited the car and approached our side. When he saw that we did not understand his Arabic comments, he spoke to us in broken English. Saleem, being the man on the scene, stepped up to translate what the *muthawen* could not communicate to us. Essentially, he wanted us to cover our hair. When we realized his demand, Lynn and I retrieved our headscarves from our bags and began to adorn them. While doing so, I simply smiled at the *muthawen* and said "*Mofie mushkala.*"

In ten years, I only had two other encounters with the *muthawen.* One was fairly comical and the other was extremely terrifying. Before I share these events, it is important to understand the "*official*" policy distributed to expatriates by the American Embassy with regard to women's attire and the *Muthawen* in the

Kingdom. *Officially*, American women are not required to wear the *abaya*, only to dress conservatively. *Officially*, Americans should avoid confrontation with the religious police; yet, if unable to avoid a situation, Americans should only respond to an accompanying police officer and call the American government relations officer as soon as possible. *Officially*, an American should never give their *igama* to a *muthawen*, only to a Saudi police officer. The bottom line, however, was to remain composed and avoid confrontation as much as possible.

Of course, the only problem with these *official* proclamations is that the American Embassy representatives are never with you when a situation would arise. You were alone and had to fend for yourself if a situation arose, using your wits and understanding of the culture to try to pull you through unscathed.

I was pregnant with Mason, and we decided to go to the *Al-Khobar* Mall to shop for baby items. Knowing that this mall was renowned for *muthawen* encounters, David and I asked my mom and dad to go with us. There is always safety in numbers. Not wanting to offend, I wore my *abaya* over my short-sleeve maternity clothes, and Mom wore a calf-length dress with long sleeves. Believing we were appropriately covered, we headed for the mall. After finding a parking space fairly near, we began walking toward the entrance. Just as we crossed the street, David grabbed my elbow and whispered.

"Hurry up," he said anxiously, "*Muthawen*. Let's get inside."

With Mom and Dad a few steps behind, we encouraged them to pick up the pace as well, trying not to cause alarm. David had seen a whole group of them turn the corner in their old dilapidated Suburban, as they do when they want to cover more ground than they could on foot. It was like a posse roaming around to find their next prey. Seeing us, the driver halted long enough for five to jump from the Suburban and head in our direction, the direction of the sinful uncovered women.

As we entered the electronic doors of the beautiful-marble laden mall, we knew for sure that we were being pursued. To avoid the confrontation, we jumped on the nearest escalator to disappear to the second floor. Unfortunately, the hunt was becoming louder and more obvious every minute. We faced forward, pretending not to hear their calls as the escalator moved us upward. With all of us huddled onto two steps, the five men followed, perhaps 15 steps behind, huddled together as well and shouting at us in Arabic. Once on the second floor, we took a left, walking briskly and aimlessly while trying to decide what to do. We actually thought of going incognito by ducking into a store and putting us all under *abaya* and veils, but dismissed the idea after a laugh. Soon the need to stop became obvious. David and Daddy took charge and decided to face the inevitable rather than continue with this absurd parade through the mall. As we stopped and turned to face the men behind us, my condition became obvious to the *muthawen*, and the older one actually seemed to mellow his tone in respect of the mom-to-be. The younger one, however, continued with his hostile quest. Speaking to David, he began.

"Sir," he said in fairly good English, "the women must cover. It is our custom," he demanded as the others continued to chatter at us in Arabic.

At this my dad stepped up, knowing that age is respected as is eminent motherhood, and spoke.

"It is not our custom," he began, beginning to get a little agitated as well. "But," he paused for emphasis, wanting to shame them in some way for being so belligerent, "we will leave your mall." And we did.

Although somewhat annoying, our mall encounter with the *muthawen* was not frightening. To this day, we still laugh as to how comical it must have looked, all of us parading through the mall with a crazy mob on our trail screaming at the top of their lungs. However, the other time I had an altercation with the religious police was terrifying, and it lasted an entire evening.

It was late December after Christmas and before the New Year. It was cold and surprisingly rainy. David and I decided to go to *Dammam* to go gold shopping. After dinner, we left our villa and arrived just after the completion of the *Isha* prayer. Unlike *Al-Khobar*, *Dammam* is much more conservative and populated by mainly *Shiite* Muslims, but it has better gold souks and prices. Because of the weather, I had on jeans, a long sweatshirt and a London Fog raincoat that reached to my calves. However, I still had my *abaya* in my bag. I never left home without it.

After parking the Suburban, we scampered across the street to try and duck under awnings to avoid the rain. Just as our feet hit the opposite sidewalk, a man stepped into our path. It was a *muthawen,* and he began ranting in Arabic. His point of contention, we assumed from his ranting, was my dress. Where was my *abaya* and headscarf? Not wanting a confrontation, we repeated, "*Mofie mushkala, mofie mushkala,*" while David insisted that I hurry as I pulled my *abaya* from my bag and put it on over my raincoat. Believing that the problem was solved, David grabbed my elbow to escort me away from the situation, when the *muthawen* began again, this time seeming to demand David's *igama.*

Refusing to give him any documentation, David, relying on the *official* Embassy policy, attempted to thwart the confrontation by telling the *muthawen* "*mofie,* police. You need police. I only talk to police." Then, as if he had been laying in wait, a police officer appeared from behind a partial wall behind the *muthawen.* Momentarily relieved to see him, believing that everything would be okay with him there, David handed his *igama* to the police officer who, without hesitation, handed it directly to the *muthawen!* Suddenly, the situation was looking problematic again. After checking our papers, the *muthawen* began to rant again. This time, through the police officer's feeble attempt to translate, we understood that he wanted me to cover my head in addition to the *abaya.* Again, hoping to end the situation, we offered to comply. However, I did not have my headscarf in my bag, and I conveyed this to David.

"I'll go across the street to that *abaya* store and get one," I said to David, attempting to convey the same to the *muthawen*. Believing we were in agreement, David and I started for the store, and the *muthawen* went crazy. He did not want us to go to that store and demanded that we follow him and the police officer.

"*Yellah, yellah, imshee,*" he shouted as he started to move.

In our minds, we were captives and felt that we must follow because they had David's *igama*. Not knowing where they were taking us, we respectfully followed, keeping quiet and hoping our compliance would help to end the situation soon. We followed a pace behind the *muthawen* and his police officer around the corner and down the rainy pedestrian path. Shortly, he stopped in front of another *abaya* store. Through his Arabic and hand gestures, he indicated that he wanted me to buy a scarf at this particular store, probably his brother's or cousin's establishment. Leaving David with the men in the rain, I ran inside to purchase the required scarf.

Honestly, I hated spending money on these items, even though I did. Hence, if I had to buy one, I wanted to buy one that I liked. So I began to shop. Requesting the prices of several scarves, I continued browsing. A few minutes later, I felt a hand on my shoulder. I turned to find David behind me; his brows were furrowed and he was quite annoyed.

"What in the hell are you doing?" he exclaimed.

"I'm buying a headscarf!" I declared.

" How can you be shopping NOW!" he yelled. Not allowing me a chance to respond, he turned to the shopkeeper.

"What is your cheapest?" he demanded. "Best price."

The shopkeeper, somewhat frightened because of David's tone, grabbed a scarf from under the counter and replied, "Fifteen *riyal.*"

"Sold." David threw the money onto the counter as he grabbed up the scarf and shoved it into my hands while we headed back to the men waiting for us outside the store.

"Put it on," he demanded as we walked, infuriated at my shopping attempt and nervous because of our situation.

By the time we got outside, I had the scarf on my head and looked to the *muthawen* for approval. Again, the Arabic ranting began. He wanted my hair completely under the scarf. Obediently, I tucked my bangs under the black cloth as well. With that, he turned his back to us.

"*Yellah, yellah, imshee,*" he bellowed yet again, while motioning for us to follow him. Dutifully, assuming we should, we followed again. After several blocks, he stopped abruptly in front of a makeshift portable trailer, *muthawen* headquarters, I assume, and insisted we follow him inside. Once inside the foyer, the *muthawen* proceeded into a room to the right, and David and I continued behind. As we reached the threshold of the room on the right, an arm appeared in front of me, not touching me, yet indicating that I could not enter. When I looked up at him, the guard motioned to the room on the left side of the foyer. "*Tieeb,*" I responded and headed for my designated room.

The left hand room was small, about eight-by-eight, completely lined with raggedy old sofas crammed end to end. It smelled. Submissively, I looked at the guard who had escorted me and sat. Acting dominant, he left. Alone, I waited for this nightmare to end.

As I sat, I surveyed the room. The wood-paneled walls were covered with posters, each either publicizing negative information about the infidels and how bad we are or how good Islam is. One commented on the wearing of eye makeup to attract men. Immediately I began wiping mine off. Everywhere I saw anti-infidel, anti-American, pro-Islamic propaganda. With frustration beginning to turn to fear, I sat down again. In the distance, I could hear loud Arabic voices, and periodically, I could hear David's faint replies.

Since a simple conclusion to our detention began to look slim, my mind began to race. I had to do something. We had told no one that we were going to *Dammam* that evening, so I could not rely on someone eventually missing us and consequently looking for us. What to do? My mind whirled with ideas on how to get us out of this mess. As I sat on the edge of the sofa, becoming more frightened by the minute, I suddenly noticed a telephone. It was an old rotary telephone hiding under some Islamic literature. I could try to call for help. As I was not sure if I would be allowed to use the phone, I wanted to make sure that the guard was not looking. Quietly, I got up and peered around the door into the foyer. I saw him with his back to me inside the doorway of the room to the right where they had taken David. He seemed absorbed in the activity there, so I silently moved back to the phone. Again, relying on the *official* Embassy policy, I dialed the American government relations officer's number that I had committed to memory. No answer, only a machine. Frustrated, I tried the American Consulate's number. Again, no answer. Getting nervous, I peered around the corner again to make sure that my dialing had not been heard. The guard's back was still to me, and he seemed to still be enthralled in the events of the other room. By this point, the right room had become extremely crowded with about 15 *muthawen* crammed into the little room around David. Knowing that I was the only one that could help us, I tiptoed back to the telephone and tried the company's government relations officer's number. Again, an answering machine. With fear now turning to panic, my thoughts turned to Madawi. She could help me; I just knew it. Even in the whirl of fear, I had enough wits about me to realize that their phones were probably tapped, and it would not be a good idea to call a princess from *muthawen* headquarters. The last thing I wanted to do was to get her in trouble, to draw attention to a royal helping an infidel. As I sat wondering what to do, my little internal voice came through, pulling up yet another point from my mom, "*They won't touch a woman.*" That was it. I had a plan.

I stood up, took an enormously deep breath to gain my courage, and walked right out the door, down the steps, and across the street! I set out with determination as the guard shouted behind me, obviously wanting me to return to my room. Ignoring his cries, I continued without looking back, resolved to get us out of this mess. I walked into the nearest shop and asked the shopkeeper to use his phone. Wanting to please, as they always did, he handed me his rotary dial from beneath the counter with a smile.

With my hands shaking, uncertain of how much time I had before they came after me, I dialed Madawi's number. Ibrahim, the palace operator, answered.

"Ibrahim," I exclaimed, extremely happy to hear a friendly voice, "*Amity*, Madawi, *mumkin*."

Recognizing my voice, he continued as he always did.

"Ah, Mrs. Teresa," he began, "*Kayf Haalik?*" He repeated in English, "How are you, Mrs. Teresa?"

"*Tieeb, Shukran*, Ibrahim," I replied and insisted again. "*Amity*, Madawi, *mumkin*." My voice must have conveyed my anxiety, as he did not attempt to continue our conversation.

"Wait, Mrs. Teresa," he responded and put me on hold.

Finally, I heard Madawi's voice greeting me.

Still unsure of the time I had on the phone and completely exasperated, I did not begin with the normal cordialities of Saudi conversations, and I went straight to the point.

"Madawi," I gasped, "the *muthawen*. They have us." I paused to catch my breath.

"Ooos," her familiar sound of expression came across the line. "What?" She exclaimed without hesitating for me to respond. "Where are you?"

"*Dammam*," I said, and then pleaded, "help me."

"Calm down," she insisted. She was always in control even when things looked bad, always the stabilizing force. She continued after a thoughtful pause.

"Tell them you want to be arrested," she replied calmly.

"What?" I screamed into the receiver.

"Yes, tell them you want to be arrested."

Acting on faith, I absorbed what she said and questioned no more.

"Okay," I responded, completely trusting her.

"It will be okay," she answered. "*Yellah*," and she hung up the phone.

I returned the receiver to the cradle, trying to process what she had just told me to do. Thanking the shopkeeper, I turned and took a deep breath before heading back to the doors of the *muthawen* headquarters where the guard was still shouting at me and waving his arms. Just as I had left, I returned. Shoulders back, confident, I climbed the stairs holding my *abaya* up so that I would not trip, not taking my eyes off my destination. Once inside the foyer, I stopped and shouted at the top of my voice.

"We want to be arrested, NOW!" I yelled as I stomped my foot. Knowing that I had done something, probably called Madawi, David stood and repeated firmly.

"I want to be arrested NOW," he yelled as he stomped his foot as well.

Knowing that action had been taken, I turned and entered my detention room. Without confronting the guard, I sat and looked at him as if daring him to say anything. He did not.

Clamor and movement could be heard from David's room. I strained to listen. Arabic chatter ensued, and then David announced again.

"I want to be arrested," he demanded over and over again.

Surprised at this revelation, the one *muthawen* who spoke broken English confirmed. "You want to be arrested?" he asked, as if we were asking for something horrible.

"Yes," David responded firmly.

With that, several crowded together by the desk. The head *muthawen*, speaking profusely in Arabic, was leading the charge while one of them wrote rapidly as the others talked. After about an hour, they stopped and stood. The head *muthawen* demanded that the guard take us to the GMC outside. We were made to sit in the third seat, in the back, while six of them climbed in the remaining seats. They passed some papers back and forth as we traveled to the police station, probably trying to make sure they had their story straight before we saw the police.

Once inside the station, we were instructed to sit on an old bench to the side. Ominously, feeling that things were getting worse, not better, we sat as the head *muthawen* and police chief exchanged kisses and greetings and enjoyed tea, naturally. Over a half an hour passed as we sat and they visited. I was the only woman there, so I sat and looked down at my lap as much as I could, not wanting to draw attention to myself. The station was a disgusting place, unclean and smelly. Finally, around midnight, they stood and it appeared as if they were completing their business. The head *muthawen* handed the police chief the paper they had scrutinized in the GMC, and they concluded their goodbyes. As the head *muthawen* headed for the door, the police chief's attention turned to us. Without saying a word, he stood, glancing to his left to ensure that the *muthawen* had left. Once so, he took the papers in his hand and ripped them in half, letting them fall into the wastebasket to the side of his desk. Then he stepped forward to shake David's hand.

"*Mofie mushkala*, Mr. Davids and Mrs. Teresa," he started. "Abdul is here for you."

Just then, in came Mr. Abdul, Madawi's trusted palace manager, with Abdullah a few feet behind him. What a relief it was to see him, to see a familiar, friendly face! He greeted the police chief and spoke with him in Arabic, and then he greeted David and me.

"Oh, Mr. Abdul!" I exclaimed, unable to wipe the smile of relief from my face. "It is so good to see you."

"I have been waiting," he replied. "Come, I will take you to princess."

He turned to David. "Abdullah will take you to your GMC, and I will take Mrs. Teresa to the palace. Meet us there," he instructed. We all departed the police station with an enormous feeling of relief.

Having heard me come in, Madawi was already on her feet as I entered the salon. She, too, seemed relieved and grabbed my hand.

"Oh, Mrs. Teresa," she cried.

"Thank you, Madawi," I whispered as we kissed the

greeting and I hugged her neck. "Oh, thank you," I repeated over and over.

"Tell me what happened!" she insisted, while gesturing for me to sit.

As we moved toward the sofa, Nora and Fatma bounced in to hear the scoop. Apparently everyone in the palace was aware of our situation and awaiting the outcome. After taking off my *abaya* and shoes to get comfortable, I breathed a long sigh of relief, trying to regain my composure after the incident. Then I retold the events of the evening as they sat and listened intently, hanging on to every word.

After the story was told, we all began to speculate. None of us could decide why the confrontation began and why it escalated as it did. Madawi did have one theory though.

"You, Mrs. Teresa ... you were the catch of the night," she declared.

"What do you mean?" I questioned.

"It is close to New Year's, and they probably thought they had caught some Westerners drinking or something," she continued with a sip of juice. "And when you followed them without saying no, you became the catch of the night ... like a fish. That's why they brought in all the rest," she concluded, proud of her take on the subject.

"That does make sense," I added. "But why?"

Ignoring my question, she continued. "When I was a little girl," she explained, "the *muthawen* were good, wise men." She glanced off as if remembering fondly. "They were there to guide people, to tell the them the right thing." Her glance returned to me. "But today," she paused remorsefully, "many of them are not so good. They are men who go off and do things they should not. Out of guilt, they then become *muthawen* to make things right with God." She stated, "They are not like they used to be." With that, the conversation turned, and the incident was never mentioned between us again.

Madawi never told me, but I later learned that she helped me the only way that she could. Sending me to the police to be arrested was the only way she could rescue me from the grasp of the religious police. The royalty has no power over the *muthawen*. They, too, are subject to detainment and control by the Committee of Public Morality. However, she could control the police, a governmental agency. Little did we know that the *muthawen* do not arrest people, they only detain people. And it is the person's right to ask to be charged and taken to the police. Subsequently, we also discovered that we did not have to follow them that evening. Because the *muthawen* have districts, so to speak, all we had to do was find out what cross street we were near and leave. Our government relations officer could have then gotten David's *igama* back for us. Oh, how little did we know. Thank God I had Madawi to call.

To the Westerner imposing Western values, the Saudi laws and their punishments of criminals may seem severe. Nevertheless, I can attest that I never felt afraid for my children and myself the entire decade I lived there. I could go downtown at any time, even alone late at night during the month of *Ramadan*, and I knew I was safe. I never felt fear until we became the target for terrorists.

ॐ *Chapter Eighteen* ॐ

The Learning Center

"*B*uild it and they will come," the classic line from
the movie *Field of Dreams,* was all I could think of as I
listened to her proposition in the salon that hot, steamy
afternoon in May of 1995. As she spoke, I became more
and more excited. I felt compelled to help, to become a
part of this ambitious endeavor. I knew that it would
be a success, but I never dreamed it would be the largest challenge, my most influencing achievement, and
lead to the eventual demise of my life in the Kingdom.

My thoughts refocused on the conversation at hand.

"Yes, Madawi," I responded, "I'm listening. Ideas are
already rushing through my head."

"It is important to me," she continued as she sipped
her tea. "If I know that one lady is sitting in a classroom somewhere, learning something, I can sleep at
night ... *Insha Allah.*" Her sincerity and passion pow-
ered through her words.

With that statement from the princess, I knew I
must dedicate myself to educating Saudi women.
Madawi dreamt of an educational learning center for
ladies within the borders of Saudi Arabia, and I decided I wanted to help her realize her dream. On that

May afternoon, Madawi bestowed upon me the opportunity to prepare a proposal for the creation of The Learning Center.

For the entire ride home as Saleem weaved through traffic, my thoughts raced at the possibilities. I was astounded that Madawi, a royal princess, wanted me to start a business for her, that she wanted me to organize a learning center for women in Saudia Arabia of all places. I thought of what it would mean to the women, how it would change life as they knew it. I thought of how it would change my life. A tremendous mission lay before me.

Like a volcano, my excitement erupted as I rushed through the villa doors to tell David. He listened intently as I recapped the day's extraordinary events.

As Madawi and I sat at the table in her salon, my shoulders were erect and my eyes focused, prepared for whatever I was about to hear. She began by explaining that many of the moms from *Al-Hamdi* had asked her repeatedly over the years when she was going to open a school for them as well. They had been so pleased with what she had provided for their girls. However, she had been unable to do anything for the mothers because she did not have the right person to take on such a challenge.

"And that is where I believe you fit in, Mrs. Teresa."

"She really said that?" David questioned with amazement.

"Yes," I replied, earnestly feeling the passion Madawi had conveyed. "Oh, David, it is so obvious that this is her dream, one that she has had for a long time."

I continued to explain as we worked our way down-stairs for some dinner. "She wants to open a place where ladies can learn."

"Here?" David clarified.

"And what is wrong with women learning?" I questioned with a touch of sarcasm.

"Nothing," he defended. "I supported you through your masters. You know I think it's great for women to learn. I just question how you are going to make it work here," he paused, "in Kingdom." He continued, "They're not really big on that, you know."

"I know," I answered solemnly. "But this time, it will work. After all, there is a princess behind it."

"A princess ... that's putting you on the front lines for her," he answered as he gave a suspicious look.

"No," I reacted defensively, "a princess who needs me to help her accomplish something."

From the day we met, I always knew Madawi had an uncanny understanding of the value of education and the benefits a good education would provide. She had been able to fulfill this dream for the girls through *Al-Hamdi*; yet she had not taken the next logical step to offer educational opportunities for the women in her community.

As David and I continued with dinner, the conversation about the proposed school ensued. This dinner topic dominated our personal lives for the next several months.

"But what about a feasibility study?" David interjected, exuding his business sense and practicality. "Do you think the women will come?"

I laughed at his question, remembering the line from *Field of Dreams*, *"Build it and they will come."* I shared this with David and he chuckled as well.

"I guess you're right," he said. "It is a leap of faith; but if Madawi believes they will come, so do I. I'll help where I can."

The following morning, I stared at the computer monitor in front of me. All of the ideas I had noted mentally in the car the day before deserted me, and an overwhelming feeling hit me. Where to start? This was an incredible endeavor to undertake. A blank slate was in front of me, and what it would become was based on what I would develop. After roaming around the villa and the garden for inspiration, I decided a mission statement would be the best place to start. The wording of this guiding document was critical. It would have to express the goal of the center … yet not offend members of the society. It had to express the academic goals of the center and incorporate an aspect of socialization for the women.

During our initial meeting, Madawi had explained to me that women in her society did not know how to interact with people from different families. She explained that up until now, women were always with members of their family, their tribe, and did not mingle with those who were from other families. Yet, their society was changing and the women were not ready for this change because they were unsure how to interact with other women. Hence, I determined at least 50 percent of the mission had to include basic socialization. The mission statement began to emerge:

A unique new place where women can learn skills that are not readily available in the area, meet other ladies, and generally enhance their well-being and self esteem through the exchange of skills and ideas.

As promised, I presented my proposal to Madawi the following Tuesday. We reviewed it line by line. The mission statement was the first order of business, as I wanted to be sure that my vision and hers were the same. They were, they always were. We were intuitive that way from the start. Secondly, I had to run my idea of a name past her. Because the basic goal of the center was to offer ladies the opportunity to learn I suggested: *The Learning Center: A Ladies Place for Personal Development.* In the years to come, the acronym TLC became well known throughout the Kingdom, which always seemed clever to me because of the Western connotation to the same letters.

Initially, the center would be a place for women to gain knowledge and skill in the fields of English Language, French Language, Human Communication, Art, Typing, Computers and various classes for personal development such as CPR, parenting and business. To provide instructors for these classes, I would look to the local market for qualified Western ladies already in the Kingdom with their husbands. This would save us money as opposed to hiring teachers and bringing them into the country.

Operating on four terms per year, the center would be organized to offer four-week workshops and eight-week courses, depending on the topic and amount of information to be presented. Each class would be held two days a week for two hours per day, allowing time for tea and socialization at the one-hour break of each class.

After approving the mission statement, the name and reviewing the proposed logistics of the center's operation, I questioned Madawi as to a physical location. "Where will it be, Madawi?" I inquired. "I didn't include this in the proposal because I don't know how it works here. Do we rent? Do we buy?" I paused momentarily. "It will have to be a place with enough space to offer classes simultaneously, yet have a large space for the women to gather and visit."

She hesitated thoughtfully at my questions. "Don't worry about the place," she stated. "Awad will help us." I never guessed she meant we would use one of the facilities governed by the airbase, a facility that would cost us nothing to use and offer us protection and seclusion.

With the structure and cost analysis of start-up determined, the issue of funding arose. Madawi explained that she had the capital; however, she preferred to obtain funding from a local bank.

"I really like it, Mrs. Teresa," she said as she closed her copy of the proposal. "Sila will call you tomorrow with the name of a bank and a man to see about the money," she continued. "Have David go with you and present this to the man," she instructed, referring to the proposal.

"I will call you by the end of the week about the building," she went on. "I'll talk to Awad tonight and see what is available."

With that, we said our goodbyes, and I headed upstairs to tutor the girls for the afternoon.

The meeting with the bank took place the following week, and we were granted a loan of 450,000 Saudi *riyal* ($120,000) to start the center. Unlike stateside banks, however, we would be required to pay the loan back in three large payments of 150,000 *riyal* over a nine-month period. The first payment was due only one month after the center was scheduled to open. Hearing these terms made my heart sink. How in the world could we cover operating costs and make this kind of payment in only one month? We were starting a new, illegal business in the eyes of the Saudi government, which meant advertising would only be by word of mouth, and we had to generate 150,000 *riyal* ($40,000) in only one month. I knew that this would be problematic, but I took the step as Madawi instructed.

Although illegal with respect to governmental agencies, there was a point to which the things we were doing in the center would be tolerated. After all, education of females is allowed, and having a princess behind the endeavor afforded us a further point of tolerance than would be allowed for a non-royal. From the beginning, I knew that if we ever crossed that unspecified line of tolerance, I would be the one to endure the consequences. After that, however, I could only rely on Madawi to protect me. We had an understanding, although never specifically stated, that I would be the face of the center, and Madawi would remain backstage to free me if necessary.

Albeit I knew that what we were doing was an underground operation, counter-culture so to speak, but I was willing to take the chance because I wholeheartedly believed in the center. I knew what we were doing was fundamentally correct. Consequently, I naively fluttered through our weakest time, the first years of the center, without fully understanding the ramifications of my actions. Many times now, I stop to consider if Madawi did. Did she know or stop to think of the jeopardy in which she was placing the two of us?

As planned, Madawi and I met the following week to view three locations that the Colonel had offered for possible use. As we went through the first one, we discussed the pros and cons. It was a single-family villa formerly used by David's company. It had nine rooms on two floors, a large, elegant living area that would work nicely for socializing, a large kitchen for refreshment preparation and a private swimming pool. All of these were good points, yet it had a major disadvantage. As Madawi quickly noted, it was in a local neighborhood and only protected by its own privacy wall. Too many people would question the number of people and cars coming and going every two hours. The location of the villa would draw attention to us, leaving us open for ridicule and possible closure. Because of security, we ruled it out immediately.

The second location was also not located on a protected compound, but it was not in a neighborhood either. Rather, it was on a major street in open sight. Currently it was empty, but it had previously been the medical clinic for our company. The few neighbors that were around were accustomed to people coming and going. Hence, it was a possibility, so we continued to investigate. It was four apartments within the same structure, divided inside by a central stairway housing two apartments on each floor. It had plenty of rooms for classes, plenty of bathrooms, and nice areas for our proposed tea times. Still, we did not feel it was the perfect choice, until later, just over a year later.

The third potential location seemed perfect almost from the start. It was located on my previous compound, surrounded by a 15-foot privacy wall with a gated entrance. In addition, the gate had a security bar that could be lowered to block entry and a huge iron gate to close if more security was required. Inside, we were offered two of the villas near the gate, leaving the other 73 villas vacant. Because we were on the compound, we would have, with permission, access to all the facilities the compound had to offer: swimming pool, dinning hall, theater, tennis courts and the like. It took us six months later to realize the potential of these additional compound amenities. Our focus in the beginning was strictly ladies' classroom learning, but in time that focus expanded to include children, sports and numerous other areas of learning. With the safety concern solved, the choice of location became a mute point.

We took possession of the two adjacent villas on DM 18, my old Western compound, for the center a week later. We utilized the villa closest to the guard gate as the administrative villa, with the downstairs accommodating reception and plenty of room for socializing. My office and two classrooms were housed upstairs in the same villa. The second villa was used strictly for classes, with the first floor completely consumed by the computer lab and three classrooms upstairs that were suitable for language classes.

With the facility selected and funding in hand, Madawi gave me the notice to proceed, and the physical, exhausting work began. It was non-stop days of shopping and nights of assembly and organization.

Although 400,000 *riyal* sounded like a lot of seed money, in actuality it was not. By the time we bought the computers and appropriate desks, televisions for the computer room, five chalkboards, 20 classroom desks, and a few artificial plants, much of our money was exhausted. Hence, we had to be resourceful. David was able to obtain unwanted desks from the base for my office and reception area. Fortunately, we were able to utilize the sofas, chairs and coffee tables that came with each villa, which worked nicely for our social area. With funds running low for additional desks, it worked nicely to use the two dining room tables provided with each villa as classroom seating for our discussion style classes.

As ready as we could be, the doors to The Learning Center were opened on November 2, 1995. The ladies loved the center from the beginning. In spite of our scavenging for furniture, it all fell together and looked elegant. It was a warm, inviting place where ladies liked to be even if they were not in a class. As the ladies entered the administrative villa, they were greeted by soft background music, a reception area to the right of the marble foyer with white upholstered sofas, and chairs positioned throughout in a way to encourage open conversation and mingling during tea time. On opening day the center was a buzz with women selecting courses and seeing who was there. Although I am sure some of the women came to learn, I feel that there was a large portion that came just to say they were rubbing elbows, so to speak, with royalty. Real excitement filled the air.

In the middle of all of the commotion of registration, Madawi pulled me to the side.

"I have a special project, Mrs. Teresa," she began with that look of hers that always indicated planning and possibly mischievousness. "Her name is Nadia, and we have to encourage her," she whispered, smiling so no one else would know the topic of our conversation. "She needs the center to fill her mind." Madawi elaborated, "She has had such misery. Many bad things have happened in her life," Madawi added with true concern for her friend as she shook her head in grief and disbelief. "She will be here today, and I will point her out to you."

"I'll be on the lookout," I answered. "Don't worry. We'll get her involved."

Before long the nod came from Madawi as she stood near the doorway. I moved from the social area and made my way to the reception desk, targeting the woman dressed completely in black. Stepping up at the opportune time, Madawi introduced me to Nadia who was completely veiled, wearing black gloves and socks as many of the more fundamental women do. As Madawi spoke, Nadia raised the black fabric from her face, revealing a tired-looking woman with no make-up and no joy. Madawi patiently presented the class offerings to her, and she eventually agreed to take the *"Starting Your Own Business"* course that debuted at the center the following day.

The dawn of the next day saw the memorable beginning of classes at The Learning Center. We had 29 ladies enrolled, five teachers, a hostess, and me, the director. To fulfill the socialization aspect of our mission, all classes would break for 15 minutes so the ladies could visit and have refreshments in the main villa. I made it a point to appear at every tea time, mainly to make the ladies feel welcome, listen and learn. On that special day, I greeted every student personally to welcome them to the center and inquire as to how they liked things so far. As expected, I saw Nadia. She was despondently dressed with no make-up and had obviously made no effort with her hair. I spent additional time with her to make sure she felt an extra sense of belonging and encouragement.

With classes just beginning and me learning as I went, many details had to be tended to in those first few days. Feeling somewhat nervous with this ambitious, illegal endeavor, Madawi felt it was important that we maintain a list of each student's car, including make, model, color and license plate number, so the men manning the security gate could make sure that we knew who was in the center and for what purpose. Hence, I developed a car registration form and proceeded to speak with each student to gain the necessary information for our files. As I made my way around the room during break time, the ladies soon knew my purpose, even those who did not speak English very well. It became somewhat of a bragging opportunity, as each woman would tell me in a rather loud voice the make and color of her vehicle. I still chuckle to this day with one particular student's response.

"I need to know what kind of car you have," I questioned, speaking slower than normal in the hope that I would be better understood. Johara, who was a student in our beginner's English class, proudly began her response.

"I have Mer—ce—dees," she stated, wanting so badly to respond correctly.

"Okay," I replied as I jotted down the make of the car. "And the color?"

"Maroony," she replied.

"Maroony?" I questioned, not really understanding what she said.

"Blue," she then stated as if clarifying.

"Oh, a blue Mercedes," I replied encouragingly.

"Yes," she responded smiling, "maroony, blue."

"I'm sorry," I said. "I think I've got it now. You have a maroon Mercedes."

She looked at me, obviously becoming as confused as I.

"Gold and black," she replied.

"Okay," I answered, yet again somewhat discouraged by my lack of understanding and fearing that I was making her feel uncomfortable. "You have a gold and black Mercedes," I said, still smiling. But she shook her head no.

Overhearing the conversation and knowing that we were both becoming frustrated, Nadia, who was much more fluent in English, intervened to help.

She stepped in between us and turned to Johara to clarify in Arabic as I waited patiently and relieved. Then Nadia turned to me.

"She has a maroon, a blue, a gold," she began looking to Johara as she spoke and counted the colors on her fingers, "and black Mercedes," she concluded as Johara nodded in agreement to Nadia's English response.

"Oh," I stammered almost stunned, "so she has a car of many colors?"

"No," Nadia laughed, "she has many cars of different colors."

Smiling wide, and completely embarrassed, I answered as I wrote down the various colors. "Oh!" drug out of my southern tongue. "I get it now!" And we all smiled and nodded to pass the awkward moment. How silly of me not to know that everyone has many cars of different colors! At that moment, it became crystal clear that I had a lot to learn about the ladies I was now associated with. They had money and lots of it. In spite of this, they did not have something I took for granted. As women, they did not have freedom, and they did not easily have the opportunity to gain knowledge, an oversight that the center was determined to rectify.

Because we were underground and not legally sanctioned by the Ministry of Education, we had to be very careful. Unfortunately, the center could not give the ladies official certification or diplomas for the classes they completed, in spite of the fact that all of our instructors were degreed in their fields. Many even held masters' degrees. We were only able to offer them our certificates to indicate that they had, in fact, taken the class and been exposed to the material. This was a shame because as the years passed our offerings were to the same standards of many stateside colleges.

Supposedly our existence was a secret, and I soon learned just how secret.

Transportation was always provided for women because they could not drive. For this reason, Madawi purchased a minivan for the center's use, complete with curtains to hide our femininity. One morning we needed supplies, but Saleem was busy with the van running teachers to and from work. Hence, I had to take a taxi to run the center's errands. Upon my return to the compound, I could not help but chuckle at the Indian taxi driver as he unloaded my packages.

"This is a new place," he began, smiling and swaying his head back and forth as Indian nationals do. "A place for ladies," he remarked, proudly showing that he was in the know.

"I know," I replied, not daring to tell him that I was the director. Then holding my finger to my mouth, I said, "Shhh, it's a secret."

"Yes, Madame, yes," he answered quickly. "It is a secret."

On November 13, 1995, the safety of our existence took a turn for the worse, directly affecting all Americans in Kingdom. Eventually, this event would affect The Learning Center. OPM/SANG, the central *Riyadh* office building housing U.S. military and civilian personnel, was bombed. Five of the six people killed were Americans, and 30 Americans were among the more than 60 injured. The explosion was deemed to "demand the withdrawal of all foreigners and foreign forces from Saudi territory," as reported by the U. S. Embassy in *Riyadh* on the 14th of November (Appendix C). The report further stated that future "isolated bombings are possible," with attacks most likely at housing installations ... foreign military or security personnel." Basically, our company fell into the listing and our security began to heighten — but only a little. None of us ever considered that any group, not even radical Islamists, would attack women and children. Casually concerned, we did take a few measures with regard to the center: we closed the curtains on the minivan and closed the huge iron gate at the entrance when it was convenient.

Our first term of classes proceeded beautifully. All of the students enjoyed their classes, coming to the center just to visit, and many brought a friend along as well to see the new place. Each day I visited with them and learned their interests so that I would know what classes to offer in the future. I was fortunate to see Nadia every Tuesday and Thursday. At first, she continued to look as she had the first time I saw her, somewhat unhappy and plain-looking in dull-colored dresses. Then after about four weeks, I was amazed one Tuesday when I was helping set out the coffee and tea for the morning break time. In front of me was a lovely lady. Her hair was curled, she had nicely done make-up, she wore a bright, stylish dress, and she was sporting a proud smile.

"Nadia?" I questioned in amazement at her transformation. I stopped dead in my tracks, still holding the teapot.

"It's me," she replied, beaming as she held her arms out for approval.

"You look fantastic!" I exclaimed.

"And it's all thanks to you, Mrs. Teresa," she remarked. "Can we sit for a moment?" she questioned. "I want to tell you something."

"Sure," I replied anxiously as I put down the teapot and moved into the sitting area.

"I want to share a story with you," she began, as we got comfortable next to each other on the sofa. "I want to thank you," she said earnestly as she reached for my hands. "You and The Learning Center saved my life," she stated as tears of joy began to fill her eyes. I sat and listened, deeply touched, as she explained.

In February she had lost her brother in a horrible car accident. Then in June her father had died either from old age or a broken heart. As if this was not enough, her daughter was in a coma and the doctors had no idea if she would regain consciousness or not.

"Oh, Nadia," I exclaimed as my heart deeply ached for this lady, "I am so sorry."

"Thank you," she answered and continued. "I was truly, truly drowning in my home ... I was dying." Nadia paused to wipe a tear. "But, I then found you, *bisme Allah*. Because of Madawi, I came even though I didn't want to at first," she explained. "And you made me feel welcome. You made me feel like I was alive again. It is because of you and the center that I am alive again!" She exclaimed, "*Shukran*, Mrs. Teresa, *shukran* from the bottom of my heart!"

It took everything I had not to break down and cry with her. I was so touched by this story and so overwhelmed with a sense of purpose. I knew then that the center was good, really good, no matter how hard I had to work to make it so. Even if I never heard another story like Nadia's, it would have been enough to know that we had helped one lady. But I did hear more stories. I heard many stories over the course of the next six years. Tales of women and their plight and how the center was instrumental in bringing positive changes to their lives. It was truly inspiring.

As our first term drew to a close, I knew we had to do something extra special for the ladies who had taken the initiative to support our new venture. I needed to think of a way to commend them on their achievements and to entice new students: we would have an end-of-the-term party.

We were able to use the dining facility of the compound to hold an elegant dinner party, an elegant dinner party that I had to pull off on an extremely tight budget. To offset cost, we sold tickets to cover the price of the catered dinner, and it was encouraged that each student bring a friend as well. Decorating, however, had to be squeezed from the center's budget above and beyond our loan payment. However, I pulled if off in spite of the financial concerns. Remembering the idiom,

KISS, "Keep It Simple Stupid," I decorated with burgundy candles of different heights, greenery from the floral shop and burgundy ribbon. Simple but beautiful, and the ladies had a ball.

During the course of the evening, we honored the ladies who had completed their coursework and focused on the center's achievements as a whole. All night, TLC was the rave. Current students discussed what classes they would take next, and the visitors talked about what classes they hoped to take. From the evening's feedback, I knew we would have a tremendous winter term to follow. Seventy-two ladies dressed in their best attire attended our end-of-the-term party, and it was the social event of the month. Again, I knew many ladies simply wanted to rub elbows with royalty. But I did not care about the motive for their attendance. I was just happy they were there, laughing, socializing and broadening their horizons.

Before The Learning Center, most Saudi women filled their days with sleeping, eating and beauty enhancement. Their nights were occupied with parties and visiting friends. The idea of attending classes and learning was almost non-existent, although I am sure some had dreamed of the opportunity like Madawi. Consequently, to convince these ladies to be more productive with their time and to motivate them to enhance their minds was not an easy task. This is where the party idea came into play. Through the parties the center sponsored, we brought the ladies to our door, and the exposure to the possibilities of learning made them stay.

After our first TLC party, Madawi, the staff and I were elated with what had been accomplished in our first term. We were pleased with its initial success and confident for the future. Consequently, we were completely unprepared for what took place. The following Saturday, the entire staff showed up for work to greet and register the new students we were expecting for the winter term. We waited and waited, but the door rarely opened. When registration was complete, we only had 12 ladies enrolled. We could not imagine what had happened? Where was everyone? At the party, they had all said that they wanted to enroll, but where were they? I became very concerned, to the point of physical sickness, as I knew we had that huge loan payment looming. What could I do? How could I keep Madawi's dream alive? Days passed and I could not help but worry.

A week later, I entered the center as I did every day in the hopes that more students would show. Again, the center was quiet and things were starting to look really bad. Then the telephone rang. It was Nadia.

"Ello, Mrs. Teresa," she began, "it is Nadia."

"Oh, hello, Nadia," I responded. *"Kayf Haalik?"*

"Tieeb, al Hamdulila. Kayf Haalik?" she questioned.

"Well, honestly, Nadia," I started, "I'm not so good."

"Why, Mrs. Teresa?"

"No one is coming to the center," I declared, finally verbalizing my frustration. "We only have 12 ladies enrolled!"

"That is why I call you," she remarked in broken English. "I want to ask you something for the children," she explained. "The children are home for the winter break, and that is why no ladies. Can you do something for the children to keep them busy, huh?"

My mind was clicking as she spoke. That was it!

"Of course, we can!" I exclaimed with excitement and relief. "I'll call you as soon as we have the program organized."

"Very good, Mrs. Teresa," she remarked, seemingly happy with my agreement to her suggestion. "*Insha Allah*, they will come, *insha Allah*."

"*Shukran*, Nadia," I answered. "Oh, thank you for the idea! This is the answer to our problem."

"*Tieeb*, Mrs. Teresa, *ma'assalaamah*," she replied.

"*Shukran* Nadia, *ma'assalaamah*." I answered and I heard a click as she hung up the phone. A new phase to the center began as Nadia, whom I referred to as my *Saudi guardian angel* from that day forward, had given me the answer to our survival. From then on, The Learning Center was structured to offer classes for ladies in the fall and spring terms and for their children in the winter and summer.

I immediately called an emergency meeting of the staff for the next morning to determine what we could offer the children. We also had to discuss whom we could recruit to teach children from the compound. Our meeting was very productive, and our first children's program, *Winter Jamboree*, was born. For a one-month period while the children were on school break, we offered English, arts and crafts, music, computers, cooking, painting and exercise. That first *Winter Jamboree* we had over 150 children enroll, and my prayers were answered, thanks to my Saudi guardian angel. All was going well when a knock came at the door two weeks into the program.

MaryAnn, a delightful older lady who had been in the Kingdom as an expatriate for over 11 years, was our receptionist. Shortly after the children had changed classes that morning, she heard a knock on the villa door, which was highly unusual as most just entered without knocking. Not sure at first if she had actually heard a knock, she turned down the music and listened intently. Yes, it was definitely a knock. Curious, she went to the door and opened it slightly. There were two Arab men standing there with long red-tinted beards sporting Western suits that did not fit them properly. Knowing our illegal status and extremely familiar with Saudi customs, MaryAnn stepped outside the door and handled the situation beautifully.

"May I help you?" she innocently queried in her Scottish accent, knowing full well that something fishy was going on.

"We want to come inside," one of the men replied in broken English, as he fidgeted in the suit that did not fit him.

"Oh," MaryAnn began in a charming way as her mind raced with what to do. "I would love to invite you in from the heat," she remarked theatrically, "but I cannot."

"Is this a school?" the man asked.

"No," MaryAnn answered, thinking quickly and smiling the entire time.

"We have children inside," she paused, "Western children." This was not a lie as we did have a few American kids in attendance. "For fun activities," she stammered a bit. Without allowing the men to respond, she continued, "Would you like to speak to our director?"

"Yes."

"I will go and get her. But you must remain outside because there are women and children here," she said as she turned to slide back through the door. Wanting to kill them with kindness, she hospitably asked, "May I get you some lemonade to quench your thirst from the heat?"

"No," they answered coldly while simultaneously wiggling in their inappropriate attire. With that, MaryAnn returned inside and locked the door before coming to me.

MaryAnn came running, literally, into my office, breathless from her trip up the stairs. Adrenaline pumping from her encounter with the men at our door, she explained the encounter so far.

I took a deep breath as I stood, adjusted my dress and assessed the situation. We were not doing anything visibly wrong. All of the ladies there were dressed appropriately, and I would just stall them until I could somehow get help. From the day the center opened, I always knew that I, personally, was on the line. I always knew that if a problem arose, it would be me that would go to jail. Hopefully, Madawi could get me out. Above all, I would not let them in or allow them to harass any of my teachers or staff. Taking yet another deep

breath for confidence, I prepared myself mentally as I
headed down the stairs to the waiting confrontation.

Pausing with my hand on the lock, making a final
attempt to gain inner strength, I released the dead bolt
and opened the door. No one was there. I looked at
MaryAnn and she at me. Extremely concerned, we
stepped out further to check the sides of the villa. Still
no one was in sight. Confused, I ran over to the gate to
speak with the guards. They had seen no one, but only
the security bar, not the sliding iron gate, had been
used that morning. We surmised that they must have
snuck under the bar avoiding the attention of the
guards. With the guards' help, we searched the entire
compound. The two suspicious Arab men with beards
and suits were nowhere to be found. They had disappeared without a trace. Following the search, I called
Madawi and explained what had happened.

"Have them close the big gates," she answered. "I'll
be there soon."

As I waited for her, I paced my office, wondering
exactly what had happened. Who were these men?
What did they want? Were they *muthawen*? Madawi
would hopefully have the answers.

Arriving quicker than usual — Madawi never gets
in a hurry — her BMW pulled in front of the center. By
this time, I was downstairs, anxiously waiting for her.
Once inside, she removed her *abaya*, and we settled
down with MaryAnn in the social salon to recount the
events. Madawi listened carefully to every detail without saying a word. When MaryAnn finished, Madawi
interjected.

"*Hiyah,*" she stated firmly. "It was the *Hiyah,*" speaking as if she were trying to convince herself.

"*Hiyah?*" I questioned. "What is the *Hiyah?*"

"They are part of the *muthawen,*" she explained. "The ones that work with Westerners."

"How do you know?" I questioned further.

"The way they acted ... their beards," she continued, seeming somewhat anxious. "They probably wore the suits to trick you into letting them in," she said as she glanced at MaryAnn. "You were right not to." She paused yet again in what seemed like deep thought. "They will come again. Next time ... they will come officially."

"What do you mean?" I questioned, becoming concerned with my own safety.

"Next time, they will bring the police," she remarked and turned to get her cell phone from her bag.

Within an hour, she had extra guards on our gate and instructed them to always use the big iron gate.

"Do not," she repeated adamantly to the guards, "let anyone in unless you know they are a student." Then she turned to me.

"And Mrs. Teresa," she began, "you make identification cards for all the students. Immediately." Seeing the look on my face, she added, "But do not scare them, huh?" and she smiled reassuringly.

"I will have them ready by tomorrow," I answered.

"*Insha Allah,*" she replied as she entered the BMW to leave. "*Ma'assalaamah,*" she called from the back seat.

"*Ma'assalaamah,*" I answered. "I'll call you tomorrow."

"*Insha Allah*," she returned, "*yellah.*" Abdullah closed the car door.

That afternoon, I held another emergency meeting with my staff. This time, however, I was not meeting to motivate them; rather, I was meeting to warn them. I shared the events of the morning and stressed the severity of the situation. I explained the steps that Madawi and I were taking for security and reassured them that everything would be okay if we all followed a few simple guidelines. Giving them the plan of action, I reinforced the need to wear appropriate clothing to work and even encouraged that they wear their *abayas* in the van on the way to work. I insisted they go on about their business; yet if any unusual telephone calls came in or if any suspicious visitors arrived, they should not confront the situation but refer it to me. Madawi called at least once a day and usually more, to see if "they had come back officially." My answer was always the same. No. Two long, anxious weeks passed and nothing happened.

"They will not come," Madawi stated firmly in my office over two weeks later. "If they have not come back by now, they won't. They must have been satisfied by what MaryAnn told them," she concluded, and we never spoke of the incident again.

Following a successful *Winter Jamboree*, we enrolled over 70 ladies in our first spring term at The Learning Center. The term saw the addition of several new courses and workshops, and our momentum began to build. Keeping pace with previous lessons learned, I developed an extensive summer camp program to follow the ladies' spring term. As the summer break came around, we were able to add swimming and tennis for the children to our repertoire. It became obvious that The Learning Center was going to remain alive, even thrive. What we were doing was good, in spite of the fact that we were doing it in a country that frowned on women learning and growing intellectually.

From the moment I entered each morning until I left in the afternoon, the center was a constant flow of activity. With our venture so new, I wore many hats in the beginning due to budget constraints. I was the director, an instructor, the hostess and receptionist, when needed. My nights were consumed as well with things I did not have time for during the day. After I performed my duties as Mom and wife, I would go into my home office and work. I produced textbooks with graphics for teachers, completed necessary financial work, organized brochures for the following term, produced newsletters and much more. Essentially, the center had become my third child.

It was the end of May in 1996, another pretty day in the desert, and I sat at my desk preparing registration material for the upcoming summer camp when the phone rang. It was David with startling news.

"Well, baby," he began, not wanting to alarm me, "it looks like you are going to have to move the center."

"What do you mean, move the center? Oh, honey! We've just gotten established ... the ladies are coming ... people know us here," I protested.

"I just left a meeting with Colonel (now General) Awad and several high ranking officers with the U.S.

Military, and they are planning to house troops on DM 18."

"Why here, for heaven's sake?" I could not help but question.

"Our security threat level has increased, and they feel that the troops can be better protected there and less conspicuous." He paused as he heard silence on my end of the line. "It's a done deal, honey. There is nothing that can be done about it."

After ingesting the news, I had questions.

"When do we have to be out?" I asked, very concerned about our upcoming summer program.

"By August first," he answered.

"Well, thank God I can get the children's program done first," I replied. "Where will we move?" Knowing me and how I think, David was ready for that question.

"DM 12."

"DM 12?" I exclaimed, not sure of where in the world DM 12 was. "Where is that?"

"Now, honey, calm down," he started. "It's the old clinic. You and Madawi looked at it before you chose your current place."

I was embarrassed that I did not know the clinic was officially DM 12. Yet I recalled that it needed a lot of work to be converted to meet our needs. David assured me he could get some of his construction crews to help and make it even better than what we had currently. Feeling relieved, I took him up on his offer to go check it out again after work.

After an assessment was made, work began to ready the new facility. Simultaneously, I had to keep our summer kids' program going. It was a grueling summer. As I went back and forth between the center and the new facility, I watched as cranes hoisted large concrete Jersey barricades along the road in front of DM 18, preparing security for the soldiers that would soon live there. The sand was shifting beneath us, and I never saw it coming.

In time and with me at the helm, The Learning Center was able to offer more classes with substance and meaning to the ladies and their children, and our following increased steadily over the course of the next five years. Step by step, we grew and became stronger along the way. Our location changed, and we persevered. We faced challenges and found solutions. As obstacles arose, we found ways to circumvent. We even faced more brushes with the Committee for Public Morality. Still we survived, only to be tripped up by unforeseen and unimaginable circumstances.

ॐ Chapter Nineteen ॐ

Terror

It was late in the evening on the 25th of June in 1996. I was exhausted from running back and forth between the old and new learning centers all day, but sleep evaded me. After getting the children and David to bed, I headed downstairs to my home office to do a little computer work for the center in the hope that sleep would finally come. There was so much that had to be done, and I had no time to waste because David and I were scheduled to go with Madawi the following morning to *Jeddah* for three days to see a new children's center that had just opened there. We wanted to take the opportunity to investigate the new facility on Madawi's request and, hopefully, acquire new ideas for The Learning Center.

Over time, I learned that the Saudis were always interested, almost enthralled, with anything new. Yet they were somewhat unconcerned and disinterested once the idea grew old. Anything new, they had to see or they had to have. At the time I was unaware, but looking back, I see that they tended to treat people the same, unfortunately. Oddly just after 1 a.m., the telephone rang. It was Madawi.

"Ello, Mrs. Teresa," she began, sounding somewhat preoccupied with what was going on in her salon.

"Oh, hello, Madawi," I answered, surprised yet happy to hear from her. "I'm almost packed."

"With all that has happened, I don't think it's a good idea that we travel tomorrow," she started. "We'll reschedule, huh?"

"What has happened, Madawi?" I questioned with concern, completely oblivious to the evening's event.

"I don't think it's a good idea to travel with the explosion," she replied.

"What explosion?"

"The government buildings exploded tonight," she answered, as if she were surprised that I did not know. "We felt it here at the house, and the girls are very upset."

"What government buildings?" I questioned with heightened curiosity.

"The ones on the *Corniche*," she replied.

"Which ones on the *Corniche?*" I queried, still oblivious to what she was talking about.

"The ones by the water," she persisted.

"Oh," I responded, still unsure but not feeling that I could ask yet again. I knew that the police station and a few other Saudi government buildings were located there, but I was not sure that they were the buildings she was referring to. "Okay," I paused, trying not to reveal my disappointment. "It's okay, we can go another time."

"We will," she responded soothingly, "when everything settles down a bit, huh? I'll call you tomorrow. *Yellah.*"

"Okay, Madawi," I replied in agreement, "I'll talk to you tomorrow."

"*Insha Allah*, Mrs. Teresa. *Ma'assalaamah,*" she replied, "*Yellah.*"

Anxious to tell David, I ran up the stairs and hopped into the middle of the bed. Shaking him awake with one hand, I grabbed the TV remote control with the other. For some reason, I had an uneasy feeling. For some reason, I did not think the evening's event was as casual as Madawi had made it sound.

"Wake up, David!" I exclaimed. "There's been an explosion."

Half asleep he responded, "Explosion ... uh ... where?"

Because of my uncertainty, I only restated, "Madawi just called and said the government buildings on the *Corniche blew* up tonight." I bounced a little on my knees to convey my assumed severity of the situation, glancing at CNN to see if they mentioned anything about an explosion in *Al-Khobar*, but nothing was reported. "David, what government buildings are on the *Corniche?*" I pleaded, trying to pull him from his sound sleep. "She said there was an explosion!" More awake, he rolled over and we began to talk.

"She's probably talking about the police station," he surmised as he took a drink of water. "You know how these people are. A TCN probably cut a gas line or something," he concluded nonchalantly, as crazy things like that always seemed to happen in the Kingdom. "I'm sure it's nothing to worry about. Why don't you get some sleep?"

"No, David," I repeated with emphasis. "I think it's something worse than that." I paused, unconvinced by his composed manner. "It must have been something worse or she wouldn't have canceled our trip!"

"Really, honey," he responded, "I don't think it's anything serious." Rolling back over, he suggested again, "Come on now, sleep. It's late."

Frustrated, I agreed to let him sleep as he obviously wanted to do, but I could not shake the nagging feeling I felt, and sleep was nowhere to be found for me. Getting a snack from the kitchen, I crawled back into bed and lay in darkness watching CNN for the next two hours. Nothing was mentioned, not a word. Over and over I heard the same headline stories, but nothing about an explosion. Then around 3:30 a.m., I was half asleep when I suddenly heard that familiar music CNN plays when they run the breaking news graphic across the screen. Immediately, I was fully awake and glued to the TV, straining to listen to the low volume I had set because David was sleeping.

"We have unconfirmed reports that there has been an explosion in *Al-Khobar*, Saudi Arabia," the announcer began as a map of the Eastern Province appeared with a red arrow pointing at where we lived. "Reuters indicates that an explosion occurred approximately four hours ago at the U.S. Military housing complex along the Arabian Gulf. At this time, we have no details as to injuries or fatalities, if any."

Shocked, I came out from under the covers and onto my knees, shaking David vigorously this time. "David ... David!" I exclaimed. "Wake up! Wake up! It was *Khobar* Towers," I shouted. "The explosion was at *Khobar* Towers!"

Startled as well, he sat up, still wobbling a bit as a person does when they quickly wake from a deep sleep. "What?"

Anxiously, I repeated. "CNN ... CNN just said that an explosion occurred four hours ago at the U.S. Military housing complex here. Although they didn't call it *Khobar* Towers, it must be. I just know they must be talking about *Khobar* Towers!" I repeated out of amazement.

More awake, he reached for the remote to turn up the volume, and we watched the TV intently. Because of shock, sleep did not come for us the rest of that night, and all we could do was wait for details. It all seemed surreal, and our watching was as if we were trying to convince ourselves to believe what we were hearing.

As we listened to the sketchy details deep into the night, all I could do was thank God that I had quit my part-time teaching position at *Khobar* Towers in April. Even though I had so much on my plate with the children and The Learning Center, in January I had decided to teach the military personnel two nights a week for the University of Maryland. My class was held in *Khobar* Towers. In spite of my schedule, I had taken on the class because I felt it was important to teach a public speaking class every now and then to stay abreast in my field. Fortunately, I had opted not to teach during the summer term or I could have been there. After thanking God for my safety, my concern turned to the men and women housed there. I prayed, prayed hard, that no one was injured as the details trickled through on CNN.

Unfortunately, the next pretty day in the Kingdom brought sorrow. CNN reported 19 American soldiers among the dead, and hundreds of people were wounded. My heart ached. Because of our inability to sleep, we were up very early, and David decided to go on in to work to see if he could help out and learn any details at the airbase.

Historically, details about events in the private world of the Kingdom do not usually make it to CNN; and if they do, they are usually squelched as soon as possible. The Saudis do not like any attention, particularly negative attention. They have no desire for the outside world to look inside their world. The November bombing of the OPM/SANG building only made the international newscast twice that I heard, essentially one day of coverage, in spite of the fact that five Americans were killed.

Still shaken after David left, I decided to go to the recreation center to see what I could hear. Leaving the children sleeping with Ann, I headed down the street on my little purple bike. This particular morning I truly needed to feel the sun on my face. Once inside the restaurant, it was obvious that the news of the bombing had spread quickly, particularly since the black smoke of the smoldering buildings could still be seen from our compound, looming over the gulf. Women were everywhere, speculating.

It all began with everyone sharing their experience: where they were, what they felt, or whether or not they had gotten a telephone line to call family in the states. Everyone had to recount the night before and how she had heard the news. Some of the women whose villas bordered the outside wall of the compound even said they heard the explosion. Others said that they felt a slight rumble but brushed it off, assuming it was fireworks or something insignificant.

After excessive amounts of tales and coffee, the conversation turned to speculation. Immediately the name Usama bin Laden was mentioned. Every lady at my table believed that the bombing had to be the work of bin Laden. Since 1993, we had heard his name and been briefed thoroughly as to his existence and his intent. When the Kingdom denied his assistance in the Gulf War, his plight soon became apparent. Simply put, he and his fanatical band of followers want the infidels out of the Islamic Holy land. There was no doubt in our minds; he had to be the mastermind behind the atrocity. Hence, the conversation about him was short-lived. The only question that remained was, would we be his next target?

Panic soon followed speculation, and the conversation quickly turned to safety. Would the U.S. government force the women and children to evacuate? If not, would the company force us to leave the country? What were we to do? How could the company protect us? How could our children be safe now? The conjecture was endless.

After a few hours of this, my head began to hurt almost as much as my heart. It was too much for me to absorb. I needed to be alone ... and think. I desperately needed to hear from David. Because he was in management, I knew he would have answers. I knew he would know what we should do.

After paying for my coffee and cordially saying my goodbyes, I left and mounted my little purple bike for home. As I rode, I took extra long breaths. I pushed the pedals so hard that my legs hurt, which was good because it made me feel alive. I rode faster and faster because I needed to feel the wind against my face. On this particular ride, I wanted to absorb every bit of the pretty day my desert home offered.

What seemed like an eternity passed before the phone rang. It was David.

"Hey, baby," he began, "how ya doing?"

"Oh, David, I still can't believe all of this," I replied, before telling him everything that was said and speculated by the wives at the recreation center.

"Everyone is scared, honey, really scared," I concluded. "What will we do?"

"I know, baby, everyone here is pretty shook up, too. It's incredible. Hundreds of Saudis were injured as well," he said with a sigh.

"Saudis?" I questioned. "How could Saudis have been injured? *Khobar* Tower houses Americans."

"Teresa, think about where *Khobar* Towers is," he replied, as if I should have known better. "The park … right next to the Towers. Because it was at night, the park was full of Saudi families. Many children and adults were hurt or killed, too," he said somberly.

"CNN didn't say anything about Saudis dying," I replied, almost shocked.

"Would you really expect them to?"

"Well, now that you mention it," I paused, "no."

"I also heard that the percussion blew the windows out of *Shula* Mall six blocks away," he added.

"You're kidding?"

"No ... really," he paused, "that must be why Madawi said that the girls were so upset. They had to have felt the percussion blast at the palace if *Shula* Mall felt it."

"Oh, my God," I answered with such sorrow and despair. "What's going to happen now?"

"Several memos have already gone out to all of the employees. I'll bring home copies (see Appendices E and F)," he said with a sigh, feeling just as bewildered as I. "There is a town meeting tonight at the theater. The company is going to fill everyone in on what's going to happen."

As I paced the villa, my mind raced with possibilities of what could happen and for ideas of what to do. Since I was in uncharted territory, the ideas were few and far between. I would just have to wait and see. Perhaps the town meeting would bring answers and relief from my indescribable stress. Either way, there was nothing I could do at the moment, and I was tired. So I curled up with the children and held them tight as I tried to push the worry from my mind so that sleep would come.

In spite of the squabbles and petty gossip, the compound community learned to know itself over the years and always stuck together when events were serious. However, the one and only time we were truly divided, unable to support each other, followed the *Khobar* Towers bombing. A group of expatriates usually united was suddenly divided.

Our division became clear the moment the American base director spoke in the theater that evening. He assured us that management had everything under control, yet there would be additional security measures taken. "Fortunately," he announced, "the American government did not order our evacuation from Kingdom." With that statement hands went up immediately, demanding answers. "What about our children?" they began to yell in unison. "Does our salary increase?" or "How are you going to protect us?" Questions were coming from every direction, as people began to stand up and demand answers.

After waiting for the incessant questions to die down, the director stepped to the podium and continued. The company would grant optional departure for those families who wanted to leave. He explained that if a family wanted to go, the employee would be paid an additional per diem of $33 per day while the family was in the United States. He added that when the company deemed it safe, the employee's family would be able to return to Kingdom. The director adjourned the meeting by announcing that everyone would receive memos and American Consulate Warden messages when necessary, and all of these would be posted in the mailroom as well.

No one left the room as the director left the podium. Everyone stood around and continued to speculate. As David and I spoke with friends, the base director, a long-time friend of ours whom we knew in the states, stepped up. After cordial goodbyes to our friends, his demeanor became more serious as he began to speak to us.

"Be careful, David," he said in a lowered voice, "things aren't always what they seem." David looked at him curiously. "If you decide to send Teresa and the kids out, do it on your own nickel."

"What do you mean, George?" David questioned.

"If the company pays ... they decide on when you come back," he responded as he secretly looked around the room.

David understood his caution, and we weighed the options. For several days we discussed what to do. As we did, the compound began to boil, but not from the outside temperature. The compound was on temporary lock-down, with the company only advising people to leave the compound if it were absolutely necessary. Couple the confinement with the mental aspect that no one had come to terms with the bombing, and a mixture for upheaval is formed. People were stressed, and rightly so. However, their fear and anxiety soon exploded. Straight down the middle, the expats on our compound were intensely divided. One side unwaveringly felt that the families should leave, and the other staunchly felt like it was okay to stay.

The following evening the telephone rang. It was Madawi. Her immense concern for my family and me was apparent. As a member of the royal family, she too felt violated by the event. She explained that they had decided to leave a little early for their summer vacation. As a result, she wanted to let me know that if I needed anything, even help with departure, that I should call the palace.

"Ibrahim," she began, "will know how to reach me and what to do." She paused, accentuating her instructions. "I wish your little Michelle were older so you could join us."

"Me, too," I replied, "but don't worry. I'm sure we'll be fine. You guys just have a great time."

"*Insha Allah*, Mrs. Teresa," she answered, "*Insha Allah*, take care, huh?"

"I will," I responded. "I'll see you in September."

"*Insha Allah, yellah.*"

As I hung up the receiver, my heart dropped. Even though I was used to Madawi traveling, it really upset me to know that she was not going to be close by. I guess it was selfish. I wanted my dear friend near, particularly now. There was no one I felt that I could talk to on the compound with all the division tension, and now, with my true friend gone, I felt very alone.

In spite of the company's advice to remain on the compound unless absolutely necessary, we had to go somewhere for sanity's sake. I desperately needed to get away from the squabbling and off the compound if only for a little while. It was Thursday morning, and we decided to take a short drive.

Looking back, I see pros and cons of the new compound, DM 22, which we had moved to right before Michelle was born. What once seemed like the epitome of luxury to me now seemed like a remote target, waiting for the hit. Built on reclaimed land from the Arabian Gulf, our compound stood isolated on a small peninsula surrounded on three sides by water. There was only one road in and out of the compound. On the one hand, this could be useful for protection. On the other hand, it could be our downfall. All someone would have to do would be block that sole entrance, and they would have an entire community of expats captured with nowhere to run.

As we pulled through the guarded gate and made our way down the road with our compound on the right and the Arabian Gulf on the left, we noticed the flatbed truck with TCNs unloading plywood and other building materials. David told me that we were going to have a second security gate soon that would check vehicles before they approached the main gate of the walled community.

When we reached the point where the new security gate would be, David pointed to the area of land that separated the compound from the mainland, and he explained that he was in the process of having a berm built. He explained that the berm would stop any truck from crashing the wall of the compound, forcing it down into the ditch. Also, he explained that because of the angle of the berm, it would force any type of explosion to go up into the air, rather than toward the compound. Sensing my fear as he talked, he reassured me that it would be landscaped and not look like a barrier at all. Boy, was that comforting!

It was refreshing to see the beautiful blue green of the gulf as we drove down the *Corniche*. On this particular pretty day in the Kingdom, it was nice to see the sun glimmer on the water, and it brought a slight smile to my face. I am ashamed to admit it, but we just had to go by *Khobar* Towers. After all, we were curious, as humans will be. As we curved around the road, following the water, the smile left me as we could see the towers rising up in the distance. When we were within two miles of *Khobar* Towers, we were stopped in heavy traffic. Lanes and lanes of cars were moving slowly to view the catastrophe, and we were stuck. Once there, I wished that we had not gone. Slowly, our car crept past the towering debris of buildings that once housed our troops. With the walls completely blown off, I could see bed sheets and other personal items hanging from the rubble. I could not help but cry.

In front of the towers was a huge hole that resulted from the enormous blast that took down these soaring structures. Later, Madawi told me that when the criminals responsible for the blast were caught, it would be in that hole that they would receive their punishment — beheading.

Not able to tolerate the sight any longer, David made a turn down a local neighborhood street as soon as possible. Surprisingly, we did not leave the sight of death and destruction. Everywhere we looked we saw shattered windows and broken walls as a result of the blast. As we drove, David told me that some of the Saudis at work told him that several people were killed or injured when their wall unit air conditioners blew into rooms with the percussion of the blast. As he told the story and my eyes viewed the destruction, my thoughts turned to all of the Saudi children that were hurt or killed while playing in the park on a beautiful Friday evening. As we meandered through the web of neighborhood streets, my tears continued to flow silently down my cheeks.

When we passed *Shula* Mall, all I could see was plywood tacked where windows once were. I suddenly felt anger towards the people who had done this to my desert home. Like ghosts weeping over the destruction, I could see faces of American troops and Saudi children as we rode past the devastation. How could these people do this? How could these people harbor so much hatred?

Although I felt we were correct to remain in Kingdom, I could not help but question our judgment. I needed to talk to Mom, and again she came through for me.

"Now, Teresa," she paused, "I don't care about what the compound people are saying. I want to know how the locals are acting. How are you treated when you go downtown?"

"What little we've gone, they have been wonderful," I responded. "They beat their hearts and repeat 'so sorry,' and 'Americee good.' "

"Then, that is all you need to know," she answered definitively. "Never forget this, Teresa … if the locals are polite to you, then you are fine. But when they shift and are no longer kind, then it is time to leave," she concluded with one of the firmest voices I had ever heard from her. Since she was a 12-year seasoned Middle Eastern expat, I felt secure with her opinion. Hence, the matter was closed, and my path was determined.

Within a matter of days, we began to be bombarded with memos from the company and Consulate Warden Messages. The memos promised various security enhancements, and the Warden Messages kept us abreast of official U.S. government policies. The communication was endless, yet appreciated. However, I was ready for action, not talk.

One company memo reported that work would begin soon to apply Mylar to the windows of each villa. The Mylar they would apply would be clear, and theoretically it would protect us from the windows shattering as a result of a percussion blast from an explosion. The memo further stated that the workers would begin on 11th Street the following Saturday. Our villa, however, was on 20th Street, completely opposite from where the work would begin. Hence, we could expect to wait at least three weeks before our villa would receive attention, if not longer.

Although I was still comfortable with our decision for the children and me to remain in Kingdom, I felt a serious need to do something ... just in case. That evening, I shared my need with David.

"You know that packing tape would provide some protection," he explained.

"What do you mean?" I asked curiously.

"You can make an X across the large plate glass windows and it will have a similar effect as Mylar should there be a blast nearby. It stops the glass from shattering. Plus, you can't see it."

"Really?" I replied, deep in thought with my hand to my chin. Within a matter of minutes, my plan for the next day was set, and I was able to find sleep.

Early the following morning, I mounted my little purple bike and headed for the compound store. One way or another, I had to feel as if I were doing something. I purchased five rolls of clear packing tape and began my mission. As I moved from window to window, I assessed each room along the way. When I reached the children's rooms, I noticed that in both rooms their beds were by the windows. As I crossed their windows with tape, I paced off a direct line from the window, as if glass was blowing in, and moved each of their beds to a place in the room that would not be in the line of fire, so to speak.

Exhausted from moving furniture and taping a dozen windows, I plopped into my recliner in the den for a quick rest. As I leaned back despondently, my hand brushed the draperies. It was not until that moment that I thought of how they could help protect us as well. Because of the blowing fine sand of the desert *shamaals*, all villas were equipped with heavy drapes made of beautiful fabric, but they were lined with a plastic-like material to keep the sand from blowing inside through the edges of the windows. They could easily stop blowing glass, too. Consequently, our draperies remained closed for several weeks that followed, blocking the sunshine of many pretty days.

Believing that I did all that I could do to protect us, I felt a little bit more at ease, but only a little, and I waited for more memos and messages. Because of the tension among the residents, I remained at home and avoided the common facilities as much as possible until the families that were leaving the country left. Every one of the women who had decided to leave strongly felt the women who had chosen to stay were "bad mothers," and they voiced their opinions loudly and rudely. They constantly made comments as to how stupid we were to stay in this "Godforsaken place." As the time passed before they could leave, it became unbearable. Amazingly, the day after they all left, the compound atmosphere seemed somewhat uplifted in spite of the remaining security concerns.

Weeks passed and daily life slowly began to return to normal, even though we remained on the compound most of the time. On the 6th of August, another town hall meeting was called for 6:30 p.m. (see Appendix G). Enough time had passed for the company and the U.S. government to determine what to do for us and to put the people in place to take additional action. Representatives from the United States Department Mobile Training Team were in Kingdom to meet with us on safety issues, and everyone was encouraged to attend.

Assuming that the meeting would follow a positive note, I was flabbergasted when I found out why the men were there to talk to us. Instead of hearing how we were going to be protected and that everything would be fine, we endured a three-hour briefing on personal security measures, surveillance recognition, attack recognition and improvised explosive devices.

Now at threat con Charlie, we had to learn a new way to survive in the desert. We were instructed not to accept mail or telephone calls from unfamiliar sources. We were told we should never take the same route when leaving the compound, and we should alter all patterns of behavior. They told us to keep a low profile, limit our contact with nationals, and avoid crowds at all times.

We learned how terrorists watch their targets for weeks, perhaps months or years, to determine how "hardened" the target may be. By "hardened," the Mobile Training Team explained that the term indicated how tight our security was, or at least how strict it appeared to anyone who may be surveying us as a potential target. Basically, how easily could a terrorist attack us? Would they receive very much resistance to an attack? Did we have measures in place to stop such an attack?

The U.S. representatives explained that as supporters of the Saudi military, we were a secondary target behind the U.S. military. However, with the U.S. military now tighter with their security enhancements, we had moved up on the list of possible targets for terrorism in the Kingdom.

We were taught how to make Molotov cocktails and utilize other household items for self-defense. They explained that a bomb could be anything from a juice box to a water truck. After enduring three hours of this information, I left the meeting with the thought that essentially we could not know what a bomb looks like because it could be anything.

After scaring us all to death, they explained that they had surveyed the security measures imposed immediately following the bombing, and they had determined what additional security measures needed to be taken to help make us a more hardened target. Saudi National Guard boats would patrol the three watersides of the compound 24 hours a day. Elevated security guard huts would be placed on every corner and manned 24 hours a day. Surveillance cameras would be mounted around the compound perimeter and monitored around the clock. They explained what I already knew from David that we would have a berm built on the inland side of the compound, along with a second security checkpoint. However, David had neglected to tell me that the new security checkpoint would be guarded 24 hours a day with a manned machine gun to greet our guests. What I used to call "Peyton Place" had become "Alcatraz."

In spite of the frightening things we had learned and the additional security measures being taken, I actually felt safer knowing them, even though I realized I could not control what would come, if it came. Outwardly, life began to feel somewhat normal again, and we slowly became accustomed to the compound's new enhancements, and eventually they became a normal way of life. However, our world was spiraling out of control. It was just spiraling so slowly that we never knew it. In hindsight, I realize that various global events preceding the *Khobar* Tower bombing and several events that followed affected our lives in Kingdom in a way that we can only understand a decade later. Naturally, we were unable to predict the things that would come, unable to understand at the time that the *Khobar* Tower bombing was the pivotal point in our stay in the Kingdom of Saudi Arabia.

ॐ Chapter Twenty ॐ

Looking Forward

As I shuffled through the enormous amount of memos and Warden Messages that flooded our mailbox on a regular basis in the summer of 1996, I prayed that life would return to the normal carefree life I had known before the bombing.

When Madawi returned in September, we were together once again, and my prayers seemed to be answered. As the years passed, I worked hard with her by my side to move the plight of women in the Eastern Province forward, and we were successful. As we accomplished these challenges, our friendship as I perceived it grew deeper than ever before. We triumphed in ways that we never dreamed possible and faced trials that we overcame. Our experiences did not end with Khobar Towers, only the direction of those experiences changed.

As mothers, we shared the lives, successes and challenges of our children. As wives, we supported each other through the good and bad times that we faced with our husbands. As women, we grew by expanding our minds. As friends, we grew by sharing these steps along the way.

For Americans, security measures tightened even more as the years unfolded, but I took these in stride because I had my friend, never noticing the subtle changes and the movement that had begun. Together, we watched as world events unfolded, yet never turned on the other as a result. Rather, we felt for each other and empathized as much as possible with the others' feelings. I guess in some way, I believed our friendship would hold tight and that we could make the world a better place by being together.

Yet today, 12 years later, I still cry with the way these shared times ended. I feel pain that my friend is no longer with me. I never dreamed that the friend I shared thousands of wonderful times with, even childbirth, would forsake me. Almost daily, I relive in my mind the events that changed what I thought was the perfect friendship. The words of caution that Dick shared with me on my first day of work with Princess Madawi vividly stand out in my mind. "Remember," he warned, "watch your step with the princess as things can end as quickly as they start when it comes to the Royal family. One minute you can be in their favor, their golden child, and the next, you can be out of the country bearing an exit-only visa."

It was not the world dictating that an American and an Arab should not be friends. It was not Islam or Christianity per se that directly caused us to break. It was the most unforeseeable and unimaginable circumstances that tore us apart — that shifted the sands of a decade of friendship. But our remaining trials and tribulations are a story, a long story, for another day.

Wind makes caves
— Hofhuf.

The "Sea of Palms," seen from the top of the caves outside the city of Hofhuf, the oldest oasis in the world.

Our picnic lunch in a remote area near the caves of Hofhuf.

A 10-riyal ride at the Hofhuf Camel Market.

Right: Emblem designed to commemorate the 100th anniversary of the Al-Saud monarchy and 100 years of the Kingdom of Saudi Arabia.

A camel sold — Hofhuf Camel Market.

Compound dining facility.

Compound swimming pool.

An ordinary way of hauling goats.

Typical gold souks.

An example of the creative gasoline stations seen around the Kingdom.

An example of the beautiful mosques that are prevalent throughout the Kingdom.

Site of the first mosque in Saudi Arabia, built in the days of Muhammad (PBUH), which is approximately 1,400 years old.

Early morning breakfast with our dear friends.

Nora's graduation party.

Nora's party.

Khobar Towers' destruction following June 25, 1996 terrorist bombing.

Family park beside Khobar Towers, where hundreds of Saudi men, women and children were killed or injured.

Appendix A

Glossary of Terms

The Arabic language is a phonetic language.
Words should be enunciated exactly as written.

Abaya – the traditional long black covering for women worn to hide one's figure

Afwan – "you're welcome"

Al – preceding a name indicates "family of"

Allah – Arabic for "God"

Allah Aakabar – essentially "there is but one God" in Arabic and is said to lead the call to prayer five times per day

Al Hamdulila – "praise be to God"

Al-Mana Hospital – the major local hospital used by most Westerners in the Eastern Province

Amity –"your highness" when referring to a female

Amir – "your highness" when referring to a male

Ashufee baden insha Allah – "I will see you later, God willing"

Asr – The late afternoon prayer call, which is one of five daily prayer calls practiced by Muslims. This prayer occurs around 4:00 p.m./ late afternoon.

Baba – "father"

Bata – an old shopping district in the heart of Riyadh

Baksheesh – basically means "kickback," yet not considered illegal in Kingdom; rather commonplace

Bedouin – the nomadic people of Saudi Arabia

Bin – "son of"

Bint – "daughter of"

Bisme Allah –"thank you, God, for the blessing"

Champs d'Elysee – a famous street in the heart of Paris, France that stretches from the Arch d'Triumph to the Louvre Museum.

Corniche — a scenic road that parallels the Arabian Gulf the length of the Eastern Province

Dohr – The midday prayer call, which is one of five daily prayer calls practiced by Muslims. This prayer occurs around 11:30 a.m. / late morning.

Dhows – traditional Arab boats, hand made of wood

Dubai – one of the United Arab Emirates on the Arabian Peninsula

Eid Al Fitr – the three-day holiday which directly follows the Holy month of *Ramadan* to celebrate the breaking of the fast

Eid Al Hada – the three-day holiday that follows the Hajj to celebrate the annual pilgrimage

Empty quarter – a region in the southeast corner of Saudi Arabia that consists solely of desert

Fagah – a small potato-like vegetable that grows wild in the desert

Fajr – The sunrise prayer call, which is one of the five daily prayer calls practiced by Muslims. This prayer occurs at sunrise each day.

Faux pas – French for "mistake"

Ghawa – "coffee"

Guthra – the traditional red and white headdress for Arab men

Hiyah – a segment of the Committee for Public Morality (the religious police) that handles dealings with Westerners

Hummus – a dip made of chickpeas, seasoned with garlic, lemon and tehina and eaten with pita bread by scooping the dip

Igal – the black band that goes on top of the men's traditional Arab headdress

Igama – the required Saudi Arabian work permit for expatriates in the Kingdom. It is your "lifeline," your identity. There is a large fine applied if you lose it or are ever stopped at a checkpoint or roadblock without it. Pictures of the man's family are included in the back.

Il est dommage –French for "It is a pity."

Imam – a scholar of the Quran

Imshee – "walk" or "follow"

Insha Allah – "God willing" or "if God wills." Muslims use this phrase constantly because their beliefs are so deeply rooted in the idea that God controls everything.

INCO – an acronym meaning "In Country Company Number," which is assigned to each expatriate employee, marking the date he enters the Kingdom for the first time.

Isha – the prayer time 1-1/2 hours after sunset

Jamboorah - a small kangaroo-like rodent that is indicative to Saudi.

Kayf Haalik – "How are you?" to a female

Kebsa – a traditional celebratory Arab meal consisting of goat and rice

Kolasse – "finished" or "stop"

La - "no"

Ma'assalaamah – "goodbye"

Maghrib – The sunset prayer call

Marhaba – "welcome"

Majlis – an open court held weekly by the King and Governors in the Kingdom

Mofie Muskala – "no problem," a very common phrase that Westerners learn almost immediately

Mubarak – an Arabic term used to offer good wishes on a holiday

Mumkin – literally translated means "possibly" but is used in conversation to mean "please"

Muthawen – the Islamic religious "police" in Saudi Arabia

PUBH – an acronym meaning "peace be upon Him" and used whenever a reference, either written or spoken, is made to the Prophet Muhammad (PBUH)

Quran – Holy Book of the Islamic Faith

Ramadan – the ninth month of the Islamic calendar in which Muslims fast as one of the five pillars of their faith. This is an extremely Holy time for Muslims.

Riyadh – the capital city of Saudi Arabia, located in the Central Province

Riyal – the name of Saudi currency notes

Sambusha – a triangle pastry filled with either feta cheese or seasoned meats

Shabah – "old, wise man" used in a fond, respectful manner.

Salla – "prayer time"

Sharia Law – the laws that guide citizens of Saudi Arabia based on their religious beliefs

Shariah – the judicial body in Kingdom

Share'a Al Khabbaz – a famous shopping street in Hofuf

Shawarma – a wrapped sandwich

Sharja – one of the United Arab Emirates on the Arabian Peninsula

Sheesha – a water pipe usually filled with dried fruits and spices

Shiite – a sect of the Muslim community that does not directly follow the teachings of the prophet Muhammad (PBUH)

Shukran - "thank you"

Shula – a popular, older indoor shopping mall in Al-Khobar

Sideeke – literally means "friend," but used by expats to refer to a homemade alcohol

Souk – "store" or "shopping area"

Souk Al Khamis – "Thursday Market"

SR – the abbreviation for Saudi Money called "Saudi Riyal." Used like the dollar sign for American money

Taif – a city located in the Southern Province

TCN – an acronym for "Third Country National," which refers to individuals working in Saudi Arabia from third world countries

Thobe – the traditional Arab attire for men, long and usually white

Tieeb – "okay"

Qadis - Islamic judges

Ulema – The Islamic authorities in the Kingdom

Wahid – "one"

Yellah – an Arabic term with diverse meaning depending on the context. It can mean "hurry," "come along" or "do something."

Zakat – the act of giving alms, which is done to fulfill the third pillar of faith in Islam.

Appendix B

Prohibited Items in the Kingdom of Saudi Arabia

- Arms and ammunition
- Alcoholic beverages or anything pertaining to their manufacture (which also includes cologne and mouthwash)
- Narcotics, unless accompanied by a doctor's prescription
- Pork or any foods containing pork
- Fireworks
- Cigarette advertisements
- Candy cigarettes
- Books or magazines depicting nudity (which includes most bathing suit or lingerie advertisements and art books.)
- Pornographic or sexual items of any type
- Chemicals
- Government symbols (e.g. flags, stickers, etc.)
- Military clothing or equipment such as hand-held transmitters and citizens band radios
- Christmas trees or decorations
- Publications which are banned in the Kingdom
- Dolls or items with pictured faces

Appendix C

Original Copy of American Consulate Warden
Message dated November 14, 1995

NOV 14 '95 16:47   SECURITY INUS D069   PAGE.02

SAUDI ARABIA TRAVEL SECURITY GUIDE

OVERVIEW & RISK RATING

Saudi Arabia is one of the safest and most stable countries in the Middle
East. It is also one of the most conservative. Foreigners are tolerated
rather than welcomed, though foreign business is well-established and is
crucial to the economy.

Risk Level Two (Vigilant).

TRAVEL RISK UPDATE

14 Nov 95

Bomb at US military office

There is no need to cancel or postpone business travel to Saudi Arabia in
the aftermath of the bomb explosion on 13 November at a central Riyadh
office building housing US military personnel. Five of the six people
killed were US nationals, and 30 US nationals were among the more than 60
injured. A previously unknown Islamic extremist group opposed to the
presence of foreign troops in Saudi Arabia has claimed the bombing, though
it is too early to assess the authenticity of this claim.

Further isolated bombings are possible. Attacks are most likely at
installations housing Saudi and US or other foreign military or security
personnel. However, extra security will act as a deterrent and there is no
indication that the attack heralds the start of a sustained anti-foreign
campaign. We do not expect bombings at foreign corporate premises, hotels
or airports.

Disruption in central Riyadh resulting from the blast is likely to last
for several days. The longer-term legacy of the bombing will be tighter
security at government buildings and official foreign premises such as
embassies.

SAUDI ARABIA FORECAST

14 Nov 95

Islamic extremist group claims Riyadh bomb

It is too early to assess the authenticity of a claim made by a previously unknown Islamic extremist group, the Tigers of the Gulf, for a bomb attack in Riyadh on 13 November. In a call to a French news agency in the city, the group warned that 'attacks will continue until the departure of the last American soldier'.

Six people - including five US nationals - were killed and more than 60 injured in the explosion outside the Office of Programme Management (OPM), where US military personnel train the Saudi National Guard. The duties of the Guard, commanded by the heir to the throne, Prince Abdullah Abd al-Aziz, are to defend the royal family from social unrest and from military coups by the regular army. The virtually unprotected building is situated in a busy area of Riyadh; parking the vehicle in which the bomb was placed was a relatively easy task.

The attack was intended to highlight the covert and semi-covert links between the Saudi regime and its Western allies and thus destabilise the state. It has dealt a major blow to the confidence of the Saudi regime and its security apparatus. Despite the government's denials of a US military presence in Saudi Arabia, more than 1,300 US personnel - both military personnel and employees of US corporations such as BDM and Vinnell - work with the National Guard.

Sources in Riyadh report that the security forces had been on low-level alert because of concern over terrorism in Riyadh since early November. Leaflets have recently been circulating in Riyadh warning Westerners not to support the Saudi regime. The little-known Islamic Peninsula Movement for Change - Jihad Wing (IPMC-JW) in July and April this year sent faxes to a London-based Arabic newspaper demanding the withdrawal of all foreigners and foreign forces from Saudi territory.

The suspects

The OPM was a target for opponents both of the US presence and the National Guard itself. Under suspicion are:

- Islamic extremists, such as the Tigers of the Gulf and the IPMC-JW, comprising mainly local 'Afghanis' - former fighters in Afghanistan. However, it is unlikely that such extremists would have acted without outside assistance, either from states such as Iran, or from foreign extremist groups;

- traditional opponents of the Saudi regime. Tribes from Qassim province have always opposed the Al-Saud dynasty. Recently, Qassimis have established anti-government groups in London using Islamic fundamentalism as the latest standard for their historic opposition to the regime. However, a bombing would be a radical departure from their strategy of media manipulation and stirring up dissent in Qassimi mosques.

Risk of further attacks

Whoever is responsible, events. . . . . .

be sustained, as the Saudi security forces are usually efficient in
rooting out extremists. Saudi installations housing US or other foreign
official, semi-official and corporate military-linked personnel are the
likeliest targets for further attacks. Tight security at US and other
foreign official installations reduces, but does not eliminate, the
chances of a successful attack. An assault on official transport similar
to a shooting attack on a bus carrying US personnel from Jiddah airport in
1991 is possible. Extremists are unlikely to target foreign companies.

Appendix D

Original Listing of

You Know You Have Lived In Saudi Arabia Too Long When...

- You enjoy camping in the sand
- You are not surprised to see a goat in the passenger seat
- You think the uncut version of "Little House on the Prairie" is provocative
- You serve coffee in a thimble
- You expect the confirmation of your airline reservation to be *"Insha Allah"*
- You think everyone's first name is Al
- You buy a falcon hood for your gear shift
- You don't expect to eat dinner until 11:30 p.m.
- You need a sweater and it's 80 degrees Fahrenheit
- You serve Listerine over ice
- You think 500 SR is a good price
- You enjoy Channel 2
- Your ideal vacation is anywhere you can eat a pig
- You have to write an official apology because your toes are uncovered
- You think cars are available only in white
- Your idea of housework is leaving a list for the houseboy
- You understand "no problem" means "follow-up"
- Your measure of success is coming home from the *souks* without a confrontation
- You think a picnic means pulling over to the side of the road with TV, carpet and a water pipe
- You own more than one Rolex
- You think black is appropriate daytime wear
- You wear a jacket inside and take it off when you go out
- You think all crimes should be punishable by beheading
- You think shopping malls are covered *souks*

- You can judge a perfect "10" by the ankles
- You think carpets belong on the wall
- Your favorite hamburger chain features a goat for a logo
- You think anyone carrying a cane is out to get you
- You turn up the air-conditioning to write Christmas cards
- You enjoy the Arab News because it has few advertisements
- You know which end of a *shawarma* to unwrap first
- You think that the further you inch into the middle of the intersection, the faster the light will turn green
- Your best friend asks to buy your Bar-B-Q grill
- You think your neighbor gives a great hair cut
- You carry an umbrella and it isn't raining
- You give directions by landmarks
- You think all gas stations are made of marble
- You think a desert storm is a war
- You look forward to the Monday edition of "Islam in Perspective"
- You think every major sale is preceded by cups of tea
- You think being liberated means sitting in the "family section"
- You think a red light means "run it"
- You think only men should hold hands in public
- You can't buy anything without asking for a discount
- You have more carpets than floor space
- You think there is a great correlation between the acceleration of the car in front of you and the speed at which you can blow your horn when the light turns green
- You think the "feminine mystique" means covering up
- You make left turns from the far right lane
- You expect gold for every birthday and holiday
- You think "Pepsi" begins with a "B"
- You measure time by the number of prayer calls
- You send friends a map instead of your address
- You expect a palace on every corner
- You think Kleenex™ belong on the dining table

Appendix E

Original Copy of American Consulate Warden Message dated June 26, 1996

Consulate General of the
United States of America
Dhahran, Saudi Arabia

Dear Wardens:

Please pass the attached Embassy Riyadh warden message immediately.

Consulate General Dhahran will open for consular services on 891-3200 x 213, 214, 215, 217, 219, 220, 269 and 278. In the event of an emergency after hours, the Duty Officer can be reached on 891-3200.

We thank the many Americans who have offered assistance, and have passed your offers to the appropriate military officials. We appreciate your support in this tragic time.

H. Bridget Burkart
Acting Consul General

Quote:

The Embassy requests that the following message be passed in its entirety by all wardens to members of the American community.

At approximately 21:55 on Tuesday, June 25, a terrorist explosion occurred in Al-Khobar in the Eastern Province directed against coalition military forces. Current reports indicate that there have been 19 American deaths and more than 80 wounded of the estimated 240 casualties. Thus far, international news services appear to be giving timely and accurate information as details surrounding the event emerge.

- page 2 of 3 -

The Embassy has suspended all routine consular services (passports, visas, and notarials) to focus on the situation and to provide essential services to American citizens. We hope to resume normal operations on Saturday June 29 or as soon as possible thereafter. Those that need to contact the consular section can do so by calling 488-3800 ext. 1130, 1117, 1119, or 1138. The Department of Defense has provided the following U.S. telephone number for relatives of affected service members seeking information: Air Force personnel: 800-253-2979; other services: 703-697-5131.

Both the Embassy and the U.S. military component of the coalition are working closely with Saudi authorities to deal with the aftermath of this tragedy. U.S. authorities will provide all needed assistance to the investigation, and the Embassy will continue to work with Saudi authorities to ensure that additional measures are being taken to protect the security of American citizens in the Kingdom. The Saudi Government has assured us of its full support and assistance.

The Embassy again encourages all Americans in Saudi Arabia to exercise extreme caution, keep a low profile, reduce travel within the Kingdom, and treat mail from unfamiliar sources with suspicion. We want to stress that Americans in Saudi Arabia should be especially vigilant of their personal security and surroundings, and should report any suspicious activities to the Embassy or nearest U.S. Consulate.

The Embassy will endeavor to keep the community informed of relevant security information and developments through the warden system. For the latest information, call 488-3800 and press 7.

Unquote

End of Dhahran's warden message - 019/FY96
- page 3 of 3 -

Appendix F

Company Security Memorandum
dated June 26, 1996

JDM-P118-96-33
26 June 1996

To: All DM-22 Compound Residents

Subject: Security Enhancements

1   As you are aware, the US Military was targeted
last evening at Khobar Towers resulting in a tragic
loss of many lives and a greater number of personnel with serious injuries. Last night we had a bomb
threat directed specifically at our compound. We
think it was a hoax, but in light of the situation it
will be necessary to take the following additional
security measures:

  a. Armed Saudi Army personnel will be stationed
  at the first guard post entry to the Compound.
  They will be asked to provide security on the
  Exhibition side of the Compound and augment
  Compound security with muscle, if needed.

  b. At this guard post, the security arm will remain
  down until occupants in the vehicle can be confirmed to be valid occupants of the compound by
  our guards.

  c. At the second and main guard post at the entrance of the compound, the guards will inspect
  under the hood as well as the trunk of the vehicle. The interior will be inspected on some vehicles. Delivery vehicles will be allowed on only
  after confirmation of the resident as to the validity of the delivery.

d. Flood lights are to be installed on some exterior compound walls.

e. Functions and visitors are to be severely curtailed until further notice. Gatherings with more than six outside personnel must be discontinued for now. Approved visitors are to have their names left at the first guard post at compound extension 6552. No visitor will be allowed on compound unless specifically approved by you when called by the guard.

2. Following are security enhancements under consideration:

a. Use of personal ID to gain entry to the compound.

b. Concrete barriers in road between security guard posts.

c. Improved surveillance from Saudi Coast Guard on water side of compound.

d. Visitors driving to the compound will surrender driver's license or igama before entering the compound.

3. I encourage each of you to give me any input that you desire relative to our security procedures during these trying times. I think they are necessary to achieve and maintain a lower profile until security returns to normal. Thank you for your patience, consideration and understanding.

Director Base Operations
Dhahran

Appendix G

Company Memorandum
dated August 6, 1996

6 August 1996

To All Members of the DM-22 Compound

Tonight's seminar by the State's Department Mobile Training Team will include the following subjects: surveillance recognition, attack recognition, improvised explosive devices and personal security measures, all subjects that we need to know in our travels throughout the world. If you cannot attend this evening, the consulate has advised that it may be possible to attend a make-up period on the Consulate grounds. Contact the Consulate as soon as possible at 891-3200, extension 217. Tonight's session is planned for three hours, I will ask the Team to expedite the training where possible to shorten the period without degrading the quality of training. See you at 6:30 in the Theater.

Company Base Director